'In this gem of a book, Amanda Ridings brilliantly marries ancient and contemporary wisdom to give the reader a detailed anatomy of what goes on in our conversations. However, this is no mere dissection of key conversational elements; the reader is skilfully led to inquire deeply into their own and others dialogic processes – and to improve them. An array of new practices and resources powerfully draws the reader into engaging fully with the central concepts in the book.

Amanda's authentic voice offers us a compelling conversation, one that encourages centred, embodied, conscious dialogue – dialogue that will hugely increase our 'collective intelligence.' From boardroom to bedroom, from professional life to the playground, we urgently need the guidance and transformative possibilities of this rigorous, profound and engaging book.

'Pause for Breath' comes at a time when globally, we are hungry for healing connection and are often uncertain how to speak both compassionately and fearlessly with each other. As the poet, David Whyte, puts it, 'People are hungry… one good word is bread for a thousand.' This book is a major contribution to our capacity to create miracles together. Read it.'

Edna Murdoch, Director, Coaching Supervision Academy Ltd.

'Amanda has adapted key features of the dialogue work, as I hoped and anticipated other practitioners might, to develop her own unique coaching practice. It is apparent to me that the curious blend of T'ai Chi, dialogue and penetrating reflective awareness she propounds in her book is practical, sensitive, effective and worthy of careful consideration by anyone working in the field of coaching and leadership development.'

Peter Garrett, Founder of Dialogue Associates and Prison Dialogue

Based in Scotland, Amanda Ridings is an executive coach, coach supervisor and T'ai Chi practitioner. In both her one-to-one work and in small groups of co-learners, she fosters the embodiment of dialogue practices. She also hosts leadership retreats, enabling those caught up in relentless activity to pause for breath and clarify their leadership purpose.

In all she does, Amanda's intent is to create spaces in which people can make contact, gently and lucidly, with their deeper wisdom so that they can draw on it in mindful service to their life and work. For more information see www.originate.org.uk

When not working, writing, or practicing T'ai Chi, she finds perspective and renewal by walking in the Scottish hills and mountains. She also loves to dance.

Pause for Breath

Bringing the practices of mindfulness and
dialogue to leadership conversations

Amanda Ridings

lip

First published in 2011 by:
Live It Publishing
27 Old Gloucester Road
London, United Kingdom.
WC1N 3AX
www.liveitpublishing.com

Publisher's Note
Every possible effort has been made to ensure that the information contained in this book is accurate at the time of going to press, and the publishers and author cannot accept responsibility for any errors or omissions, however caused. No responsibility for loss or damage occasioned to any person acting, or refraining from action, as a result of the material in this publication can be accepted by the editor, the publisher or author.

ISBN 978-1-906954-23-9 (pbk)

Dedicated to...

Kay, Lorna, Louise and Susan –
my first dialogue practice development group.
Without your trust my dialogue journey may have stalled.

Sifu Ian Cameron
and
Five Winds School of T'ai Chi Chuan
From whom I truly learned the nature and spirit of practice.

Paldron
Inspiration, aspiration.

'Foster and polish
The warrior spirit
While serving the world;
Illuminate the path
According to your inner light.'
Morihei Ueshiba

Contents

Preface   13
Part one – Preparation and beginning   17
   Chapter 1   **Introduction**   18
   Chapter 2   **The journey on offer in this book**   25
   Chapter 3   **Setting the scene for the practice of mindfulness**   32
   Chapter 4   **Setting the scene for dialogue – advocacy and inquiry**   38
   Chapter 5   **Why become aware of our conversational habits?**   45
   Chapter 6   **Pause for breath**   54
Resource list for more on different forms of conversation   57

Part two – Mind and conversation   59
   Chapter 7   **Introduction**   60
   Chapter 8   **First person inquiry with kindness and fascination**   64
   Chapter 9   **A simple frame for conversational exchanges**   69
   Chapter 10   **Taking a look inside the black box**   75
   Chapter 11   **A structured framework for the black box**   88
   Chapter 12   **Internal dialogue – why mind and conversation matters**   102

Chapter 13   External dialogue – why mind and conversation
                 matters   108
Chapter 14   Pause for breath   116
Resource list for inquiry into processes of the mind   118

Part three – Body and conversation   119
Chapter 15   Introduction   120
Chapter 16   Handling difference   125
Chapter 17   Difference and our physiology – fight, flight and freeze   131
Chapter 18   Embodied mindfulness – centre   139
Chapter 19   Skilful advocacy, inquiry and pause   148
Chapter 20   Internal conflict   160
Chapter 21   Why body and conversation matters   168
Chapter 22   Pause for breath   175
Resource list for inquiry into impact of physiology   178

Part four – Spirit and conversation   179
Chapter 23   Introduction   180
Chapter 24   Spirit as individual essence   185
Chapter 25   Spirit as collective energy   196
Chapter 26   Spirit in the face of challenging conversations   206
Chapter 27   Cultivating spirit as practice/discipline   219
Chapter 28   Pause for breath   227
Resource list for more on cultivating your finest leadership spirit   230

Part five – Versatility in conversations   231
Chapter 29   Introduction   232
Chapter 30   Kantor's four players and linked frameworks   236
Chapter 31   Moves, direction and authentic voicing   252
Chapter 32   Opposes, integrity and respecting   262
Chapter 33   Follows, service and listening   272
Chapter 34   Bystands, perspective and suspending judgement   280

Chapter 35   Silences, mindful presence and pausing for breath
              – a speculation   288
Chapter 36   **Pause for breath**   296
Resource list for more on the principles and practices of dialogue 299

Part six – Towards dialogue   301

Chapter 37   **Introduction**   302
Chapter 38   **Preparing for important leadership conversations**   307
Chapter 39   **Leading others into a different kind of conversation** 315
Chapter 40   **Arriving, beginning, connecting**   320
Chapter 41   **Sharing responsibility for cultivating a container** 330
Chapter 42   **What now? Building your practice**   338
Chapter 43   **Last touch**   354

Acknowledgements   358
References   360

List of practices

Practice 1   awareness in conversation   23
Practice 2   awareness of learning process   30
Practice 3   a first practice in mindfulness   36
Practice 4   awareness of advocacy and inquiry   43
Practice 5   awareness of energy fields in conversation   52
Practice 6   pause for breath   56
Practice 7   awareness of thinking   62
Practice 8   reflecting with kindness and fascination   67
Practice 9   fieldwork to explore intent and impact   73
Practice 10   awareness of preferences and filters for incoming
              information   86
Practice 11   awareness of assumptions and underlying paradigms,
              beliefs and values   100
Practice 12   left hand column activity   106
Practice 13   fieldwork with a wicked issue   114
Practice 14   pause for breath   117
Practice 15   fieldwork on observing physiology   123
Practice 16   attending to the language of difference   129
Practice 17   attending to the physiology of difference   137

Practice 18	developing a centring routine and cultivating a centring habit	146
Practice 19	attending to your energy and physicality in conversation	158
Practice 20	raising awareness of your internal dialogue	166
Practice 21	reflecting on the influence of fight/flight/freeze	173
Practice 22	pause for breath	177
Practice 23	noticing individual and collective spirit	183
Practice 24	cultivating individual spirit	194
Practice 25	cultivating collective spirit	204
Practice 26	encountering complexity	217
Practice 27	attending to, and nourishing your spirit, based on an approach by Tom Crum	225
Practice 28	pause for breath	229
Practice 29	authentic voice, based on a practice from Wendy Palmer	234
Practice 30	cultivating dialogue practices	250
Practice 31	moves, direction and authentic voicing	260
Practice 32	opposes, integrity and respecting	270
Practice 33	follows, service and listening	278
Practice 34	bystands, perspective and suspending judgement	286
Practice 35	silences, mindful presence and pausing for breath	294
Practice 36	pause for breath	298
Practice 37	awareness of attitude to learning and practice	305
Practice 38	fieldwork on the impact of setting on conversations	313
Practice 39	first touch in leading a conversation	318
Practice 40	the impact of check-in	328
Practice 41	contracting	336
Practice 42	taking stock	350
Practice 43	pause for breath	357

Preface

*'In the beginner's mind there are many possibilities,
but in the expert's there are few.' Shunryu Suzuki*

In the last few years I've been having a bit of a love affair with writing. I know that I want to write, I know that the process of writing completely absorbs me, and I know that in some ways writing is my most complete expression of myself. I've written some short stories and started a novel. I write a journal and write reflectively for my learning. I write letters and emails, reports and presentations. I simply love to write.

A key strand of my recent development has been recognising and playing with this love of writing. Another important strand has been exploring the field of dialogue, prompted by a friend who gave me *Dialogue and the Art of Thinking Together*[1] by William Isaacs. The approaches outlined in this book captured my imagination and inspired me. It is a deep, intense book, challenging and full of hope; it spoke to my optimism and to my ideals, and I knew I wanted to work with this material. In this way, a long-distance walk began. In the years since, I have participated in courses, done a lot of reading, tentatively begun to introduce the ideas and approaches into my coaching and facilitation work and, finally, started to stake a claim to my own practice, partially through a link-up with another coach and co-learner, Steve Marshall.

One thing that has become apparent on my journey, is that there is an immense gap between being excited by the idea of something and bringing it into practice. It has taken many years for me to acquire a sense that I am even scratching the surface of bringing the practices of dialogue into my conversations. This slow learning has helped me become clear about the way in which I want to support others in increasing their versatility in conversations. To me, developing capacity for dialogue is a practice, similar to practising a golf swing or practising scales on a musical instrument. Erich Fromm, in his book *The Art of Loving,*[2] describes an art as a body of theory and practice; in looking to leaders in the field for theories and frameworks, I aim to guide fellow travellers in their learning and practice.

Over time, I have deepened and clarified my approach to creating the conditions that catalyse different kinds of leadership conversations. As I've done this, I've felt an increasing need for 'something like a book' to support and guide my clients to explore their practice further. Through written material they can reflect on, and make meaning of, their conversation practice in their own time. Thus, my love of writing and my work in dialogue collided to offer the opportunity (and challenge) of creating a book.

The final inspiration to set myself to this task came from a development programme called Journey to Centre, which took place in the Rocky Mountains, Colorado, with Tom Crum and his associates. I joined the programme because I was beginning to look at the potential for working with the martial art of T'ai Chi in leadership development and dialogue settings. Tom's principal martial art is Aikido, which shares many principles with T'ai Chi, and he is established and revered in the work that he does. Tom's mind-body-spirit approach reached me in ways that other development programmes had left untouched, and I came away energised and inspired on many levels. I also began to read the books that Tom and his colleagues have written, and in them I saw a style that was deeply personal and congruent with their values and approaches. I was powerfully engaged by each of their stories and saw how I might write about dialogue and why it is at the heart of my coaching and consultancy work.

The scene was set. The result is this book, in which I explore how leadership conversations might change through bringing the practices of mindfulness and dialogue to them. By mindfulness, I mean pausing for breath and responding to the present moment; releasing any shadows of history or lures of an imagined future. Through this book, I share some of the concepts, tools, experiences, models and practices that have helped me become a little more mindful in my own conversations.

I know that as I write, I will change my understanding of the material. As in so much of life, I'll be working with a moving target. However, what will remain constant is my intent to engage you in such a way that you begin your own exploration of the practices I introduce. I encourage you to adopt them if they work for you and let them go if they don't. I invite you to hold lightly the perspectives and stories I offer and to inquire into your own perspectives and stories. I hope that you will be drawn to make changes in your own approach to, and engagement in, conversations and, through this, deepen and enrich the relationships in your life and work.

In working with mind, body and spirit in conversation, I draw on many sources and have benefitted from the guidance of many teachers. Key to the mind aspect, the theories and practices of dialogue, are Peter Garrett, Jane Ball, David Kantor, and the participants of my dialogue practice development groups. A profound contribution to my development has come from the physical realm, and I am deeply indebted to my T'ai Chi teacher, Ian Cameron – without his patience in the face of a mind-clever but body-illiterate student, I might not have truly begun this rich and challenging journey. This aspect of my growth accelerated with Tom Crum and his colleagues and has continued with many other inspiring teachers including Johnny Glover, Judy Ringer and Wendy Palmer. Beyond these teachers there are many people who have been important to my learning, and although not named here, I do not forget them: I hold each of them in deep gratitude.

In writing a book to share my experiences of making sense of, and using, the models and concepts of others, I intend to be both respectful of the work of others and honest with my own learning process. In bringing the ideas and approaches of others into my practice, I've often adapted the models or language to support me in working authentically. I apologise unreservedly where, or if, in doing this, I have misunderstood or misrepresented original intentions. I make clear references to the original work and I encourage you to access original sources and embark on your own sense-making process – if my mistakes help you in this, I'll be delighted.

Finally, I believe the blend of components in this book to be unique, but there is nothing fundamentally new in the underlying material and I've done my utmost to credit sources where I know of them. However, I have not researched the field systematically and so it is possible that I have inadvertently used a phrase, word or motif that others claim as theirs. My intent is only to share my experiences and provide a resource; if I have adopted your words without acknowledgement then it is simply because I am unaware of your material. If you let me know, I will put it right.

Amanda Ridings, May 2011
Fife, Scotland
www.originate.org.uk

Part One

PREPARATION AND BEGINNING

Chapter *1*   Introduction

Chapter *2*   The journey on offer in this book

Chapter *3*   Setting the scene for the practice of mindfulness

Chapter *4*   Setting the scene for dialogue – advocacy and inquiry

Chapter *5*   Why become aware of our conversational habits?

Chapter *6*   Pause for breath

Resource list for more on different forms of conversation

Chapter *1* Introduction

*'You talk when you cease to be at peace
with your thoughts.'* Kahlil Gibran

I have always been fascinated by space, astronomy and our solar system, and newspaper articles and television programmes about these things catch my attention. I work as an executive coach with a strong interest in conversation, and so when I hear something that connects space travel with conversation, my ears prick up. Apparently, one of the challenges in sending people to Mars is that, with current communications technology, there would be a twenty-minute time lapse between transmission and receipt of voice signals. In truth, I haven't checked whether the twenty-minute delay is for a 'return journey' of words, or if it refers to twenty minutes 'each way.' It doesn't matter much, because even if it's the shorter time, can you imagine how such a delay influences an exchange between two people?

I began to wonder how I would change the content, style and tone of what I said if I knew that words had taken ten minutes to reach me, and that it would take a further ten minutes before my response reached the original speaker. If there were absolutely no other means of communication, words might become a luxury item, scarce and of high value, which would prompt me to consider them carefully. I would want to be sure that my words accurately conveyed my meaning, and would seek to use them potently and sparingly. I'd be thoughtful about their consequence and would want any questions I posed to be purposeful and precise. I wouldn't want to squander my opportunities to speak and I would be careful to elicit understanding from what I heard. I would want, literally, to weigh the significance of each contribution in an exchange.

Bringing my thought-experiment back to earth, I wonder how conversations would change with even a one-minute pause between words being spoken and heard. I can envisage some disastrous scenarios – some people wouldn't stop talking and others would be saving up their thoughts for the next opportunity to speak, regardless of what is being said in the meantime. Others again would be so carefully weighing up their words, meaning and possible consequences, that they would either speak too late or never get around to it. You may recognise these descriptions – they are behaviours that are often present in conversations, and their impact would be magnified and made more obvious by a time delay. Which of them is most likely to apply to you?

Despite these potential challenges, and our experiences of time lapses in some existing modes of communication such as email, the dreamer in me sees beyond the problems, and imagines what might be possible if we had a culture of conversation that was both more frugal in words and more rich in meaning. Imagine the possibility of conversations in which we listen more carefully to understand, because the consequences of misconstruing what we hear are more profound. Imagine conversations where more questions are genuine and are stimulated by curiosity and a desire for more information or fresh perspectives. Imagine conversations in which we cultivate the habit of pausing for breath before jumping to conclusions or assuming we have all the answers. Imagine conversations that are more mindful, in which we are lucidly aware of what is happening, as it is happening, and in which we have relinquished our intent to achieve a preconceived outcome.

The good news is that these kinds of conversation do take place. I've participated in them and witnessed them. When such a conversation unfolds, I experience a profound sense of calm, as if time stops and nothing else matters. This contrasts with more habitual conversations, where I am often anxious to speak or to be heard or I have a sense of urgency and/or utility pressing on me. In conversations where everyday imperatives and drivers fall away, I find a deep sense of congruence within myself, and an intense sense of connectedness with others; I am completely present in the conversation. As this happens, any topic or agenda seems, astonishingly, to take care of itself.

These kinds of conversation are slower and more spacious than habitual interchanges, in the way that 'slow food' is different to 'fast food' or 'ready meals.' With slow food, time is taken to select fresh ingredients which are mixed carefully and offered when properly cooked. In slow conversation, time is taken to examine and select thinking and feeling responses by connecting to the present conversation, rather than recycling habitual and ready-formed thoughts, opinions and beliefs. I think of this time as pausing for breath, rather than reacting instantly to the thoughts and opinions of others.

Slower, more reflective conversations have been written about in great detail and depth, often (but not exclusively) being described as dialogue. The theories and practices of dialogue are well-developed and I draw on them for my work with conversations, in which I invite people to become more aware of their habits of thinking, speaking and listening.

For those who wish to develop capacity for these more spacious conversations and to explore the practices of mindfulness and dialogue, I believe it is important to cultivate awareness in three aspects of conversational practice:

1. Awareness of self-in-conversation
How refined is my awareness of the way that I experience the world, then process that experience and express myself? What do I tend to pay attention to;

20

what attracts me; what do I avoid; what do I tend to discount or distort? Do I typically rush headlong into conversations, or do I have a way of pausing and gathering my responses? How can I add to my current repertoire of practice in conversations? Questions such as these begin to cultivate awareness of how thinking and feeling influence self-in-conversation.

2. Awareness of others-in-conversation
What do I notice about exchanges between people and how others respond to change or challenge or support? How refined is my awareness of any patterns in conversations and the consequences of them? What do I notice about the quality of relationships between people? What do I notice about the way silence is handled in a conversation? Questions such as these begin to cultivate awareness of others-in-conversation and start to create opportunities to use some of the practices of dialogue.

3. Awareness of conversation energies or fields
What do I understand about the factors that shape patterns in conversations and their influence on how people talk together? How refined is my awareness of the energetic tone of conversations, the ebb and flow of their 'music?' What do I sense about the shape and space a conversation occupies? Questions such as these begin to cultivate understanding of some deeper structures in conversations.

   In becoming alert to these three aspects of conversational practice and how they influence what unfolds, we begin to cultivate the potential for making changes to embedded habits, patterns and routines.

As we embark on our exploration, it is important to note that each of us will be starting from a different place. We have each developed our own strengths and foibles in conversation over many years. For one person it will be a stretch to access their emotional repertoire with the same agility as they access their reasoning. For another, the reverse will be true. For one person, learning to challenge clearly and effectively will make a crucial difference. For another, learning to support constructively will be key. For many of us, it will be important to learn to probe the world of others and to take much less at face value. Equally, for those who come quickly to conclusions and voice their 'answers,' a learning edge may be to share their inner 'workings' at an earlier stage. Wherever your starting point, I believe you will discover room to enhance or refine the ways in which you contribute to conversations.

Practice *1* – awareness in conversation

Reflect for a moment on a recent conversation with one other person.

Where was your attention? Mainly internal, on your own agenda? Mainly on the other person and what they were saying?

What was the pattern of exchange?

Did only one person speak? Did one voice follow another immediately, or when someone took a breath? Was one of you speaking over the other? How did you know when to speak and when to listen?

Were there any silences or pauses in the conversation? If so, how would you describe the quality of them?

Now reflect more generally – what is your most usual mode of being in a conversation? Speaking? Listening? Agreeing? Disagreeing? Challenging? Accommodating? Initiating? Responding? Or something else entirely?

Notes and reflections

24

Chapter 2 The journey on offer in this book

*'If learning is not followed by reflecting and practicing,
it is not true learning.' Thich Nhat Hanh*

In aspiring to bring the practices of mindfulness and dialogue to leadership conversations, we must first become more aware of our current conversational habits and practices. In doing this, we may also raise our awareness of how others are participating in conversations. This, in turn, may offer opportunities to adjust or amend our own contribution in ways that influence the energy and contribution of others.

There are many routes to introducing new habits, and to do this successfully, it is helpful to understand our personal foibles in resisting change. For example, I might believe in my mind that I am willing to try something different, but if my experience of trying new things has caused me pain or distress, I may subtly sabotage my good intentions. To accommodate our frailties as we journey towards change, it is important to begin to acknowledge and articulate our own processes for adopting new approaches. This may be illuminated by Peter Garrett's framework for container development,[3] which is an approach to growing capacity. Garrett's model may be applied to short-span growth or to whole life-cycles. I introduce it here to act as a guide to how you might purposefully use the material in this book.

In the first phase of Garrett's model, you notice that some new possibility, approach, knowledge, concept or skill is catching your attention. You might read about it, hear about it, see a demonstration of it or experience it. Your curiosity is engaged and you start to explore further; perhaps you think about it, or you talk about it, or research it, or write about it, depending on your preferences and style. Garrett calls this process 'realising yourself,' and it tends to be relatively private.

In the second phase, you might start to 'try out' the new material and experiment with it in some way, test your grasp of it or your skill with it. You start, in a small way, to go more public, to take a controlled risk or two. Garrett calls this 'showing up,' where you are beginning to make a statement about taking a new approach.

In the third phase, you effectively 'declare for' the new material and begin to bring it into practice habitually, refining and honing your capability. Others begin to recognise the approach as part of the way you live and/or work. Garrett calls this 'occupying the ground.'

These three phases or 'learning containers' are one way of describing the process of adopting a new practice or habit. There are challenges in moving through the phases, such as the perceived risks associated with using new material and not being sure of the outcome. The process is therefore a gradual one of building capability, capacity and confidence. For example, my own process is to do a lot of reflective thinking about new ideas at first. It can take me quite a long time of mulling things over before I try them out. Then, I will probably hedge my bets a bit by talking through new material with others, perhaps testing out my understanding and their responses. I might then try some 'thought experiments' or try out a new approach in a low-key situation to see what happens, or do some light action research. Eventually, over time and practice, I adopt some things and make them part of how I work or live.

Take a moment and reflect: what is your process for adopting – and putting into practice – new approaches?

Practice development activities appear at the end of each chapter and are offered as an integral part of this book. For readers who want to work steadily through the material over time, these may be helpful in making links between ideas and practice. For others who prefer an uninterrupted read, there may be too many practice activities, or they may seem too detailed. In this case I encourage you to try only those that engage you and to skip the others – you can always return to them later.

The practices are largely experience-based, rather than something to understand intellectually. Doing them will take time. In addition, the longer practices may require a few attempts in order to include all the steps. A useful reference for engaging with these activities may be to recall learning to drive, where a conscious mirror-signal-manoeuvre stage preceded the ability to drive smoothly and automatically.

In the spirit of slow conversations, I invite you to consider reading this book slowly, taking time to work with the practice sessions. For example, over six months or a year, you might consider dedicating a month or two to each part of the book. This will create space to assimilate the material and time to do the practices, providing a foundation to integrate mind, body and spirit as you engage with each chapter.

Take a moment and reflect – how might you balance moving quickly through the ideas in this book with moving more slowly to make sustainable changes in your practice?

The potential benefits of actively working with the practice sessions are:

- raising awareness of your contributions to, and impact in, conversations;
- exploring and trying out alternative ways of engaging in conversations, reflecting on any changes that result;
- expanding the range of contribution that you are able to make to challenging or delicate conversations;
- increasing your capacity to do this in 'bad weather' (adverse conditions); and
- becoming more aware of your 'internal dialogue' and how it affects your interactions with others.

You will gain the most from this book if you are interested in generating richer conversations and are ready to examine your own patterns in conversations and to experiment with them. The aim of cultivating awareness and new practices and habits is to increase versatility in conversations. Versatility gives us choices; when faced with a frustrating conversation, I can choose to let my frustration dominate my contribution or, with practice, I can choose to pause, acknowledge my frustration and create space for more curiosity about the other person's point of view.

I think of these moments as 'sliding doors' moments, after the film of that name. In the film, we see the heroine's life unfold along two different paths, essentially determined by whether or not she manages to pass through the sliding doors of an underground train. The difference between catching or missing the train in the film is accidental, but it offers an effective metaphor for recognising that what happens in a split second can change the outcome of what follows.

As you become familiar with the ideas and practices in this book, see if you can become sensitive to the 'sliding doors' moments in your conversations; the moments where you have a choice as to whether you let any building energy of irritation, frustration or enthusiasm determine what you say next, or whether you pause for breath and find an alternative response.

I conclude this chapter with a note on being your guide. The principal lens through which I see this material is informed by my background as a leader and an executive coach. My language is therefore organisational, and is grounded in leadership, projects, meetings and teams. However, those who have explored this material with me in workshops and practice development groups have found it to be of as much (if not more) value in their non-work lives. This is congruent with my beliefs about leadership, which I see as a much broader concept than being a leader in an organisation. I believe we all have opportunities to demonstrate leadership in many settings – in our families and our communities, as well as at work. Most fundamentally, I believe that cultivating self-leadership is crucial to the impact that we have in the world. My sense of leadership includes an ethical and moral element, a call to stand up for what is right. So when I speak of bringing the practices of mindfulness and dialogue to leadership conversations, I include all settings in which leadership can be displayed, even though my principal focus is in organisations.

Practice *2* – awareness of learning process

Call to mind something that you have recently changed in the way you go about things. It might be a variation in shopping habits, a different golf swing or tennis stroke or a change in the way you relate to someone. It might be that you have taken up something new. It might be that you have stopped doing something that once suited you, and no longer does.

How did it come to your attention that you might try something different? Perhaps something you did had unexpected results and you got curious? Perhaps you needed to respond to a change in circumstances – a loss, a birth, an illness, a change of boss, a new job?

How did you then choose what to cultivate or to change? Did you simply try something new to see what happened? Did you think about it for a while? Did you follow your instincts, your heart, your head? Did you talk things through with friends, family or colleagues? Did you do nothing and see what turned up? Did you make an immediate change or take your time?

How did you judge whether the new approach suited you? If it did, how did you make it habitual? If it didn't suit you, how quickly did you recognise this and what did you do then?

Now reflect on the example(s) you have chosen:
- *Which parts of your process for cultivating something new were largely private and internally focused, involving thinking, feeling, processing ideas?*
- *Which parts involved the outside world of people, environment, books, actions, senses?*

From this reflection, what hypothesis would you put forward for how you learn to do something differently? In light of this, how might you most fruitfully use this book?

Notes and reflections

Chapter 3 Setting the scene for the practice of mindfulness

'Mindfulness is remembering to come back to the present moment.' Thich Nhat Hanh

In embarking on the journey to engage in dialogue, or the 'slow conversations' evoked in the first chapter, we need to develop the capacity to be really clear about what is relevant and important in the context of a conversation, and to edit out any 'noise' in the system. Such noise might be the history of our interactions with the people we are talking to, a related issue that suddenly springs to mind, remembering that we need to buy some lemons on the way home, or myriad other thoughts, emotions or experiences. I'll be developing this theme further, but for now I simply want to float the possibility that unrelated noise in our thoughts and emotions often influences our response to a current conversation. A simple example might be that I snap at a friend because I've just had a run-in with a colleague. My anger and frustration belongs with the colleague, not my friend, but it spills into my conversation with my friend when I am not mindful that it is present. If I had noticed it, I could have edited it out, and engaged with my friend in a way that was more appropriate.

This notion of being alert to what is genuinely relevant to the moment links with my understanding of mindfulness, which is the act of paying attention to circumstances as they actually are, rather than as we'd like them to be, imagine them to be, or fear them to be. Simple though this approach may seem, it is often not our usual practice. Left to chance, human attention tends to alight on something of interest, perhaps something we admire or desire, perhaps something we fear or find distasteful, or perhaps something that reminds us of a potent memory. This hook of interest sets imagination in motion, travelling quickly through time. For example, we may create a mental future of how life will be when we acquire an object of desire, or of what will happen when our worst fear unfolds. Or we may revisit our past, reliving a memory or recalling the last time we witnessed something that evoked similar emotions or thoughts, be they threatening, pleasurable or distasteful. In this imagined world of what has happened or what might happen, we lose contact with the current moment and what is actually taking place right now.

Odd though it may seem, to stay in contact with the present moment, alive to it and curious about it, requires a deliberate act. It requires that I notice that my mind has flitted off to planning the future or reliving the past, and that I then gently bring it back to what is currently happening, what I can see, what I am hearing, what I am feeling and experiencing. As an example, think of a time when you've missed part of what someone said because your mind was elsewhere, or a time when your attention wandered off.

Mindfulness is therefore an intentional choice of attention; in being mindful I choose to remain present to the moment. One definition of mindfulness, offered by my yoga teacher, is:

'Being aware of what is happening, as it is happening, without preference.'

Mindfulness is the practice of noticing what is going on in both our external and

33

internal worlds, and accepting what we notice without the influence of our likes and dislikes. Simply notice and accept. The practice of mindfulness therefore requires us to suspend judgement. This means holding lightly the stories, memories and reactions that our memory drums up to explain what we are experiencing. It means acknowledging that these creations of our mind are not 'real' or 'true.' Paradoxically, words can get in the way of mindfulness because once a human mind has 'named' an experience, labelling it as known, attention tends to move efficiently onto categorising or naming the next thing or experience.

To get a sense of what 'without preference' might mean, the next time you find yourself thinking the weather is too hot, too cold or too rainy, gently pause for breath, park your thoughts and experience hotness, coldness or the wetness of the rain. As an example, I am often out walking in Scotland where it rains a lot. I used to grumble and wish that the weather was otherwise. I'd quite often change my plans and not set out for fear of getting wet and cold. Or I'd cut a walk short. Nowadays when it rains, I put my waterproofs on and pay attention to the rain. I feel the softness and coolness of the drops as they connect with the skin on my cheeks. I notice the tickle of droplets as they run down my nose and perhaps collect in a drip on the end. I taste the rain as it moistens my lips. I hear the drumming rhythms on my hood. I observe my vision becoming impaired as my spectacles mist up and notice how what I can see (or not) changes. I notice my body, still warm within my waterproof, and my fingers tingling in my gloves. I notice how most of me is dry and warm. Sometimes the rain brings an eerie, misty, silent stillness with it. Sometimes it comes on the squalls of a noisy and turbulent wind. Sometimes it brings a damp smell, sometimes a fresh one. Each sense brings different qualities to the moment, a different experience for me as a walker. No rainy day is the same as another. As the rain continues, or not, I pay attention to my experience of the rain, as it is. If I do this, I am more likely to make a mindful choice either to continue to walk on, or to decide, 'not for me, today' without regret.

So how do we develop the quality of intentional attention? One way is to use the process of breathing as a mindfulness practice, intentionally guiding our mind to observe our breath. Why use breath? Part of the answer is that breathing is a continuous process and so is always available as a reference point. It is also useful in the context of conversation because breathing is largely unconscious and automatic, yet it can be brought into consciousness and be modified intentionally. It therefore offers a metaphor for speaking.

We each have many years of practice and experience in both breathing and speaking. We are already 'experts' and may imagine that we have nothing more to learn in either realm. Both processes are automatic and natural and yet, on the whole, we use each in a limited way. With attention and practice, we can extend the range of both our breathing and our talk. A practice for mindfulness of breathing is found at the end of each section of this book.

This short chapter on mindfulness offers only a flavour of a deep and rich area of practice. Internally, mindfulness can be applied to our thinking, our feeling, our physiology, and our energetic presence. Externally, we can bring mindfulness to our interactions with others and to our responses to our circumstances and environment. In bringing mindfulness to our conversations, we can aspire to be more aware and discerning in our exchanges with others.

Practice 3 – a first practice in mindfulness

I invite you to do some gentle research into your habits, and start to notice when you mentally 'check out' and how often in a day it happens.

Notice when you miss part of what someone has said, because your mind is elsewhere. Can you recall what caught your mind's attention so that it followed a stream of thought that took you away from the current moment?

Notice under what circumstances your attention wanders – what sparks it? Boredom? Frustration? A pressing need to focus on your own agenda?

Try this for a day and be curious as to how, when and why you tune out of conversations. And then become curious as to what happens to bring you out of your reverie and back into the current conversation. What patterns do you notice?

In the longer term, repeat this practice from time to time. As you develop your understanding of when you get distracted from the present moment, try to cultivate the habit of noticing this when it happens and then intentionally bring your attention back to the present moment.

Notes and reflections

Chapter 4   Setting the scene for dialogue – advocacy and inquiry

'True words aren't eloquent; eloquent words aren't true.
Wise men don't need to prove their point; men who need to prove
their point aren't wise.' Lao-Tzu, translated by Stephen Mitchell

There are many words for describing conversation, of which debate, discussion and dialogue are probably most frequently used. There are many books and articles that explore different conversational forms in detail and I list some of these at the end of Part One. The roots of my thinking and practice lie in dialogue as described by Senge, Isaacs and others. From these roots, I approach conversation through a lens that distinguishes between taking a position (advocacy), and being open to possibility (inquiry).

One thinker in the field, Chris Argyris, offers clear definitions of advocacy and inquiry:

- *Advocacy* is speaking what you think, speaking for a point of view; and
- *Inquiry* is looking into what you do not yet know, what you do not yet understand

To expand these descriptions, advocacy is associated with speaking your truth, with offering your opinion, with taking a stance. It tends to move towards closure and certainty in the form of action, answer or decision. It is linked with forming judgements, reaching conclusions, agreeing on tasks. The conversational form of debate is strongly connected to advocacy in that it can be seen as an exchange in which positions are stated and pitted against one another in order to test their robustness. The root of the word debate is 'to beat down,' which evokes an image of hammering out the details to make a robust case for decisions. This clearly has enormous value for many aspects of leadership; for example, in shaping coherent strategy, agreeing rigorously reasoned actions, or justifying investment.

However, advocacy and debate may serve other situations less well. Without care, debate can become a simple trading of positions or point-scoring. A risk with debate is that what starts with intent to beat down an issue can easily slip to beating down a person, confusing their opinion with their identity, raising the stakes of an encounter and discounting the potential value in their position. Skilful advocacy sees a point of view in a wider context and balances the discipline of being purposeful with being open to the perspectives of others.

In contrast, inquiry is associated with seeking to discover what others see and understand, especially when that differs from your own point of view. It means surfacing difference, accepting and probing it, getting inside it and searching for the creative potential of it. An inquiring stance sees another person's world and perspective as legitimate. Inquiry is associated with curiosity, with exploration, with opening out possibility and with broadening perspectives. It involves holding ambiguity, difference and uncertainty and rummaging around in them for fresh connections, for new information or insights.

Inquiry tends to open out a conversation, and therein is a risk. Just as advocacy can become overly focused on prevailing, inquiry can lose focus and so lose relevance to current circumstances and agendas. Skilful inquiry balances the potential of curiosity with awareness of the agreed context and purpose of a conversation.

Both advocacy and inquiry have value and purpose, and Argyris defines dialogue as a conversation that balances advocacy and inquiry. This is the definition of dialogue that I use most often, as it is a practical model with which to get started in raising awareness of styles and shapes of conversations.

In the West, it is widely accepted by writers, researchers and thinkers in the field that our dominant mode of conversation is advocacy. We tend to take positions and see progress as taking decisions and implementing them. Conversations that are advocacy-led are eminently suitable for many situations, such as those where problems are clearly defined and options are few, or where expertise is high and needs to be applied, or where procedures are known and understood. However, in situations where there is significant uncertainty, or the problem is new or not readily described, then a conversation based on positions, with intent to make decisions and move to action, might quickly limit possibilities. Advocacy may also have limitations in situations with multiple stakeholders holding diverse interests and points of view, or where circumstances are changing quickly or unpredictably. An appropriate response to complexity of this kind must include inquiry, so that the impact of diversity, volatility and uncertainty can be embraced. Dialogue, in balancing advocacy and inquiry, is the form of conversation most suitable for gaining a shared understanding of complexity.

Dialogue can take place between two people or amongst many, and in a variety of settings, from family systems, to industrial relations, to conversations representing whole systems. My approach is to draw on these theories and practices to help inform and expand everyday leadership conversations, inviting leaders to become more aware of factors that influence internal thinking, feeling and speaking, both in themselves and in others.

As leaders, we can aim to become clearer about our intent in contributing to a conversation, and more alert to reading, and being curious about, the impact of what we say. We can cultivate awareness of how we take in sensory information and how our body, mind, emotions and energy respond to our experiences. We can notice any tendency to advocate; in being more aware, we may be able to hold even our most fervent opinions lightly, making room in our hearts and minds for difference and for contrasting or conflicting perspectives. A real challenge in doing this, is that it then takes time to explore and navigate these differences, and we may feel that we don't have time to do this. However, for important conversations, failing to take this time up-front may result in using even more time (and energy) to resolve later misunderstandings.

In acknowledging that it can be deeply challenging to set aside the demands of performance and 'efficiency' to create time and space for mindful conversations, it may be helpful to reframe the relationship between talk and action. In *The World Café*,[4] Juanita Brown and others describe the traditional view of talk in organisations as having only one purpose, which is to lead linearly, and efficiently, to action. This is essentially an advocatory view of talk. An alternative paradigm offers the opportunity to balance advocacy and inquiry, proposing that conversation is a core process, weaving through everything we do in organisations. Rather than focusing on action, this approach sees talk as central to:

- exploring issues;
- sharing perspectives;
- harvesting discoveries and insights;
- formulating options, strategies and approaches;
- planning for action and putting plans into action;
- assessing impact; and
- reflection, review and re-working our approach.

In this frame of reference, conversation is seen as a complex adaptive process that is integral to formulating and implementing sustainable responses to key

41

leadership responsibilities. This perspective invites a fundamental shift in how we see the role of talk in organisations. It will be challenging to commit to, and enable, this paradigm in results-oriented, time-poor cultures. However, understanding and acknowledging the strength and impact of the existing paradigm may enable you to build capacity to hold to a different approach in the face of sceptics and detractors.

In seeking to bring a new tone to leadership conversations and to balance advocacy and inquiry, the leadership challenge is to become more mindful in our conversations. This means fostering the capacity to listen deeply and to speak our truth in a way that acknowledges that others will see or experience things differently. Dialogue is a 'roomy' conversation, with space enough to breathe, to think, to be silent, to respect difference, and to select words that convey your intent as well as you are able, in that moment, in those circumstances. In bringing the practices of mindfulness and dialogue to leadership conversations, we bring an intent to be open, exploratory, alive and present. This kind of conversation is not a conversation in a hurry; it evolves as a sense of connectedness is cultivated between the people involved.

Practice 4 – awareness of advocacy and inquiry

Chris Argyris offers the following definitions:

Advocacy *– speaking what you think, speaking for a point of view.*

Inquiry *– looking into what you do not yet know or understand, seeking to discover what others see, and understanding that it may differ from your point of view.*

In your conversations over the next few days, begin to notice how much you advocate and how much you inquire.

Notice where, when, and under what circumstances you advocate and with whom? Notice where, when, and under what circumstances you inquire and with whom? What are the patterns? Do you tend to advocate in one setting and inquire in another?

Observe some of the conversations around you. What is the balance between advocacy and inquiry? What is the nature of most conversations?

When you are next in a conversation that is principally advocatory in nature, experiment with making a contribution that is inquiry-based. What happens?

When you are next in a conversation that is principally inquiring in nature, experiment with making a contribution that is advocacy-based. What happens?

What are you noticing about advocacy and inquiry?

Notes and reflections

44

Chapter 5 Why become aware of our conversational habits?

'Your pain is the breaking of the shell that encloses your understanding. Even as the stone of the fruit must break, that it's heart may stand in the sun, so you must know pain.' Kahlil Gibran

Before setting out on a journey to become more aware of the way in which we inhabit conversations, you might ask, 'why bother?' In response, I offer a framework adapted from work developed by Otto Scharmer, William Isaacs and Peter Garrett, which can give a sense of how we might get caught, and held, by energy patterns in conversations. The framework provides reference points for experiences in conversations, describing a sense of dynamics that may be present.

Scharmer describes four fields of conversation,[5] which represent different kinds of conversational energy. I imagine the fields as conversational currents or tides, a rhythm or pulse of waves, shallows, depths and hidden undercurrents. They describe the nature of a conversational 'sea' that we may find ourselves immersed in. The fields are bounded by two axes, a vertical that distinguishes between reflective thinking and non-reflective thinking, and a horizontal that distinguishes between attention on the collective (or whole system) and attention on the individual (or parts of a system). I prefer to reference the vertical axis on mindfulness and habits of thought and action. The axes delineate four energy fields:[6]

Fields of Conversation

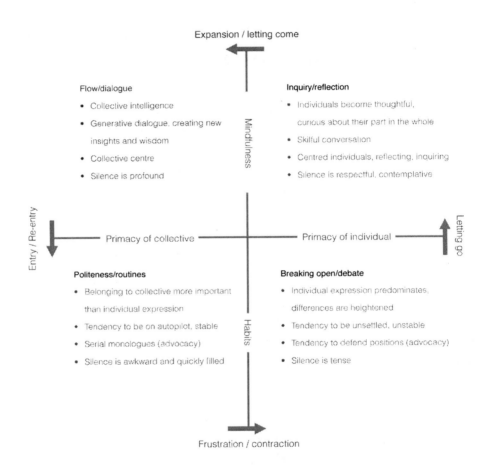

Adapted from C Otto Scharmer et al

The diagram describes some of the characteristics of each energy field and also indicates a potential for movement between one field and another. It provides some navigation points with which to read conversational territory in terms of energy, dynamics and the quality of exchanges between people. Using a map of conversational energies offers potential for understanding the tenor of a conversation in the moment, whilst also giving a context within which to choose how we might contribute. We can choose to support the existing energy or to seek to influence a conversation to move towards another phase. As you read the descriptions set out below, bear in mind that movement from one conversational field to another is not necessarily smooth and linear: a conversation may bobble between one kind of energy and another.

Politeness/routines

The field in the bottom left hand quadrant is bounded by primacy of collective and habits of thought and action, and has the label 'politeness.' This field holds a conversational form that is familiar, governed primarily by social and conversational norms. The routines of conversation in this field hold in place, and confirm, these norms. This is a field of habit, of predictable exchanges. If you are familiar with the patterns and conventions of a conversation, this field can feel comfortable, and participants can tend towards operating on autopilot. Sometimes a conversation in this field doesn't join up: it's a series of monologues in which each person states their position and withdraws.

Conversations with this energy preserve social niceties, and they are suitable for many purposes. There is some safety and protection in established customs for dealing with issues, which support stable and known conversational patterns.

However, there is a risk that a conversation remains in this comfortable energy, even when this form no longer serves a collective purpose. Many leaders recognise this experience in regular meetings within their organisations; a meeting gets into a groove and it may be difficult to speak out. Have you ever felt stifled, masked, frustrated, or unheard in a conversation that feels as if it is going through the motions in circumstances where more depth and authenticity is warranted?

The energies that hold conversations in established routines are powerful, and are not always constructive. In one leadership team I worked with, part of their unspoken intent was to minimise the length of time of a meeting and to minimise the risk of interference in their patch. There was little collective intent, and meetings did not often serve a useful purpose. In using this model to raise awareness of a pattern, the team had to choose whether to change the pattern or to knowingly continue in a routine that they described as 'a waste of time.'

Breaking open/debate

The second field, described by the bottom right hand quadrant, is bounded by primacy of individuals and habits of thought and action. Scharmer named this field 'breakdown,' but I prefer to call it 'breaking open' to reflect the creative possibilities in being liberated from the need to fit in with social norms. In this field, individual expression replaces the urge to belong, and habits of thought and speech continue to govern contributions to a conversation.

The energy for this field develops as individuals experience the field of politeness/ routines as increasingly unsatisfactory for addressing a presenting issue. Some people start to sense their stifled voice pressing to speak, perhaps fuelled by rising irritation or frustration. They may become increasingly focused on what is going unsaid, or unheard. If this pressure in an individual comes to matter more than social cohesion, it will be voiced, confronting unspoken, and perhaps unpalatable, perspectives. If a confronting voice is joined by others in the same spirit, differences are likely to surface and the energy of a conversation may increase rapidly. Led by individual voices, the conversational energy is breaking open.

In this second field, advocacy predominates and inquiry may be in short supply, or may be discounted or ignored. It is a field of high energy and challenge and, with skill and presence, it can be highly productive. Without skill and presence, the experience in this quadrant is often one of tension and awkwardness. Conflicting perspectives and dissent are out in the open, with people increasingly likely to steamroll, or defend their positions, as the protection of accepted norms dissipates.

48

The dissolution of norms can feel deeply uncomfortable, and some of those present may move quickly to try and reinstate them, minimising dissonance and attempting to recreate the apparent harmony of the field of politeness/routines. In the field of breaking open/debate, egos may emerge, buttons may be pushed and frustrations may flare into irritability or anger.

However, if those present can sit with the discomfort of this heightened energy, the potential of this field is that mindfulness replaces habits of thought and actions and so contributions become thoughtful and reflective. Cultivating the capacity to be present in sometimes dissonant conversations, and to hold the energy of difference impartially, is crucial in developing potential for dialogue. Developing the capacity to be present in unpredictable settings requires that we understand, and are able to work with, our mental, physical, emotional and energetic reactions to confrontation, pressure and stress. This perspective is at the heart of my approach to dialogue practice.

Inquiry/reflection

The third field, in the quadrant bounded by primacy of individuals and mindfulness, is named 'inquiry' or 'reflection.' Individuals are more aware of their habits of thinking, speaking and acting, and are reflective about the impact of these. In being mindful, they respond to the present moment, without preference.

After the relative turbulence of the energy of breaking open/debate, the energy of inquiry/reflection may initially feel like calm water; peaceful and still. This conversation is characterised by attending, both internally and externally. This means listening profoundly and paying careful attention to both internal and external experiences, seeking to understand what is taking place. As more of those present come to this kind of presence, a conversation slows down, there are longer silences, there are more exploratory questions, more reflection, and there is a palpable sense of people mentally chewing over what is being said. Whilst intent in this field may be more reflective, individual interests still dominate and so there may be a sense of serial inquiry, a seeking to meet personal needs rather than to serve the collective interest. Don't imagine, however, that this field is low in energy. It can have intensity, a calmness and stillness charged with the importance of the topic and the vitality of curiosity and genuine thinking. In this field, synapses are firing and engagement is high.

To reach this quality of energy, a kind of amnesty is required: a laying down of opinions and defences, with a surrender to the possibility of being open to the truth of others. In this field, people begin to listen more carefully, to accept, include, and be influenced by, the views of others. Our sense of the conversation, the possibilities and ourselves, expands. This is the beginning of the 'roominess' that I described earlier. In laying down the weapons of our opinions, we let go of the idea that our opinions are synonymous with our identity, and so remove internal limits on the range and scope of information that we are open to receiving.

Flow/dialogue
The fourth field is the quadrant bounded by primacy of collective and mindfulness. Relationship and a sense of inclusion are central. A sense of collective intelligence develops as the practice of mindfulness enables habits of individual thinking to dissolve. In this field, insight and wisdom emerges that is not possible from a solo perspective.

The conversation in this field can feel intimate, which can be uncomfortable or incredibly natural, depending on circumstances, the relationships, and the way the conversation has evolved. The conversation can feel quite fragile, or perhaps delicate, or tenuous. None of these words are quite right; perhaps spellbound is a better word. When I'm in a conversation that has this quality, I feel it is precious and full of meaning. I feel I mustn't make a sudden movement, or say anything careless in case the spell is broken. I am a beginning-practitioner in this space and so it still seems somehow magical. There is a collective sense of being part of something, without fully understanding that experience. Bohm describes this kind of dialogue as an entity in itself, a conversation that is unfolding through the people present. Individual voices and positions seem to have no meaning in this

50

field. It is as if those gathered are one organism, pooling their wisdom, and creating the conditions for entirely new thinking to arise.

In summary

In being aware of these four conversational fields, we can begin to discern whether a conversation in which we are engaged is energetically fit-for-purpose. In politeness/routines, we are unlikely to liberate new thinking, a factor that may provide the impetus for developing our capacity for the practices of mindfulness and dialogue. If we intend to nudge a conversation from its comfort zone, we must cultivate our capacity for holding, and working within, the heightened energy that follows. In my view, doing this means increasing our awareness of our habits of mind, body and spirit, so that we become more aware of our energetic impact.

An individual may experience a different energetic state in each of the four fields. In the first field, there is a tendency to operate on autopilot; thinking, speaking and acting in familiar, habitual ways. In the second there is a tendency to defend or attack positions, as those present react to difference and uncertainty in the pattern of conversation; and in the third field individuals let go of their position and develop a sense of vital and alert ease. Later I will call this state of vital and alert ease 'centre' or being present. It is a mindful state in which we can be comfortable with our own fallibility and can be open to the views of others. In the fourth field, the notion of individual is less relevant, as the sense of collective becomes a powerful experience. In cultivating awareness of our habits of thinking and physiology, we are able to be mindful of their impact and so will be able to change our energetic presence as we engage in conversation, thus influencing those around us.

Practice 5 – awareness of energy fields in conversation

For this practice, use a regular meeting you participate in, and pay attention to the dynamics and energy. Which of the four fields seems to best describe the qualities of the conversation? You might attend to this on a few occasions. What patterns emerge?

Pay attention more generally to conversations, and get a sense of the kind of energy that predominates. What metaphors might you use to describe different kinds of energy? Find your own descriptors so that you can more quickly identify particular experiences as they occur.

If you think you might be participating in a conversation in which accepted norms and habits are challenged and begin to change, notice what happens. Who expresses irritation or frustration first? How is it received? What is your internal response when this happens? What happens next in the conversation?

Notes and reflections

Chapter 6 Pause for breath

'The pauses in our life make our experiences
full and meaningful.' Tara Brach

In these chapters, I have raised the possibility of different kinds of conversations, exploring the potential impact of slower, roomier exchanges. To expand our repertoire and increase our versatility in conversations, we need to become more aware of how we think, speak and act, so that we can make choices about whether our current habits serve us. In doing this, it may help to have a sense of what might be possible, and models can assist us to imagine where we might refine our strengths and to begin to articulate those things that might not yet be part of our practice.

Models can suggest things that might be missing. They can help us to explain our experiences, which may make it easier to replicate them or change them, and may also enable us to articulate them and share them with others. But models are just models – they may help us think and understand, but they are no substitute for trying things in practice. This explains my focus on practice; trying out words and approaches in real situations, particularly when we are under pressure, is often challenging and always revealing. Trying something out helps us to find our own understanding of it, makes a concept real and begins to translate the unfamiliar language of a model into known experience.

To do something unfamiliar requires concentration and effort. To do something familiar under pressure also requires our full attention. To bring full engagement to a moment, a word, a response, it is helpful to pause and gather our resources and resilience. To this end, I invite you on a journey towards expanding your repertoire in conversations (adding the unfamiliar), and towards handling familiar conversations more skilfully in charged circumstances, simply by beginning to practice pausing.

To begin, I invite you to notice and enjoy the 'between' moments. The moment between hearing someone speak and responding; the moment between the phone ringing and picking it up; the moment between getting into the car and starting the engine; and the moment between an inhale and an exhale. In these moments, can you simply pause for breath and collect yourself, rather than rushing straight onto the next thing?

Practice 6 – pause for breath

This foundation practice appears at the end of each section of the book.

Sit in a comfortable upright posture, so that your feet are firmly planted on the floor and you are supporting your own back, rather than leaning against a chair. Rest your hands on your thighs, palms down.

Become aware of the contact between your feet/shoes and the floor. Become aware of the contact between your hands and your thighs. Become aware of the contact between your thighs and the chair. Become aware of the sitting bones, the bones at the base of the pelvis, pressing into the seat.

Notice your strong base, formed by your feet and sitting bones, and allow your spine to grow to its full length by gently imagining each vertebra lifting slightly from the one below. Sense lightness and spaciousness in your spine. Notice that your neck becomes long at the back, your chin tilted slightly towards your chest.

Now bring your attention to your breath. On each inhale, imagine your breath seeping into the spaces in your spine, allowing it to lengthen just a little bit more. On each exhale, imagine your breath flowing down through your chest and belly, softening any tension. Follow your breath for a few moments.

Now mentally scan your body and notice any places of tension, aching or discomfort. Choose one and, for a few breaths, imagine your inbreath soaking into this place and, on a longer exhale, imagine your outbreath dissolving any discomfort and carrying it out into the air around you, letting you rest.

After a few breaths, become aware of the contact between your sitting bones and the chair, between your hands and thighs, and between your feet and the ground.

Rise gently and stretch. You are ready to re-engage with the world.

Resource list for more on different forms of conversation

On Dialogue, David Bohm
Dialogue – a Proposal, Bohm, Factor, Garrett, http://dialogue-associates.com/published/
  dialogue-a-proposal/
Dialogue at Work – Making Talk Developmental for People and Organisations, Nancy Dixon
From Debate to Dialogue – Using the Understanding Process to Transform our Conversations,
  Deborah Flick
Dialogue and the Art of Thinking Together, William Isaacs
Time to Think, Nancy Kline
Theory U, Leading from the Future as it Emerges, C Otto Scharmer
Difficult Conversations, Stone, Patton, Heen
A Simpler Way, Margaret Wheatley, Myron Kellner-Rogers

Other sources of related work:
The World Café, Juanita Brown, David Isaacs et al
Synchronicity and the Inner Path of Leadership, Joseph Jaworski
Appreciative Inquiry for Change Management, Lewis, Passmore, Cantore
The Fifth Discipline, Peter Senge
The Fifth Discipline Fieldbook, Peter Senge et al
The Dance of Change, Peter Senge et al

Part Two

MIND AND CONVERSATION

Chapter 7   Introduction

Chapter 8   First person inquiry with kindness and fascination

Chapter 9   A simple frame for conversational exchanges

Chapter 10   Taking a look inside the black box

Chapter 11   A structured framework for the black box

Chapter 12   Internal dialogue – why mind and conversation matters

Chapter 13   External dialogue – why mind and conversation matters

Chapter 14   Pause for breath

Resource list for inquiry into processes of the mind

Chapter 7 Introduction

'Thinking is speech in mind.'
Thich Nhat Hanh

What is the relationship between our experiences, what goes on in our minds and how we talk? How aware are we of our thinking and what we're embellishing or editing out? What part do emotions play in what we attend to or discount?

We now explore how we might begin to raise awareness of what is happening within the complex system that is 'me.' With awareness comes the opportunity to bring deliberate attention to our experience, to the ways in which we recognise and make sense of it, and to the influence this has on how we express ourselves. With deliberate attention comes the opportunity to pause and make a choice: if I notice what I am embellishing, I can choose to reflect my experience more directly; if I notice what I am editing out, I can choose to include what I tend to ignore or avoid.

As we grow in awareness of what happens within ourselves, we may also find that we become more curious about how others perceive, and make sense of, the world. We may become more mindful of different ways of experiencing, thinking and feeling and as this happens, it's hard to believe that our future conversations will be unchanged.

First, I will clarify my stance on the links between mind, body and spirit. Although mind, body and spirit appear as separate in the way I have organised this book, I regard them as fundamentally connected. They are different facets of the energetic entity that is 'me.' This reflects Eastern philosophies. For example, in Tibetan Buddhism, mind and heart include one another. In a Western paradigm, I might say that the best decisions and actions are those that are congruent with both logic (mind) and values (heart).

My approach to exploring the relationship between experience, attention, mind and talk is to invite you to engage in empirical first person inquiry – by this I mean an experience-based curiosity about, and a gentle objective examination of, self. Self is a good starting point for influencing conversations, because it is the realm in which we have most sway, and so is where the most far-reaching difference can be made.

In inviting you to enter into this kind of inner scrutiny, I emphasise that the aim is to learn about yourself and how you participate in conversations. It's a process of discovery, potential and wonder (a stance of skilful inquiry), not a process of labelling whatever you find as 'right' or 'wrong' (a stance of unskilful advocacy). I invite you to notice what you find and reflect on the consequences of your current styles of thinking, feeling, listening and talking, so that you can use them with poise and skill where appropriate.

Practice 7 – awareness of thinking

Reflect for a moment on a recent conversation with one other person.

As you listened and responded, how much of your thinking and reaction did you share with them? What did you edit out? What did you embellish? What were your reasons for editing or embellishing? What judgements and assumptions did you make about how the other person would receive what you said?

Now reflect more generally – what is your most usual approach to sharing your thinking and reactions? Are you inclined to edit a lot? Embellish a lot? What are your assumptions and beliefs about what you have to contribute and how it will be received?

Notes and reflections

Chapter 8   First person inquiry with kindness and fascination

'Grant me serenity to accept the things I cannot change, courage to change the things I can change, and wisdom to know the difference.' St Augustine

The aim of first person inquiry is to look at ourselves as we are, and as far as we're able, 'without preference.' This means seeing clearly and impartially our tendencies, such as our likes and dislikes, the ways we build ourselves up or knock ourselves down, or our propensity to attack or defend. I invite you to become intensely curious about how you perceive your world and about the impact that this has on your conversations.

In a spirit of discovery and learning, I encourage you to approach first person inquiry with kindness and fascination. I suggest fascination because bringing a sense of wonder to the scrutiny of our unique ways of going about our lives generates a rich and endless source of study, full of possibilities for growth. I suggest kindness because the chances are that you will stumble on attitudes and behaviours in your current habits that don't immediately impress or inspire you. When I unearth these idiosyncrasies in my own listening, thinking and talking styles, I find that they are often habits that I have developed to serve me well in previous situations. Without thinking, I've called them up again, perhaps inappropriately. For example, when I worked in dealing rooms I used acerbic humour as a defence in a fairly brutal environment. I no longer need this strategy, but if I am socially uncomfortable it can leak out. Paradoxically, this is an unskilful attempt to make a connection. If I reflect on my behaviour with kindness and fascination, I can understand what prompted it and so seek to be more skilful another time.

Another reason for bringing kindness to first person inquiry is that what is done is done: wishing it were different changes nothing. This reflects an important aspect of mindfulness; seeing things as they are and being clear about where it is helpful to direct attention and energy, and where it is fruitless or even unhelpful. I learned this lesson in a powerful way in one of my first engagements as a trainer. I had been invited to design and deliver four half-day workshops to a cohort of twelve clinical directors. I was nervous and excited about the assignment. I designed the programme with care, and felt quite pleased with the way the first session went. However, when the feedback sheets were returned, one of the doctors had found fault with almost everything I'd done and listed many things that, in his judgement, I had failed to do. His final comment was just one word: appalling.

As a rookie trainer, I was shaken. In those days, my habit, when criticised, was to beat myself up and to analyse what I should have done. I had been less than perfect and therefore I needed to correct something. Ashamed of my failure, I would search relentlessly for that something, investing energy in self-recrimination. On this occasion, I was lucky to get support from the person who commissioned the training. She supplied kindness and helped me to pay attention to the positive and supportive feedback from eleven of the doctors, setting the comment of 'appalling' in perspective. Less attached to the awful feelings of failure, I was able to review the day for the things I might improve for the next session, without fruitlessly rehashing what I could have done differently this session.

Bringing kindness to self-reflection minimises the risk of beating ourselves up for our errors and immeasurable failings. If we berate ourselves, it can colour what happens next. If I had been harsh on myself in light of the comment of 'appalling,' I might have withdrawn from future sessions or tried too hard in delivering them, overcompensating for my perceived flaws. On the basis of distorted perception and self-criticism, I could have jeopardised possibilities for positive future experiences.

I know, from both coaching clients and friends, that I'm not alone in this tendency to 'lock on' to criticism and to discount affirmation. When we 'lock on' we reduce our capacity to think clearly, narrowing and distorting our perception of an event or circumstance. When we're kind to ourselves, we are able to hold lightly the things that others see as our failings. This allows a more generous consideration of our circumstances, widening our sense of what might be possible and increasing the prospect that we will make good choices in what we say or do next.

The purpose of first person inquiry is to bring more of 'self' into awareness, distinguishing actual experience from embellishment or editing. It's about seeing, hearing and experiencing self with gentle lucidity, seeking to build on current capabilities and awareness, adding to what is possible. It's a process of expansion, rather than correction, aiming to increase our options and versatility in conversations. In cultivating a broader repertoire, we may use current habits less often, but this doesn't mean that they are without value or utility.

Practice 8 – reflecting with kindness and fascination

This practice session builds on the practice for awareness of advocacy and inquiry in Part One (Practice 3). Reflect on your responses from that session.

On balance, do you tend to use advocacy or inquiry? What is your default:

- *making statements or suggestions, sharing your opinions, offering advice?*
- *listening, curiosity, probing, wonder and discovery?*

Whichever tendency is habitual, reflect on the benefits it brings to you and those around you. Aim to identify at least five benefits.

When you have five benefits, think of one example where your favoured habit (of either advocacy or inquiry) didn't serve you well. What was your aim or purpose in using your favoured approach? What was the result?

Now imagine that the same situation arises again tomorrow – keep the same aim, and speculate about how you might use the alternative approach. How might the result be different? What can you learn from this example that will give you more options if you meet a similar situation again?

Notes and reflections

Chapter 9 A simple frame for conversational exchanges

'I've learned that people will forget what you said, people will forget what you did, but they will never forget how you made them feel.' Maya Angelou

This chapter outlines a deceptively simple frame for our exchanges with others that can help us to notice what is unknown in a conversation. In *Difficult Conversations,*[7] the authors distinguish between the intent of words (or actions) and the impact of them on a recipient. To explore this distinction, think of a time when you made a comment, or asked a question, and were completely surprised by the response you got: something seemed to have been lost in translation. As you read the next few paragraphs, recall other incidences where you have experienced a mismatch between what you said and the reaction or response you got.

Consider a short exchange between two people. One speaks, ('the speaker') whilst the other listens, receives and responds ('the recipient'). This framework considers what the speaker knows through direct experience and what they are piecing together from the response they get.

We only know half the story

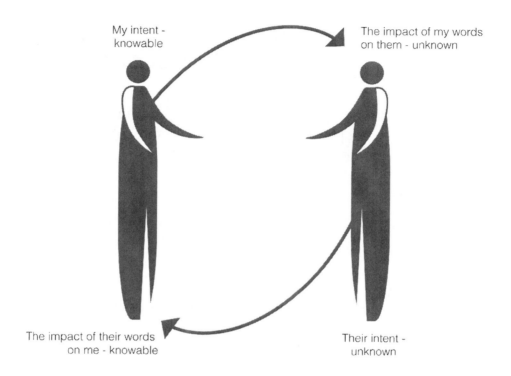

The speaker will have an intent in speaking. Their intent may be clear or confused and may or may not be in immediate awareness, but if asked, 'what was your intent?' a speaker is usually able to access or construct this intent. The way their words are received and the impact of them on the recipient is largely unknown to the speaker as a direct experience.

For example, a speaker may intend to offer a helpful suggestion, but a recipient may experience this as interfering or irrelevant. Similarly, a speaker may intend to seek clarification of an issue through a question, but a recipient may experience it as a challenge or obstruction.

70

The recipient takes in what has been said and makes a response. Sometimes that response is frank, but it can be masked by convention or circumstance. For example, when I am asked to change a coaching appointment at short notice, I will usually reply with a professional, 'of course.' However, the impact of the request can be extensive in terms of rearranging my diary and travel. There may also be a financial hit, such as a delay in cashflow, unless I charge for cancellation, which might be detrimental for the relationship. The impact of the request and the mental juggling that I do to assess what is reasonable is unknown to my client. They hear only my light, 'of course, when would suit you?' What is an equivalent experience in your world?

To return to the diagram: the recipient replies. The original speaker largely infers the recipient's intent, based on how they experience the impact of the response. However, impact is not always straightforward, as the recipient's words may trigger mental, emotional and physical memory banks, which then colour the current experience. For example, if a coaching client is in the habit of changing an appointment at short notice, I am likely to be irritated by yet another disruption and this may influence my response. I will remain professional, but I may be less flexible in what I offer as alternatives. This, in turn, will have an impact on them.

Distinguishing between intent and impact can help us see that we only ever have direct access to half a conversation. Unless we ask, we tend not to know our impact on others and we mostly assume that we know their intent from our interpretation of their words.

What's happening is that, as human beings, we undertake an enormous amount of rapid internal processing as we take in what someone is saying (and not saying). Both intent and impact are more complex than they first appear, each coloured by a lifetime of character and experience. I think of our internal processing as a 'black box' busily storing data exchanges. A very real challenge is that we're not only

71

unaware of what's happening in the black boxes of others, we're also largely unaware of what's going on in our own. Given this reality, every conversation is a potential recipe for comedy or drama as meanings diverge.

It's easy to understand how conversations wander from original intent, as we guess what another person means from their words, tone and facial expressions. Have you ever found yourself in a conversation at complete cross-purposes, only realising later? I find it amazing that we ever manage to communicate at all, and yet most of the time we do, with sufficient connection and skill that we understand and are understood.

The occasions when things go awry provide impetus for inquiry. In recent years, much has been discovered about what goes on in the black box of a human mind, both in terms of the pure science of neurons, synapses, chemicals and other physiological aspects of our brains, and in terms of behavioural and sociological narratives such as emotional intelligence; how we learn, how we make meaning and how we think. These narratives give rise to models and frameworks to explain how we speak and act, which, whilst not being scientific, can bring our attention to things that are so familiar we often overlook them.

Practice *9* – fieldwork to explore intent and impact

Next time you are in a meeting, listen for occasions when you don't fully understand what someone has said. Also listen for times when you think people may be talking at cross-purposes. Try asking, 'can I check my understanding of what you said?' or, 'what is your intent/motivation/ purpose in saying…?'

What happens?

Try a similar approach if you witness a response that puzzles you or seems disproportionate to what has been said.

What happens?

Next time someone says something that frustrates or irritates you (adverse impact), consider what question you might ask to understand or clarify their intent.

What happens?

Try a few different phrases to get more information whenever you are provoked, and see if you can find a stock phrase that helps you get beyond the immediate impact of irritation/frustration.

Notes and reflections

74

Chapter *10* Taking a look inside the black box

'A man hears what he wants to hear and disregards the rest.' Simon and Garfunkel

In the last chapter, I used the idea of a black box to account for what happens, often usefully and in an instant, as we take in a situation and react or respond to it with actions or words. To explore the workings of the black box, we'll consider inputs, processing and outputs or, in human terms:

- What we hear or receive, including how we take in information;
- How we process and begin to formulate responses; and
- How we express those responses, in speech/silence or gesture/stillness.

To gain a working understanding of the complexity of these receiving, processing and responding routines, we'll scrutinise them frame-by-frame, as if in slow motion.

Receiving – senses and attention – what are we taking in?
In each and every moment of our lives, we are faced with more sensory information than we have time to notice, process and make some meaning of. If we think of our bodies as futuristic sensory satellite dishes, in any instant there is a plethora of visual, audio and tactile experience available, not to mention tastes,

smells and other signals such as energy. In the business of living we simply can't take it all in and, in any case, we don't need to. We take in a proportion of what we experience, and bring into consciousness only part of that. In some way, we are selecting what we pay attention to, sometimes from choice or preference (conscious or unconscious) and sometimes because, over our years of evolution, we have become programmed to focus more on some things than others, simply as a matter of survival. For instance, we notice loud noises, sudden movements or things out of place because these represent possible danger and put us on alert.

If we consider an everyday experience of a moment, perhaps this moment, as you read, we can ask what we're paying attention to. We might also ask what we're skipping over. Had you noticed before I asked? Are you aware of any sensations, such as contact between your leg and your chair or a breath of air on your face? Any tastes or smells? In briefly checking your current experience and sensory intake, you become more alive to the moment.

An aspect of sensory awareness is that we favour some senses over others. To explore this, call to mind a recent time of pleasure and happiness. What form does your remembering take? Is it visual? Visceral? Do you hear again sounds or words? Are there any scents or tastes associated with the memory? Which senses are sharpest and in what order do you recall them?

This activity draws your attention to how you tend to take in and store sensory information and how you access it to 'recreate' the past. In becoming aware of what you notice, you can begin to frame a working hypothesis about how you tend to favour information that is available to some senses, whilst tending to filter out that which is available to others.

Sensory filters are only one aspect of the ways in which we select or edit the information available to us. Our attention and energy and our level of engagement and interest in a topic provide another sifting process. There are subjects that attract our enthusiasm, which we will tend to take account of, and remember. There are subjects that we wish to actively avoid, that we fear or hate and, paradoxically, we will tend to pay more attention than we wish to these subjects. And there are subjects that neither engage nor repel us, those that bore us and hold no interest for us. On the whole, we notice little about these subjects, switching off when others talk about them, skipping over articles in newspapers and habitually editing them out as not relevant.

Tony Buzan, creator of mindmapping, is fascinated by how the mind works and by what we attend to and recall. In a workshop he illustrated the impact of the filter of interest using the hundreds of us in his audience. He asked us to write down the names of all the planets in our solar system in order of distance from the sun. He gave the answer and asked those who got at least two correct to raise their hands. Lots of people did. Then he asked those who identified at least three to leave their hands raised, then at least four and so on until the only raised hands belonged to those who remembered them all. Next he asked us to lower our hands if we had a special interest in the solar system or related topic at some stage in life. A large proportion lowered their hands. He then asked those remaining to lower their hands if they hated or actively disliked everything to do with the planets. Nearly all lowered their hands. He drew attention to this and then returned to the large number who had identified either two or three planets correctly, asking them to raise their hands again. When he asked those who had no interest in the planets and solar system to lower their hands, not a single hand remained in the air. Tony Buzan's message is that lack of interest, or apathy, is far more limiting to what we hold in our minds than attraction or aversion. We pay attention to, and store, both things that we find interesting and things that niggle or antagonise us. More generally, we pay attention to, and remember, things that engage our emotions in some way. Why do I remember this five minute activity so well? You might recall that I declared my interest in the solar system at the beginning of the first chapter.

Tony Buzan's demonstration offers compelling motivation for being clearer about what engages us, positively or negatively, and what we tend to overlook. We will tend to include those things that engage us in our deliberations, filtering for them. In doing so we can create a reinforcing loop that makes us even more likely to miss the things that don't engage us. In cultivating our capacity for mindfulness, we become more aware of our habits of attention and are more often able to listen to the people, topics and senses we tend to discount. We are also more able to moderate our preference for what we already know or have a map for.

For example, if you tend to filter for task-related issues and skip over human factors, it is helpful to know this and to compensate for it. Or perhaps you like to cut to the chase and get the details right, switching off during inconclusive conversations about policy or strategy. You may be attracted to change, seeking it out, whilst discounting the value of current systems and practices and those who speak for them. Equally you might be attracted to the status quo and dismiss or edit out signals indicating that change might be needed. These possibilities are neither exhaustive nor right or wrong; they are just examples. If you cultivate an understanding of your habits, you can choose whether to stay in a familiar groove or to listen and respond differently when it will serve you better to do so.

To develop awareness of filters, preferences and other ways in which we tend to discriminate for or against certain information, we can cultivate the habit of first person inquiry. There are also many tools and inventories available to help us understand how we engage with the world and we can use these to supplement the empirical process. These instruments can increase self-awareness and cultivate understanding of difference and diversity. They can provide perspectives of how others see you (feedback you may be blind to), and can act as a mirror in revealing attributes that may be so familiar and automatic that you don't know you have them.

The importance of filters and preference is their impact on what we perceive in our lives and work. We might become curious about the risks associated with, and the consequences of, the things we discount or miss altogether. One of the implications of our known human process for taking in information is that we are always (yes, always: a heavyweight word) consciously perceiving only partial data from all that is available. Whether in awareness (consciously) or out-of-awareness (unconsciously), we only ever (yes, ever) have part of a story. And yet how quickly we believe we are all-knowing, and worse still, right. In recognising the reality of our partial perspective, and taking steps to examine what we tend to take into account and what we tend to ignore, we are sowing the seeds of becoming more aware of our habits and their impact.

Processing – what happens next in the black box?
What do we do with the partial data from our current experience? What happens next in our frame-by-frame approach to understanding our black box? A relevant and accessible narrative of how we process information and the potential consequences of this is outlined in an article from the Harvard Business Review,[8] entitled *'Why Good Leaders Make Bad Decisions.'* The authors explain how recent neuroscience shows that as quickly as we perceive information about a current situation, we are checking it against our store of previous experiences to see whether we can draw on existing patterns of response. Neuroscientists call this pattern recognition. We're effectively checking for a best-fit template that has already served us well. This process is efficient and supports speed of response; the risk is that we force-fit an accessible template that is a poor match for a current scenario.

As we draw down previous experiences, we also connect to any emotional memory that is attached to them. Neuroscientists call this emotional tagging. This part of the process helps us decide whether or not to pay attention to something. Just as the process of re-using templates has upsides and downsides, so does emotional tagging – we might be over-confident of success in a current situation because our best-fit template brings with it an adrenalin rush of

79

previous achievement. Similarly, we may be deterred from speaking or acting by imagined fear linked to a best-fit template associated with a previous failure.

I witnessed an example of this when I was out walking with a friend in the Scottish highlands. We were heading for a remote and beautiful waterfall. About half a mile from the falls, we became aware that an all-terrain buggy was meandering about behind us with two men in it. It was deer-stalking season and likely that the men were estate managers, but it was slightly disconcerting. In an attempt to lighten the situation I said, 'it gives a whole new meaning to stalking!' My friend turned, clearly distressed, and said, 'that's it, I'm going back' and she started to head back down the path. I caught up with her and tried to reason with her – the men had gone past, we were so close to our destination, there was no danger. But she was overwhelmed with fear, because she had been attacked on a hill in her youth. Her template was so powerful that it was her reality, even though there was no current danger to us. I reluctantly followed her back down the hill, accepting that I would not change her mind and should not let her return alone.

It's clear how the innate processes of pattern recognition and emotional tagging serve us, and equally clear that they can distort our perception and nudge us in inappropriate directions. The latter tends to happen when current circumstances are different in a critical way from a previous template, or when we displace emotion from a memory into the present. We cannot stop these processes, and would not want to. What we can do is pause for breath, raise our awareness of them and, in important situations and conversations, take steps to identify the links we're making with stored events and experiences so that we can be more discerning about whether they are relevant, appropriate or helpful in the current scenario.

In our rapid search for a best-fit template, the factors that influence available templates will be many and varied, from family values, cultural beliefs, practical experiences, schooling and training, to travel, reading, hobbies and interests and, perhaps, genetic make-up. We've each been storing these templates all our lives and some are more often-used and more easily accessible than others. A marketing consultant, Ross Smith,[9] introduced me to the idea that we have a 'mindshelf,' an easy-access area of memory in which a range of handy images, ideas and solutions are readily available. He aims to place his brands on people's mindshelves so that a generic reference sparks recollection of a particular brand. For instance, a reference to 'luxury car' might bring a particular model into your mind, as an image, as a brand name, or as a memory of an occasion that you were in such a car. This is the brand on your mindshelf for luxury car. If you had no immediate response and spent a few moments ranging through a few brands, this suggests you don't have a luxury car brand on your mindshelf. What does this indicate about your interest in luxury cars?

I am curious about the notion of mindshelf in our responses to everyday events. Some experiences, beliefs, attitudes and patterns of speech and action are more readily, and immediately, available. Imagine a mindshelf as an open kitchen shelf that holds jars of staple ingredients, or as a shelf in a workshop where tools are laid out. Our mindshelf for templates holds our staple responses or our most-used tools for speedy access. If we can begin to identify our personal mindshelf templates, we will better understand the lenses through which we habitually see the world, and will be more able to consider whether they are serving or hindering us. For example, a certain washing-up liquid sits on my mindshelf, associated with a laughing baby figure. However, I actively choose to ignore this prompt and buy a detergent with an ecological pedigree.

How might these constructs of pattern recognition, emotional tagging and mindshelf shape our conversational style? What is the impact of these internal processes on our hearing, our thinking and feeling, and then on our speaking? How do the workings of our black box influence advocacy and inquiry? It is my view that each of these constructs represents a form of inner advocacy; they are each inner statements of position, speaking for a point of view from the past. I am reminded of television chefs pulling a finished dish from the oven saying, 'here's one I prepared earlier.' Each template, emotional tag and mindshelf belief or filter is prepared earlier: a response or solution cooked in the past, offering a ready-made answer for the present.

The potential downside of this inner advocacy is that it runs the risk of excluding alternative perspectives and responses. With mindshelf templates you get more of the same. Accepting a point of view with no questions asked denies the benefits of inquiry. In challenging circumstances, even an expansive mindshelf belief such as, 'it'll all work out' has limitations. It may bolster confidence and courage, but may lead to glossing over, or over-riding, an evaluation of any downsides. Other mindshelf filters may result in premature closing down of possibilities and options. Examples are beliefs such as, 'no-one else will do it properly;' 'we tried it before and it didn't work;' or, 'it's not worth challenging the boss, because she never listens.' If, as a coach, I challenge these kinds of beliefs when they are spoken, the response is often self-justifying, such as, 'I'm only seeing things as they are,' or, 'I'm only being realistic.' It's a tricky balance of judgement – sometimes beliefs such as these are appropriate and do predicate results. Yet sometimes they are distortions; if they can be reframed, different outcomes are possible. What internal 'realistic statements of fact' do you routinely take off your mindshelf and use to limit what you do and say?

A further risk of best-fit templates is that they often introduce assumptions into our thinking. In particular, we may introduce an assumption that 'now' is the same as 'then.' If such assumptions are not made explicit, they may result in fundamental flaws in assessing a situation. In addition, the convenient presence of the template can make us lazy: we can avoid looking more deeply into a situation. Using a template for navigation may mean that a leader can avoid saying, 'I don't know.' Leaders are expected to have answers – to know – but not-knowing may open a gate to inquiry which may, in turn, lead to a more rich and robust framing of a presenting issue.

If the narrative of pattern recognition is a good-fit model for the way our minds habitually operate, then much more of our thinking than we're aware of is advocatory in stance. If we aspire to introducing the practices of dialogue into our leadership conversations, then a crucial foundation is the cultivation of more balance in our internal advocacy and inquiry. This brings increased awareness and curiosity to the way that we construct our view of the world. This, in turn, may open the way to exploring the inferences and assumptions on which the advocacy of others is founded. How healthy is your internal dialogue? What is the tone of your thinking, feeling and sensing? How many certainties or judgements arise? How often are you genuinely curious, questioning, noticing and wondering how something came to be so?

As you begin to be clearer about the nature of your internal dialogue, I invite you to be curious about its influence on your contributions to conversation. For example, my internal process is largely inquiry-based, wondering how things came to be this way and exploring possibilities. However, those around me would be hard-pressed to identify this, because my external style is mainly advocacy-based. When I question the intent of my advocacy, I often find I am testing hypotheses externally and generating new information, perceptions, connections and points of view to include in my internal processing. This can be misunderstood by those around me because they hear my statements as conviction and certainty. My learning curve is therefore to bring more of my internal inquiry processes into my external conversation. What are your own habits of thinking and speaking? Are you most likely to advocate internally or externally? When are you most likely to inquire? How are your inner and outer styles related?

Responding – moments of choice in action

The interfaces between our internal processing and our external speech and actions are important. These are the 'sliding doors' moments in our conversations. We have a choice whether to speak or to be silent. We have a choice in the quality of attention we give to others in listening and being open to what they are saying or trying to say. Each of these choices in the external world has a mirror image in our internal world. In the practice of dialogue, in balancing advocacy and inquiry both internally and externally, how do we navigate our choices with poise and skill?

How do we weigh the balance between speaking and holding silence for others? If we speak too much or lack care in the way we speak, we deny the legitimacy of others. If we keep too much silence, we deny our own legitimacy. If our attention is overly outward, we may fail to notice the influence of pattern recognition and emotional tagging in prompting what we say or do. If our attention is overly inward we may be caught up in our own stories or preparing for our next opportunity to speak at the expense of truly hearing what another is saying. In important conversations, the choices we make at this interface are crucial; if we draw on the practices of mindfulness and dialogue we can be more effective in achieving appropriate balance.

Feeling for balance amongst so many factors might seem overwhelming. There is potentially a lot to juggle. One solution is to focus on intent. A key challenge for the participants in my dialogue practice development groups is adjusting to the notion that developing the capacity for dialogue is not about skills, tools or techniques. Yes, there are frameworks that provide some guidance on how they might expand their repertoire in conversations, but putting these into practice consistently and gracefully is another matter.

Tom Crum, in his Journey to Centre programme, emphasises intent, rather than skill, in making effective contributions to important conversations. When participants feel that their early forays into using new practices are clunky, I pass this message on. The principle is that if our intent is good, those around us will sense this, even if the details of our communication lack refinement. For example, if I am offering feedback, I can feel uncomfortable, especially if I am not sure of the best way to approach the other person. If I worry over the details of what I will say, I may quickly become derailed because I will not be able to predict the impact of my feedback. However if I focus on cultivating a clear intent, I will have a clear reference point for whatever unfolds. Why am I giving the feedback? Who will benefit? What is my motivation with regard to the other person? If my intent is to support the person, to enable learning and to benefit the wider system, my feedback is likely to be given and received in this spirit, even if my words are clumsy. If my intent is to correct the person, or is self-righteous in some way, it won't matter how skilful I am.

Intent has more impact than finely crafted words. This may mean that, for the workings of the black box, the response, or output, is the least important aspect. However, it is where we tend to put most effort, at least in the early days of learning new approaches. The risk of emphasising output over input and processing is that we may feel self-conscious and uncomfortable as we try something unfamiliar. This can bring pressure to be perfect, or to try hard, so our attention is on our delivery, taking it away from our internal awareness and processing.

When we are focused on getting something right – whether the 'something' is inquiry or advocacy or another skill – we tighten up, our heartbeat increases and our breath becomes shallower. This tension or contraction then spills into our relationship with those we're talking to, affecting the quality of the conversation. If, instead, we can focus on our intent and on our way of being in conversation, then external measures of performance fall away. We then tend to be more relaxed and open, and these qualities flow into our relationships with others.

Practice *10* – awareness of preferences and filters for incoming information

In your next few conversations, pay attention to some of the following questions. Notice which questions you select and which you skip over.

How do you 'listen?' What senses do you use most – your eyes? Your ears? Your kinaesthetic senses such as touch, smell, taste? In what combinations do you use them?

What do you habitually listen to, or for? Words? Facts? Metaphor? Expression and tone? Pace and timbre? Emotion? Reasoning? Pattern? Relationships? Detail? Qualities such as congruence and authenticity? The positives? The downsides?

What habitually is the intent of your listening? To acquire information? To help? To understand? To discover? To gather evidence? To explore? To identify the problem? To find an opening for your own point of view? To make connections? To be present? To get the gist of something? To get to the point?

What do you tend to skip over? When do you tend to lose interest? Particular topics? When particular people speak? In particular situations? When conversations get too detailed? When conversations go off at a tangent? After ten minutes, whatever the topic? When you have something urgent to do? When someone challenges your thinking or actions? When someone gives you praise?

When you have gathered some data, set yourself the following challenge:

What, specifically, might you deliberately pay attention to in the next week that will enable you to include information you usually discount? How can you more generally expand the range of information that is available to you?

Notes and reflections

Chapter *11* **A structured framework for the black box**

'A wonderful fact to reflect upon, that every human creature is constituted to be that profound secret and mystery to every other.' Charles Dickens

A structured framework for a deeper understanding of the processes outlined and explored in the previous chapter is set out in *The Fifth Discipline* Fieldbook.[10] The 'ladder of inference,' developed by Chris Argyris, is shown below. It can be used in ascent to construct a sense of how, as individuals, we take in data and experiences and then process and act on them. It can also be used in descent as a framework for inquiring into our perceptions of actions, situations or opinions with the aim of uncovering assumptions, beliefs or values.

Broadly, as we process our experience, we move quickly away from what actually took place. As we pack and store our experience, editing, deleting, discounting, or acting on it, we make rapid connections to existing useful references and lose original detail and nuance. This means that, by the time we're acting in response to an originating stimulus, we're already some distance from reality. By the time we're re-telling a story or recalling it, it is more fairy tale than fact, and if re-told several times, it takes on the polish and tenor of legend or myth. For example, a rule of thumb for disagreements between two people might be that there are at least three truths – one for each person and what actually took place. This can be a helpful template to have on your mindshelf when you are listening to tales of righteous indignation.

The ladder of inference

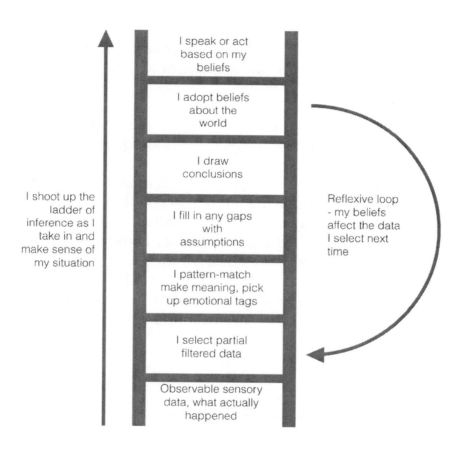

Chris Agryis (adapted)

Ascending the ladder of inference
In exploring the ladder in ascent, we already have a sense of the first two rungs: 'observable sensory data' and 'partial filtered data.' These two rungs support the

89

idea that we have only a partial perception of an encounter or experience. In the previous chapter, we explored our tendencies to filter sensory data. The same principle applies, of course, to more tangible data such as facts and figures. Painful though it may be to admit, we are as selective with numbers and other concrete data as we are with sensory data. A particular figure catches our attention because it supports our existing opinion or because it surprises us. We lose the context for it and remember only our storyline. Do you remember my starting point in Chapter 1? I recall the measure of twenty minutes but can't say exactly what it applies to.

In reflecting on how we favour some data and disregard others, we must also consider that our view of most things will come from a particular angle. Our professional background and experience will colour what we prioritise in our automatic selection process. For example, an accountant may have all the finance data required to conclude to their satisfaction that a project should be axed. However, colleagues may be paying more attention to human factors, or to reputation, and may prioritise these over figures, coming to a different conclusion. We may also be influenced by our beliefs, such as a conviction that a certain project or division is crucial to the success of our organisation. If we hold this belief, we will tend to filter for data that supports it and, as leaders, we need to be mindful of the risk that a belief may be misplaced.

The third rung of the ladder adds meaning, in which we pattern-match our data snapshot for previous reference experiences and storylines, with associated emotional tags. With our match comes the risk of failing to notice where and how the fit between template and current reality is poor. If we miss these discrepancies, we start to include inappropriate assumptions in our perceptions, based on what happened in the past or what we extrapolate will happen in the future.

Consider an example where a colleague doesn't greet us as we pass them in the corridor. We note that their head is down and their eyes remain fixed on the floor. They seem tense and distant. We say hello. They don't respond. We might assume that we've done something to upset them and react accordingly. On the other hand, they may just have been given some bad news that is distracting them, or they may be absorbed in thinking about a pressing problem. There are many possible explanations, but our general background experiences (for example, beliefs about what is rude) and our specific previous experiences with that colleague (positive or tricky) will significantly influence our initial interpretation, pulled from our mindshelf. If we quickly conclude/assume that our colleague is blanking us for some reason, we trigger a train of thought that searches for possible mistakes and unintended slights and we soar into fantasy. Can you imagine how this vein of thinking might influence our next encounter with that colleague? At best we are likely to be slightly wary.

The fourth rung of the ladder introduces assumptions. We start to fill in any gaps in our knowledge of a situation based on the meaning we have attributed to it. An example of this stays with me from my early career in the City. I was miserable in my role as a swaps trader and had worked out that if I took the early lunch shift from 11.30am to 1pm, most of the others lunched on the second shift and so I usually got another hour or so where I could read, avoid contact with people and effectively absent myself from my job. I knew I was cheating the system but I was so unhappy I didn't care too much. One day my boss's boss asked me to see him in his office – 'now.' He didn't often speak to me and my immediate thought was that my slacking had been noticed and I was about to be hauled over the coals. The meaning I gave this request was, 'the boss's boss won't speak to me unless there is a problem' and so I assumed that I'd been caught. I flushed and stammered and felt completely panicked. I can't remember the innocuous reason for his summons, but I do remember that guilt fast-tracked me several rungs up the ladder of inference on no information whatsoever. I wonder now whether he even noticed my uncomfortable demeanour.

The process of inadvertently adopting assumptions is a key step of inference and may be our best opportunity to catch ourselves as we create an increasingly compelling 'truth.' We are conjuring this truth from potentially flawed data and assumptions and sometimes simply asking the question, 'what else might explain this?' can unlock us from mistaken certainty.

Expanding possibilities on the fourth rung of the ladder may be critical, because on the fifth rung we nail down our explanation and give it substance as a conclusion, judgement or decision. We solidify our story as truth and it becomes a statement of position, advocacy. Things move quickly now. Based on this truth, we take action in words or deeds (the seventh rung). We might also generalise our conclusions, creating and adopting beliefs (the sixth rung), which then influence the data we select in future and become part of our pattern recognition and emotional tagging processes.

In summary, we take action based on partial data, added meanings, unconscious assumptions and the potentially flawed conclusions that follow. Incredibly, we run this process largely without mishap several times in every second of our lives. However, as leaders, our words and actions have far-reaching consequences and we sometimes need to pay more attention to this process; a critical skill of leadership is to cultivate the ability to discern the situations in which this is necessary.

Once we're aware of the ladder of inference model from the lowest rung upwards, we can sometimes recognise how a person, a word or an action sends us up the ladder in a routine, and therefore potentially predictable, way. Do you recognise this happening in your life? If so, where does it happen most frequently? I hazard a guess that it's in your closest relationships. At home a hasty trip up the ladder may be sparked by the cap of the toothpaste, the toilet seat, a forgotten errand or anniversary, or by clothes strewn across the floor. At work it may be sparked by being kept waiting for a meeting, lack of response to an email or voicemail, missing papers, borrowed equipment or an overly-used phrase (one that I remember is, 'what you need to understand, Amanda, is…'). Whatever the trigger that shoots you up the ladder, your response, in the context of one incident, is disproportionate because it's actually a response to an accumulation of incidents, possibly exacerbated by frustration rooted in being ignored on earlier occasions. These predictable patterns (at work or at home) offer an opportunity to pause for breath and practice mindfulness. In becoming more aware of a familiar sequence of stimulus-and-response beginning to play out, we can pause and consider whether our usual reaction will be helpful or unhelpful. This is the mindful moment that brings the possibility of making a choice.

Sometimes it's easier to see someone else shoot to the top of their ladder of inference than it is to catch ourselves in the act. We see the impact of a word, a phrase or an action on a colleague or family member and witness their habitual response. If this happens in a meeting, or in another situation where we have a legitimate stake in collective goings on, we may wish to intervene in what we see being played out. This is when it can be helpful to use a descent of the ladder as guidance for the questions we might ask.

Descending the ladder of inference
Many of our interactions with others take place at the level of the top rung of the ladder of inference, particularly those exchanges that are advocacy-based. The other person's words, tone and timbre of delivery, their physiology and actions, are our only clues as to what they are trying to convey. The impact of the non-verbal aspect is often greater than we are immediately able to take into account; we feel the energy that results from the other person's speedy trip up their ladder of

inference, without knowing their intent, and this triggers our own hasty dash up the rungs.

To swap metaphors, I sometimes characterise conversations as tips of icebergs, with 90% of the iceberg unseen. After a rapid-fire exchange about a complex issue, the assumptions, knowledge and expectations that we didn't explicitly share or explain lurk beneath the surface until they meet, and clash with, someone else's unspoken and contradictory 'below the surface' stuff. For example, we might think that all our colleagues are in agreement about a decision taken in a meeting, and then a chance remark reveals that a number of incompatible assumptions are in play and consensus quickly unravels. I sometimes think of organisations as seething seas of submerged icebergs of assumptions and diverse meanings, waiting to hole the ships of decisions and projects, inadvertently sinking them.

The stark reality of how we process our experience, coloured by our life-to-date, means that most conversations have as many versions 'in play' as there are participants. At the close of a meeting where six people think they have understood an issue and agreed on a course of action, there will in fact be six variations on a theme of understanding and agreement. For important issues, we ignore this truth at our peril. In general, except in highly formulaic exchanges (such as deals in the money markets), I suggest that the shorter a conversation about an issue, the greater the likelihood that a misunderstanding lies dormant. What is uncertain is whether the misconception is critical to future outcomes. There was recently a tragic story in the news of a young physician who misheard the name of a drug to be administered to a child. He proceeded to comply with all the prescribing rules for the drug he was administering, but the child died because he was following protocols for the wrong drug.

A root cause of varying understanding of an agreement reached in a meeting is that leadership conversations often favour advocacy over inquiry. As an instinctive advocator, when I want to make a point, I don't usually 'show my workings,' which can cause problems because my 'point' doesn't make much information available to others. If I show my workings, giving some sense of how I came to my point, listeners can get a feel for my reasoning. The idea of showing your workings comes from answering maths questions in exams; if you simply write down the answer, it will be either right or wrong. You'll be marked at 100% or zero. By showing your workings, even if your answer is wrong, you'll get credit for your approach, if it is broadly on track. This neatly applies to advocacy, which is a verbal form of giving answers.

For example, if I advocate a change, such as bringing the practices of dialogue into our conversations, I offer little information, just my opinion. It is unskilful advocacy. There will be varying interpretations of the meaning of dialogue and some people will believe they already engage skilfully in it, whilst others will switch off because they're not sure what I'm talking about. Showing some workings, such as explaining the difference between advocacy and inquiry, and saying that dialogue balances these approaches, offers much more scope for engagement and understanding.

Similarly, in a meeting where some feel strongly that a project should be progressed quickly and others advise caution, there is potential for a very narrow range of advocatory exchange, quickly escalating in tension. In unskilful advocacy, we offer only the tip of our iceberg of knowledge, experience and understanding. We mostly think we don't have time to offer anything else. However, if we explain our thinking and show our workings, we open the field for others to add facts or perspectives we've missed, question the opinions we thought were facts, and explore where there may be room for manoeuvre. For important matters, the quality of collective understanding is improved and so there is greater likelihood of subsequent actions being compatible with an agreed collective intent.

When we encounter advocacy, a descent of the rungs of the ladder of inference offers a framework to move away from the pointy tips of icebergs. To reveal lurking dangers of materially different assumptions or essential missing expertise or knowledge, we must ask questions that uncover beliefs, values, blind spots and any past experiences that are influencing our thinking. This style of conversation is different to that which many of us routinely inhabit.

In becoming more curious about how others are constructing their perspectives, we can take some steps down the ladder of inference by asking some of the following questions:

- Have any of us been in similar situations before? What does it remind us of?
- What is different this time?
- What are our interests? What is influencing us?
- What might we be avoiding or overlooking? What, explicitly, are we taking into account?
- What is the balance of risk in making a decision now, or deferring it?

Questions such as these offer the opportunity to surface frames of reference, uncover assumptions and understand initial conditions, accessing as much original data as possible.

Examining our own ladder of inference is a useful practice in any situation where we find ourselves provoked, irritated, frustrated, resentful or pressurised. When we find ourselves reacting strongly to something, we might take some steps down the ladder to explore exactly what has pressed our buttons and why. What are we reminded of? What assumptions have we made? What else might be going on here? What, precisely, has provoked us? In doing this, we raise awareness of how much of our reaction is triggered by current circumstances and what part is based on beliefs, values, preferences or past experience. In stepping ourselves down our ladder, we can explore alternative interpretations of what the other person has said or done. What is the most generous interpretation we could attribute to their words or actions?

An incentive to slow down, to pause, is that we often store more original information from a situation than we immediately recall. With calm awareness we can retrieve additional facets of memory. I had an experience of this when I was living in London, working in my first job. My monthly salary covered my rent, my travel pass and not much else. One morning, I stood at Finchley Central and watched the train approach. I travelled to Bank station and, as I approached the exit gates, I realised that I'd left my cardigan on the train, with my travel pass in the pocket. I went to report my loss; I was anxious and upset as I could ill-afford to buy a new pass.

In a small office, two men in London Underground uniforms looked bored. They were not interested in the problem of yet another person leaving something on a train. They asked which train I was on. Wondering how you tell one from another, I started by trying to give the time the train might have arrived at Bank. Trains arrive every minute in the rush hour – the men looked dismissive. I tried the time the train left Finchley Central – still no flicker of interest. I stood in despair, recalling the train as it approached the station. Suddenly I said, 'it was train number 111.' The men swung into immediate action. Now I was talking their language and giving them distinguishing information within their frame of reference. My pass was located and retrieved.

What had happened? As the train approached I'd seen the number on the front – interesting, but not relevant or useful to me, and so I hadn't kept it on my mindshelf. The information wasn't accessible in my initial distress but as I gave up and calmed down, I accidentally retrieved my visual memory.

In a diverse group of people, an awareness of the ladder of inference enables us to be thoughtful about how each person's unique background might influence their perception and processing. For example, as an accountant-to-trade, I can quickly home in on the finance, risk and governance aspects of any proposal or situation to the possible exclusion of the impact on people. How does your professional training and background influence how you perceive the world? What are the potential blind-spots and their possible risks?

The prevailing culture of an organisation or setting may have a significant influence on a ladder of inference. When this is the case, it is particularly important to ask questions in order to understand what is taken for granted in the culture, and to explore how this might influence perception. How does the culture constrain thinking? What may be the collective blind spots? What is the most counter-cultural proposal that can be made? For example, in universities, the culture is dominated by research. Status is strongly linked to having a successful profile in a particular field of research and so it is challenging to accept leadership from someone without this track record. Universities therefore tend to be limited to finding leadership from within a relevant research field.

In summary, the ladder of inference approach can be used as a support when people seem to be talking at cross-purposes; when we witness or experience a disproportionate response to a situation; when a conflict brews despite good intent; when we have a gut feeling that something is not quite right; or when someone appears to act in a way that undermines a decision we thought had been agreed. The model can be used to guide us in discovering 'what is really going on here,' leading us to uncover the intricacy and richness woven into human thought and speech.

Our challenge in a pressured and busy world is to make time and space to become fascinated by our own intake of information and black box processing:

what is their influence in our communication? Then we can seek to become intrigued by the equivalent workings in other people. If this sounds like a lot of hard work, it is to begin with. In time it becomes a new habit, a practice motivated by genuine curiosity about what is really happening when people talk together. The good news is that we don't need to apply this kind of attention to every conversation – just to those that matter.

Practice *11* – awareness of assumptions and underlying paradigms, beliefs and values

As you engage in conversations in the next few days, experiment with mentally pressing a 'pause' button in different situations and asking, 'what is happening right now?'

What is happening in your own internal processes? What assumptions are you making? What preconceived ideas are in play? What template might you be using? How are you limiting your options for a more far-reaching exchange?

What might be happening in the minds of others in the conversation? What assumptions might they be making? What might you inquire into?

If you find yourself in a conversation that seems to be stuck, try one of the following approaches:

- *leave the conversation for a moment, leave the room if you are able, and let your mind wander. What changes?*
- *invite everyone in the conversation to pause for a moment, take a few breaths and look at the issue afresh. What changes?*

Now spend some time reflecting on a general question you can ask yourself whenever a conversation seems stuck.

Notes and reflections

101

Chapter *12* Internal dialogue – why mind and conversation matters

'We all have many voices. Instead of deciding which one is right, find out what's right about each of them and practice being more fluid in moving among them.' Judy Ringer

So far, our focus has been mainly on the conversations we have with others. However, we are also participating in continuing conversations with ourselves. As human beings, we don't have a unique and coherent perspective or a single 'voice.' Earlier, I referred to my background as an accountant, and the attention I pay to numbers, risk management and governance. Yet I am also an executive coach, embracing learning, development, risk-taking, potential and possibility. Sometimes it's hard to imagine two more disparate stances – one often oriented to evaluate and contain, the other to liberate personal vision and expression. Yet these two voices live within me, alongside others. For instance, my first love is mathematics and so an important part of me favours sparing elegance and coherence. However, my experience is that life is messy, unpredictable and incomplete. As a consultant I work with change – if I put too much store in my mathematical ideals I will be disappointed, as I meet resistance, difference and the unexpected. And yet complexity sits easily with my mathematical nature, which has honed my clarity of thinking, enabling me to be clear about ethics, boundaries and order in messy situations.

So how does any person hold the many incompatible 'truths' that live within? This is a facet of our functioning that is important to explore and understand because if we don't, our unresolved internal clashes or incongruities tend to spill into our external exchanges, often with frustration. When I'm experiencing internal conflict, the first clue that I'm essentially holding two opposing points of view at the same time often shows up casually in my language. I might say, 'I'm in two minds about...' or, 'part of me thinks...and another part of me thinks...' and each phrase indicates that I am not settled within myself. If I am to bring mindfulness to my conversations, I need to consider how to fully hear my internal dialogue and to navigate the contradictions and conflicts I find there.

It is important to say a little more about 'voices.' When I first met the concept of internal dialogue, I felt alienated by it. The words 'internal dialogue' had no meaning for me initially. When I was asked about my internal voices, I said I didn't have any, that I have a pretty silent mind. I now understand the matter differently – I do have internal voices but they are not verbal. I'm not sure I can even describe the form they take. However, I know that I have some form of internal process through which different experiences and points of view within me become settled when I make up my mind. Equally, I sometimes get clues that my inner voices are in conflict, or are dissonant, because my words and actions in the external world become inconsistent or erratic.

As far as I can tell, from conversations with others, internal voices can take many forms. For some people, they are spoken sounds, often with different characters. For others, they are expressed in visual form, so the 'voices' are something like images. For others again, they are sensations, sometimes in specific parts of the body. Internal voices may be experienced as energies, as abstractions, scents, tastes or emotions, as flickers in the mind or as vibration in the body or in the air around. Each person, as they inquire into the nature of their internal dialogue, finds something unique to them. When you are in

103

conversation with yourself, thinking things through, coming to a settled state, what is the nature of the activity within you? What is your experience? How many different facets or energies can you identify within?

What is the connection between internal dialogue and what we say in conversations with others? When internal voices are in conflict, other people might experience a mixed message or might distrust us. This is because we are not aligned, and our incongruence is leaking out in a subtle or nuanced way. Equally, when we are congruent, those around us experience our authenticity and are likely to trust what we say. So, how do you know when you are subtly holding incompatible truths about a situation? How can you begin to understand the impact of this on others?

There is a helpful practice tool for examining internal dialogue, especially when in a conversation with another person. It's called the 'left hand column' approach and is an activity to bring to the surface 'what I'm thinking and feeling but not saying.' It was developed by Rick Ross and Art Kleiner and can be found in *The Fifth Discipline Fieldbook.*[10]

Choose a conversation you want to reflect on, and create two columns to write in. In the right hand column, record the conversation as if it were a play: I said, he said, I said, he said and so on. Write what was actually said, as far as you can recall, but don't get too hung up if you can't remember exactly. In a way, you are exploring what you think was said. In the left hand column, write down what you were thinking and feeling but not saying. If you are frank, you may find that there is a certain amount of irritation, frustration, anxiety, arrogance, hurt or resistance in your left hand column. It can be quite hard to acknowledge these feelings in black and white and yet you may find that even

104

attempting to engage with your left hand column sheds some light on what took place.

If you wish to inquire more deeply, you might ask what your intent was for each thing you said, taking into account the information in your left hand column, and then speculate about the impact you had on the other person. You might also examine the impact of their words on you and wonder what their intent might have been.

Other lines of inquiry include:

- what stopped me from expressing my truth as set out in my left hand column?
- what additional information could I have asked for?
- what judgements am I making about the other person?
- what if my judgements are misplaced, distorted or unjust?
- what am I discounting in what the other person is saying?

In preparing, and reflecting on, a left hand column, the aim is to use the 'nudges' of your internal dialogue as useful information and to find alternative routes through the encounter. In paying attention to the thoughts and feelings we edit out, we have additional rich information to work with. In paying attention to our internal dialogue through the left hand column process, we raise the possibility of becoming more aware of it in real time and so being able to change the course of a conversation as it happens.

Practice *12* – left hand column activity

Next time you have a conversation that doesn't quite go the way you imagined, take some time to reflect on it using the left hand column approach developed by Ross and Kleiner.

Make two columns on a piece of paper or in an electronic document. In the right hand side, and as far as you can recall, record the actual things that were said by you and by others, as if writing a scene from a play. Then in the left hand side write everything you were thinking and feeling but not saying, (even if you feel you are making this up to some extent).

Review what you have written and note with an 'A' where a speaker is advocating, and with an 'I' where a speaker is inquiring. Note also whether your left hand column thoughts and feelings are advocating or inquiring in nature. What is the balance of advocacy and inquiry in the whole conversation? In your part of the conversation?

Now review the conversation, reflecting on each part.
- *What was, or might have been, the <u>intent</u> of whoever was speaking?*
- *What was, or might have been, the <u>impact</u> on whoever was listening?*
- *At what points could you have said something differently, or asked for clarification, or stayed silent?*

How do you feel about the conversation now? Do you need to do any follow-up?

What have you learned about the nature of your internal 'voices?'

Notes and reflections

Chapter *13* External dialogue – why mind and conversation matters

'Problems cannot be solved at the same level of awareness that created them.' Albert Einstein

To some extent, I've asked you to take the inquiry into mind and conversation on trust. Why do we need to develop our faculties in these matters? How will increased awareness of intent, impact, internal dialogue and inference affect your conversations, your influence and your activities? When is it most necessary to bring heightened awareness into play? This chapter outlines three situations where awareness of these matters might prove important.

Pattern mismatches

In the article *Why Good Leaders Make Bad Decisions* (Harvard Business Review[8]), the authors say:

> *'The daunting reality is that enormously important decisions made by intelligent, responsible people with the best information and intentions are sometimes hopelessly flawed.'*

The article outlines some high profile and startling examples to demonstrate this, and draws on the work of neuroscience to explain what happens. You will recall that as quickly as we perceive our current situation we are checking to see if we have any previous similar experiences to draw on (pattern recognition) and that these reference points come with associated emotions (emotional tagging).

In decision-making or judgement calls, the two main risks are that we mismatch a template of previous experience to our current predicament, or that the emotions attached to an earlier event colour our perception, potentially creating a blind spot.

The matters raised in this article resonate with another framework, that of situational awareness. I was introduced to this concept by my colleague, Steve Marshall, a former fighter pilot. Drawing on the work of Mica Endsley of SA Technologies, he explained that research into faulty decision-making shows that errors in judgement occur principally in how a situation is perceived, and which data are noticed and included as relevant. In fact, 76% of decision-making errors lie in this part of the process, corresponding to the first two rungs of the ladder of inference. A further 20% of errors occur as we construct mental models of the situation, corresponding to the middle rungs of the ladder or the 'pattern recognition' phase of our neurological process. Only 4% of errors are attributed to the end-game of understanding the implications of the possible choices we might make. Steve Marshall puts it this way:

> 'When we understand our current environment, working out what might happen next is comparatively straightforward.'

To make consistently good decisions, we need to cultivate our capacity to perceive and understand more fully what is happening around us. We must cultivate our situational awareness.

The implications for conversations are profound and make a compelling case for bringing the practices of mindfulness and dialogue into leadership conversations. Many conversations trade solutions, exploring the consequences and impact of different options for action. These conversations are closest to being conversations about the end-game and so only risk-manage 4% of potential errors. To be more effective in managing the risks of pattern mismatches and emotional tagging, we need to be in more conversations that explore how stakeholders perceive an issue. The more complex an issue, the more crucial this is.

Complexity and wicked issues

A second reason for paying attention to intent, impact, internal dialogue and inference is to harness their influence in conversations about intractable issues ('wicked issues') that seem resistant to a leadership team's efforts to deal with them. These are the issues that return time after time; you think you've resolved them and then find the matter re-opened. This tends to indicate that the type of conversation being used by the team isn't a good fit for the type of issue they are trying to address.

To understand what type of conversation might be a good fit, we first need to understand the type of issue we are facing. A useful frame for assessing the complexity of an issue is outlined by Mike Pidd.[11] He distinguishes between puzzles, problems and wicked issues as illustrated in the table below.

	Puzzle	Problem	Wicked issues
Formulation/ framing	Agreed – a single formulation	Agreed – a single presenting frame	Arguable – multiple perspectives and no agreed frame
Solution/ response	Agreed – a single solution	Arguable – a range of appropriate solutions	Arguable – multiple responses

In this grid, a puzzle is something where both the framing question and the solution are agreed, such as sudoku, crosswords or jigsaw puzzles. Everyday conversations are mostly fit-for-purpose for puzzle-type predicaments.

For problems, there is general agreement on the issue to be tackled, and there are a range of appropriate responses to it. Depending on the range of stakeholders in a problem, an everyday conversation might suffice or some higher order collaborative skills such as influencing, negotiating and conflict-handling might be required to find a shared response and to co-ordinate action.

For wicked issues, there is ambiguity in the nature of the presenting issue; different stakeholders tend to perceive the situation from different angles. This is the realm of dynamic complexity or complex adaptive systems: with each step in a response, the system adapts, and the frame of the issue changes. There is a very real challenge in communicating frequently enough, clearly enough and deeply enough to continually make new sense of what is going on. Conversations need to focus on exploring the nature of the issue from as many angles as possible, surfacing and holding difference. The practices of mindfulness and dialogue are essential for conversations that relate to wicked issues.

To gain insight into the relationship between different kinds of conversation and wicked issues, we can revisit the four energetic fields of conversation,[5] introduced in Chapter 5. In the first field – politeness/routines – current habits and patterns routinely play out and there tends to be a preference for advocacy, most often in the form of serial monologues. Each person states their position from a place of habit, without particular reference to each other or to the whole system. Questions can be seen as opposition, and may be discounted or ignored. There is a general absence of inquiry and so any complexity that individuals have taken into account in forming their view is not shared. Constrained by politeness and the norms of the group, there may be a number of unacknowledged differences in play and any apparent agreement may founder on differing assumptions. If challenge is routinely discouraged, those who have unwelcome, yet highly pertinent news, might stay silent. The collective is poorer in intelligence as a result. Conversations in this field are of limited use in generating coherent responses to wicked issues.

In the second field – breaking open/debate – potential solutions to the problem are usually traded and fought over, with the most powerful voice potentially emerging as the preferred response. Debate may generate a more robust response than serial monologue, with some opportunity to uncover incompatible assumptions, but there is no real opportunity to get a shared view for framing an issue because the conversational effort is focused on solutions and action.

In the third field – inquiry/reflection – different paradigms, assumptions, beliefs and values can be surfaced and explored, with the possibility of finding some shared ground for framing the presenting issue. This offers the potential for considering coherent responses. However, conversation is governed by individual interests and this may mean that the inquiry does not reach the depth required for a truly collective response.

The fourth field – flow/dialogue – offers the possibility of generating fresh insights into framing an issue and of creating the conditions for systemic responses to unfold.

Being clear about whether a presenting issue is a puzzle, problem or wicked issue will give a clear indication of the type of leadership conversation that is required.

Complexity and misinterpreted meanings
There are some situations in which we actively need to minimise the risk of misunderstandings. These situations tend to be complex and involve multiple

stakeholders with diverse cultures, backgrounds, interests and points of view. This scenario increases the likelihood that a word with one meaning in a particular setting will mean something different in another. A simple example of this occurred when I was doing my MBA. A lecturer explained that the change process he was outlining should be used 'transparently.' As I listened to him in a few lectures I kept getting a sense that he was contradicting himself or that I was misunderstanding something. Eventually I asked what he meant by using the model 'transparently.' He said that it should be see-through, transparent like glass and therefore invisible to clients. In my consultancy practice, I use the word transparent to mean that a process is open and overt, laid out for all to see. One word, two meanings – imagine the impact of this if a leadership team agreed that a change process should be transparent. In a situation in which it would be important to be seen to be working together, the process might be overt in one function and unseen in another.

In managing this risk in conversation, we need to listen carefully for any indication that participants might be talking at cross-purposes, or not fully understanding each other's jargon. It's not easy to ask, 'what do you mean by that?' especially when checking on a word in common usage. It may also be challenging to admit to 'not knowing,' in a technical conversation, for instance, for fear of being the only 'stupid' person present. In bringing mindfulness to conversations, we attend to the possible consequences of confusion, lack of understanding and silence, and then overcome any fear to ensure that the meanings of important aspects of an issue are clarified and shared.

Practice *13* – fieldwork with a wicked issue

Reflect on a meeting that you regularly take part in and identify issues that seem to be permanently on the agenda or which return and re-open again and again, when a collective decision has apparently been made.

Use the model of puzzle, problem and wicked issue to try and categorise any such issues. Repeat this until you find an issue that you believe to be a wicked issue.

The challenge of a wicked issue is that its framing is 'arguable' meaning that there are multiple ways to describe the issue, the crux of the problem. At your next meeting, negotiate some time to explore how the issue is being perceived. Invite each person to describe the problem from their point of view. Imagine also how external stakeholders might perceive the issue. Ask yourselves what you might not yet know or might need to discover. Speculate what the issue might look like to a complete outsider. Imagine metaphors for it.

Keep this conversation open; invite your colleagues to refrain from any consideration of solution or response until you feel you have genuinely seen this issue 'every which way.'

Debrief the conversation with your colleagues. How was this different? What have we learned? What is needed now?

You might conclude this exploration with new insight, or with an agreement to reflect on what you have learned, or with an acceptance that you need to spend longer on understanding the situation. This is okay. Rushing at the problem with solutions hasn't worked so far, so what have you got to lose?

Notes and reflections

Chapter *14* Pause for breath

*'Do you have the patience to wait til your mud settles and
the water is clear?'* Lao Tzu, translation by Stephen Mitchell

In these chapters, the focus has been on the part of our brain which is largely occupied with getting the job done. It's the part of the brain where we are busiest, strategising in response to whatever we encounter (or imagine we will encounter) in the world. In becoming mindful of these activities, we are challenging ourselves to cultivate a sense of impartial witnessing as we observe our mind-habits. We might imagine we have an autopilot mind and a mindful, witnessing mind; often the former drowns out or over-rides the latter. In exploring the links between mind and conversation, we have been developing our knowledge and awareness of our mindful, witnessing mind and creating space for it to be more available to us.

This mindful, witnessing mind has a quality of stability and brings curiosity, fascination and kindness to our experience. In doing this, we pause for breath, allowing a calmer, slower and roomier perspective to unfold. If we want to cultivate the availability of this aspect of our mind, we can focus on our breathing for a few breaths, bringing us into the present moment. In bringing our mind to our breathing, our attention shifts to our body and this opens a new line of inquiry, into the links between physiology and conversation.

Practice *14* – pause for breath

This foundation practice appears at the end of each section of the book.

Sit in a comfortable upright posture, so that your feet are firmly planted on the floor and you are supporting your own back, rather than leaning against a chair. Rest your hands on your thighs, palms down.

Become aware of the contact between your feet/shoes and the floor. Become aware of the contact between your hands and your thighs. Become aware of the contact between your thighs and the chair. Become aware of the sitting bones, the bones at the base of the pelvis, pressing into the chair seat.

Notice your strong base, formed by your feet and sitting bones, and allow your spine to grow to its full length by gently imagining each vertebra lifting slightly from the one below. Sense lightness and spaciousness in your spine. Notice that your neck becomes long at the back, your chin tilted slightly towards your chest.

Now bring your attention to your breath. On each inhale, imagine your breath seeping into the spaces in your spine, allowing it to lengthen just a little bit more. On each exhale, imagine your breath flowing down through your chest and belly, softening any tension. Follow your breath for a few moments.

Now mentally scan your body and notice any places of tension, aching or discomfort. Choose one and, for a few breaths, imagine your inbreath soaking into this place and, on a longer exhale, imagine your outbreath dissolving any discomfort and carrying it out into the air around you, letting you rest.

After a few breaths, become aware of the contact between your sitting bones and the chair, between your hands and thighs, and between your feet and the ground.

Rise gently and stretch. You are ready to re-engage with the world.
117

Resource list for inquiry into processes of the mind

Why Good Leaders Make Bad Decisions, Campbell, Whitehead, Finkelstein, HBR article, February 2009
Six Thinking Hats, Edward de Bono
NLP at Work, Sue Knight
A Path with Heart, Jack Kornfield
Gifts Differing, Understanding Personality Type, Isabel Briggs Myers and Peter B Myers
Diamond Mind, Rob Nairn
Theory U, Leading from the Future as it Emerges, C Otto Scharmer
The Fifth Discipline Fieldbook, Peter Senge et al, especially the sections on Mental Models and Personal Mastery
Difficult Conversations, Stone, Patton, Heen
Coming to our Senses, Jon Kabat-Zinn
Wherever You Go, There You Are, Jon Kabat-Zinn

Part Three

BODY AND CONVERSATION

Chapter *15*   **Introduction**

Chapter *16*   **Handling difference**

Chapter *17*   **Difference and our physiology –
fight, flight and freeze**

Chapter *18*   **Embodied mindfulness – centre**

Chapter *19*   **Skilful advocacy, inquiry and pause**

Chapter *20*   **Internal conflict**

Chapter *21*   **Why body and conversation matters**

Chapter *22*   **Pause for breath**

Resource list for inquiry into impact of physiology

Chapter *15* Introduction

'Mr Duffy lived a short distance
from his body.' James Joyce

What is the relationship between our experiences, what goes on in our bodies and our talk? At what level are we aware of our physiology and its influence on our mind, words and actions? To what extent do we ignore or suppress what is going on in our bodies?

It is fruitful to explore our bodily awareness in conversation because the emotional tags that accompany pattern recognition are somatic experiences, visceral body memories. They are often subtle in presence, yet powerful in influence, and awareness of them brings an opportunity to attend to the impact of them.

A further reason for cultivating curiosity about the role played by physiology in our conversations is that when things get heated, energy rises and tension escalates, giving a tangible experience that more than our mind is involved. If you are in the midst of a charged exchange, it is unlikely that you remain untouched by it; you may become tense, your stomach may churn, your palms may become sweaty, or you may experience some other indication of physical unease. This unease may then significantly influence your next contribution.

When things get heated, perhaps when someone imposes on us, physically or with words, what reactions are triggered? Habitual patterns are fight, flight or freeze; to engage aggressively, to disengage, avoid or run, or to feel like a rabbit in the headlights. When these adrenalin-prompted conditions arise, we're less able to bring the practices of mindfulness and dialogue to our leadership conversations. To be effective, we need to access ways of steadying ourselves sufficiently to be skilful in our talk, even when under fire.

It is an inconvenient truth that evolution has equipped us to be highly sensitised to difference and the unfamiliar, reacting to them with efficiency and efficacy through our fight/flight/freeze system. When faced with difference, uncertainty or the unknown, this system bypasses our thinking mind and puts us into a state of heightened alert, shutting down creativity and other processes that are not essential for immediate survival. This can be unhelpful in organisations because successfully handling diversity of perspective and opinion is crucial in collaborative working. Equally, successfully handling uncertainty and the unknown and their impact on people is the very stuff of leadership. Primitive though it seems, physiological factors often play a significant and unhelpful part in interactions between people, and when we are caught up in this outside our awareness, a scenario that is already challenging can quickly escalate.

Our physiology is more relevant to our conversations than many of us acknowledge. Cultivating awareness of our body sensations brings the potential for choice. If we notice how our body is reacting, we can pause for breath and choose a considered response.

Our focus now is on increasing our capacity for having 'good conversations in bad weather.' If we find ourselves in a conversational storm, battered by rain and struggling to stay upright in the wind, how do we remain on our feet and access a calm place in the eye of the storm? When we are able to do this, what is the impact on others? How do our conversations change? In exploring the power of our body and the programmes that have evolved to protect us, it is again important to remember to bring the qualities of kindness and fascination to our inquiry.

Practice *15* – fieldwork on observing physiology

Next time you're in a meeting with several people, spend some time paying attention to each speaker and notice their impact on others. Observe and make notes of any changes in facial expression or any physical response such as an involuntary hand or foot movement, or moving a chair back, or leaning towards a speaker.

If you want a narrow focus for your observations, simply observe and make notes about eyes – open or closed? Where directed? Blinking or unblinking? Steady gaze or flitting from one place to another?

Then spend some time noticing the impact of different speakers on you. You might start with attention to your eyes, similar to the observations suggested above. Then pay attention to the muscles in your face – are you aware of clenching your jaw, or beginning to frown? Then move to your body – notice any tensions or sensations that arise. What do you learn about the impact of different speakers on you?

When you are speaking, scan your listeners and see what you notice. How do you assess your impact on others?

Notes and reflections

Chapter *16* Handling difference

'Your opinion is your opinion, your perception is your perception – do not confuse them with 'facts' or 'truth.' Wars have been fought and millions have been killed because of the inability of men to understand the idea that everybody has a different viewpoint.' John Moore

When advocacy meets advocacy, we are immediately into the realm of handling difference. A statement of position meets another statement of position and they are often not even close in perspective or worldview. While some opinions appear similar on the surface, intent or motivation may be very different. As a listener, you may find yourself agreeing with a position, and then further on in a conversation, discover that the direction of travel has taken an unexpected turn. This is often because the meaning you made was not what the speaker intended. Sometimes two people think they've said the same thing and are in agreement, only for difference to emerge when later actions seem incompatible with the agreed position. When we agree a 'what' we may not be agreeing a 'why' (direction or purpose) or a 'how' (process, words, actions). The way we handle difference has a significant influence on how our conversations unfold.

Apparent agreement can be more problematic than obvious disagreement, because expectations of collaboration have been kindled. I once heard a saying that, 'an expectation is an upset waiting to happen'. Expectation can be a breeding ground for frustration and disappointment, which can escalate into irritation and anger. This is the story of many management team meetings.

So, I repeat, when advocacy meets advocacy, we are immediately into the realm of handling difference. This is advocacy on my part; check your response to both my original statement and my repeating it. What was your initial response? Did you agree? Disagree? How did your agreement or disagreement affect how you read my explanation? Did it further convince you? Did you change your mind?

How did you respond when I repeated myself a couple of paragraphs later? If you disagreed with me the first time around, my guess is that the repeat heightened any nascent irritation. Did you notice how this arose in your body? If you agreed with me, the repeat might have evoked an impatient, 'yeah, got it the first time.' Perhaps you then hurried over the next bit. Did you experience a reaction in your body? The point is that, if you agreed or disagreed with my statement, you were meeting my advocacy with advocacy of your own. How does it feel when this happens?

My next piece of advocacy is that when advocacy meets advocacy a conversation tends to narrow in scope and focuses on an immediate topic. Rather than judging this to be right or wrong, ask yourself, 'how do advocating patterns influence conversations?' In coming to understand the extent to which advocacy focuses a conversation, you may gain a sense of whether advocacy serves your intended purpose in a given situation. Better still, if you can remain curious about the impact of advocating patterns, you'll cultivate an inquiring attitude into how conversations unfold.

Perhaps you neither agreed nor disagreed with my opening sentence. You may have been thinking something like, 'okay, interesting statement; not sure I agree. I wonder why she thinks that?' You received my advocacy for what it is – a statement of my position – and used it to stimulate your curiosity and interest. You held my statement lightly, being unsure of your own position and, crucially, you wondered how I might have come to mine. This models the stance of inquiry, of hearing, receiving, and holding an opinion lightly, whilst being curious about what you don't know. How did you experience this in your body? In meeting advocacy with inquiry, you hold the possibility that my (current) opinion is true for me, and that if you were to understand it, it may influence your thinking. In conversation, inquiry broadens and expands the exchange.

If we hold lightly that advocacy met by advocacy places us in the realm of handling difference, what might we need to discover and understand in order to navigate diverse opinions in a way that serves a collective purpose? If we handle difference skilfully, we open possibilities for multiple perspectives and ideas, for new thinking or insights and for creative ways of putting things together. We create opportunities for growth and learning, for developing robust and resilient responses to our predicaments and challenges. If we handle difference less skilfully, we may short-change any potential in a situation. At best we may close down possibilities and miss the significance of the impact of our ideas and actions on others. At worst, we may start to fight the ideas of others and develop an intent to win. At some stage, without awareness, this may evolve to winning at all costs. Battle lines will be drawn. We will campaign for our idea, we will marshal our troops and arm them with information and skills to outwit the 'enemy,' (our colleague down the corridor who heads up a sister department in our organisation).

I hear leaders in organisations use words such as battle-lines, arming and troops to describe their options when their passionate advocacy of a position meets equally passionate opposition. All-out 'war' can ensue from such adversarial positions, and over time a leader may lose sight of their original purpose or objective. This is the danger of advocacy without awareness and perspective. We get attached to winning the argument, rather than finding a good response to circumstances.

When difference becomes entrenched, it's often described as conflict which, in organisations, seems to be a polite term for disagreement, out-and-out fights or power struggles. What is curious, is that leaders often deny being in conflict with a colleague, even when others, such as their team members, describe a charged and challenging relationship. When asked about this, leaders remain polite, often describing the relationship as 'fine.' It seems that conflict, even when it's obvious to onlookers, feels unacceptable to those involved. Conflict is paradoxical; we say that it is healthy, and then go out of our way to avoid it or to deny that we are party to it. Perhaps we need to be clearer about the nature of conflict; when is it healthy and when not? Perhaps our response to difference determines whether conflict is fruitful or unproductive.

What most influences whether we handle difference skilfully or less skilfully? My view is that understanding our physical responses to differences and cultivating the capacity to moderate them is fundamental. If we are physically at ease, we can call on the full range of our experience and creativity. If we are uptight or jittery, we will tend to add our tension to a situation.

Practice *16* – attending to the language of difference

How we talk about conflict is important – the metaphors we use tend to indicate whether conflict is seen as generative or combative.

Consider your organisation, your team, or your family, and begin to note the language used when people encounter difference.

Note the type of difference that is presenting: different or competing points of view, different communication styles, difference in terms of gender, ethnicity, status, function, role, power, or difference in the form of a change being proposed.

Then note the language being used in relation to difference.

What are the principal metaphors or images evoked? What might this indicate about any underlying assumptions and beliefs that are in play?

Now attend to your own language when faced with difference – what phrases do you habitually use? What images and metaphors do you evoke? What are your underlying assumptions and beliefs about difference?

Now pay attention to how difference is typically handled. Is it welcomed as an opportunity to be collectively creative and constructive? Do you collectively diminish possibilities in a mix of frustration, hurt, fear, anger or desire to win?

What qualities and conditions are present when conflicting perspectives are handled well?

What is absent when difference deteriorates into a polite, or not so polite, fight?

Notes and reflections

Chapter *17* Difference and our physiology – fight, flight and freeze

'As soon as there is life, there is danger.'
Ralph Waldo Emerson

My inquiry into the nature of conflict and our responses to it began in earnest when I went to Peaceful Valley, Colorado, for a programme led by Tom Crum. Tom is an Aikido master and uses principles from this martial art to support people in their personal development. I aspired to do something similar with T'ai Chi. I hadn't thought much about conflict before that programme. I was often in arguments and was quite good at winning verbal fights, so it hadn't really occurred to me that understanding the nature of conflict might be important.

Tom's teaching focused on cultivating resilient responses to stress and conflict. These two states are linked through the workings of our autonomic nervous system, the physiological response that snaps to fight/flight/freeze when we are 'threatened,' and that soothes us and returns us to relaxation once danger has passed. I put 'threatened' in quotes because the level of threat that we typically experience today in the Western world is very different from the level of threat our system evolved to deal with. To illuminate this, Tom introduces the concept of the sabre-toothed idea, explaining that our flight/flight/freeze system evolved as a response to protect us from the threat posed by sabre-toothed tigers and the like. In this day and age, this system responds to anything we perceive to be threatening, which is quite often an opposing point of view or idea. I describe it as my mind, body or spirit flinching when I am surprised, or when something unanticipated or unfamiliar happens.

Broadly, our fight/flight/freeze system evolved to scan our environment for anything out of place or different, because this might represent a potential hazard. For our forebears, an unfamiliar movement, a sound, a smell, a taste or a sensation might mean danger, and so our bodies prepare immediately, making us ready to fight, to flee or to freeze. These are our three basic survival strategies – overcome the threat, outrun it, or stand so still it won't notice that you might be a tasty lunch. Our challenge in the modern world is that a system that evolved to protect us from predators is now triggered by anything we perceive to be different, threatening or overwhelming.

This system is vastly over-specified for those that live in the Western world today. When we hear or see something unexpected, unwelcome or alien, our physiology prepares to attack, to run, or to be still. Our heart rate goes up, our breathing shortens, our attention contracts to focus on the threat. We are primed. A real problem in everyday life is that many of us have been primed since the alarm clock interrupted our sleep (startle reaction). This is then exacerbated by some combination of, for example, a phone call from our boss, colleague or PA before we even get in the shower (anxiety and/or performance pressure); a traffic jam on the way to the station (frustration); a dash for a train (anxiety and/or time pressure, plus getting our heart pumping); a standing room only crush (irritation); a car that backfired (startle reaction) as we crossed the road to the office. Throw in a little caffeine and we are wired before any sabre-toothed idea is even an inkling in our least-favourite colleague's mind. It is not surprising that a red mist of anger descends as once again, she overrides or ignores the needs of our team, pressing for advantage for hers.

Okay, so I'm exaggerating – but not by much. As we become aware of this pattern of progressive tightening in our body, mind and spirit, there are changes we can make to return to a more resourceful state. First we need to tune into the sensations that we experience as tension increases: where do we feel this in our body? Where does it start? How does it develop? In becoming familiar with how it feels, we will be able to recognise it earlier, pause for breath and adopt a more resourceful state. In the sequence described in the previous paragraph, it is easier to avoid 'red mist' moments if you address your rising sense of stress earlier in the day. If you can catch yourself as you begin to tighten up, perhaps you can calm yourself sufficiently to choose a different response, handling difference more constructively and, perhaps, less predictably.

We can contrast this human condition of escalating tension with what happens in the natural world. Kabat-Zinn and his colleagues[12] describe an optimal fight/ flight/freeze response to a state of alarm. Imagine a herd of grazing animals on the plains of Africa, heads down, doing what they do, grazing. Something alerts them – a warning call, a smell on the breeze, a movement. Their heads lift, they are alert, still, attending, ears twitching, nostrils flared, primed and weighing up whether they need to run. A predator makes a move. The herd runs – a burst of adrenalin-fuelled speed. The predator brings down one of the herd. What happens next is most illuminating; once a kill has been made, the danger is past, and even though the predator probably remains within sight, the rest of the herd just put their heads back down and graze. In seeing how the fight/flight/freeze system is supposed to work, we might begin to envisage what is needed to handle ourselves differently in a modern human world, where the alarms come one after another, with no time to soothe and rebalance our physiology.

In understanding our personal tendency to fight, flee or freeze, a first step might be to inquire into our reaction to alarm. What does that look like and feel like? Until recently I thought that everyone reacted similarly to surprise or threat, and in some ways this is so. For instance, we tend to focus on the source of the alarm, rather than on the bigger picture. This is true whether perceived danger is a predator or a proposed change in working environment. Chip and Dan Heath[13] explain that police officers describe this as 'weapon focus' where a crime victim can often give a detailed description of a gun but cannot give even the most basic description of their assailant. This is because attention is fixed on the object that evokes fear. A parallel occurs in conversation when we fix on a point that is being made, rather than remaining aware of the context and becoming curious about how others are seeing the world.

There are general tendencies in fight/flight/freeze reactions and from Wendy Palmer (another Aikido master), I learned that we each develop a unique variation on fight/flight/freeze themes, and it serves us to know our own pattern. Wendy uses physical partner work to explore how and where our body contracts and tenses under pressure. Under threat, which parts of my body disengage and try to flee the situation, and which over-engage, preparing to fight? When I am overwhelmed, how do I become frozen between the part of me that wants to attack, and the part of me that wants to run?

In my case, when I'm put under pressure, my head moves forward slightly, to engage or fight, my shoulders and chest retreat and contract to protect my heart, and my hips turn slightly to prepare to run. This is not an aligned place from which to respond; my pattern signals both fight and flight, which may trigger confusion in those around me. As a leader, being misaligned physiologically, however subtly, may be perceived as a mixed message.

Working with a partner, our reactive pattern can be demonstrated through a gentle push. In conversation, the push could be an opinion that is seen as a threat, pressure to say a particular thing, or the stress of holding multiple and conflicting points of view. In organisations, the push might be pressure to deliver or perform. It might be a deadline or volume of work or multiple and conflicting requirements from more than one boss. All of these situations represent things pressing on us, and as our senses notice each imposition, our fight/flight/freeze system kicks in. What is in question is whether we notice that a perceived danger is past and therefore return to 'grazing' and a calmer physiological state. For many, this calming part of the cycle doesn't happen – I've certainly experienced being in a heightened state of alertness for long periods of time, never recovering a sense of relaxed and unconcerned 'grazing,' particularly when I held senior positions in organisations.

In our modern world, our fight/flight/freeze system is often permanently 'primed' by our distracted way of living and working, and so any obstruction, mild threat or simple miscommunication may ratchet up our state of readiness to attack, run or close down. This can feel explosive, terrifying or overwhelming. Meantime, in organisations, we know that extreme reactions such as erupting tend to be career-limiting and so we cope by suppressing the physiological build-up within us. In doing so, we add to the tension of our already heightened state, and then displace it on the squash court or in the gym, soothe it through massage or relaxation, or release it on our unsuspecting family. While these tactics may provide some relief in the short term, a more sustainable strategy is to deal appropriately with the autonomic nervous system as it is triggered, and we will explore this in the next chapter.

In our leadership conversations, what are the implications of our survival physiology? When handling different ideas and perspectives begins to feel like a conflict, our physiology quickly, and often subtly, gets involved. The energy of a conversation begins to rise. Voices may speed up, or get louder. People may talk over the top of each other, or interrupt. The stakes are rising – emotions are engaged by an issue or principle which really matters to someone. Perhaps a particular outcome or result is believed to be vital, and there is momentum to come to a decision quickly. Perhaps there is performance pressure, anxiety about a looming deadline, or a sense of wanting to protect a team or a service that has been carefully nurtured over the years. Under any of these circumstances, it is challenging to keep a conversation open and exploratory; it becomes alarmingly easy to race up our ladder of inference and to make assumptions or judgements about what another person says.

Under these conditions, we may find ourselves moving towards full engagement in a conversational fight. Alternatively, we may weigh up the risks of such a fight and choose to flee, taking steps to minimise conflict or leave the conversation completely. We might find ourselves unable to form or articulate a view (freeze), or switching from one position to another, without consideration, which is a dynamic form of freeze, or paralysis, which one of my clients calls 'faffing about.' Any of these scenarios suggests tension is rising (enjoyable to some) and indicates that physiology is now in charge, rather than mind or spirit.

This sort of experience reflects the second field of conversation, introduced in Chapter 5: breaking open/debate. If we can bring the right kinds of qualities and practices into play at this stage, we can hold heightened energy in a way that offers the possibility of moving into a conversation of curiosity and inquiry. Using the practices of mindfulness and dialogue, we can engender conditions in which difference can be held, explored and made creative. This requires resilient leadership presence. How do we cultivate this resilience and increase our capacity to sit comfortably with the energetic consequences of conflicting opinions?

Practice *17* – attending to the physiology of difference

As you go about your workplace, notice and note the physiology of others when they are faced with difference.

Note the type of difference that is presenting, as in the previous practice. Then note the language around it and any changes of physiology or expression occurring. In particular, notice whether there is a flinch of some kind – it might be a very small movement, such as a slight clenching of the jaw, or a slight change in skin colour – followed by some sort of recovery or masking to 'manage' the flinch.

Now attend to your own physiology when faced with difference, particularly an unwelcome difference.

Where do you flinch, mentally, physically?

Which parts of your body contract in readiness for fight or flight?

Which parts of your body advance to fight? Or turn away/retreat, ready to flee?

How and where do you freeze or get caught between fight and flight, oscillating from one to the other?

Notes and reflections

Chapter *18* Embodied mindfulness – centre

*'Centre is a place where decisions
are known, not made.'* Tom Crum

Our fundamental reactions to pressure, stress and perceived threat are deep-seated. Not only do we have the legacy of fight/flight/freeze, we also have our templates and emotional tags, embedded over years of use. It is therefore difficult to imagine changing our reactions. We can only become aware of them, accept them, and notice when they are manifesting. In doing this, we create the opportunity to pause for breath and choose a more skilful way of being.

An arena in which this process is explored explicitly is martial arts. One aim of martial arts training is to develop a steadiness of mental and physical presence in the face of an incoming threat. We can draw on practices from martial arts to develop our capacity for calm resilience under pressure. When we are composed in both mind and body, we inhabit a powerful presence. Cultivating the practice of mindfulness begins to develop the capacity of a stable mind: we now explore how to cultivate steadiness of physical presence, especially when we are in charged situations.

The key to steadiness of physical presence is the practice of centring, or being grounded or rooted with a sense of dynamic balance. Centring is an aspect of all martial arts and is crucial to creatively handling incoming pressure. When faced with an attack, martial artists train to respond in a way that moves with the prevailing energy, redirecting it. This kind of response requires maintaining balance and poise, or centre, as a martial artist moves towards, and joins with, someone else's momentum and desired direction of travel. Maintaining centre, the aim is to deflect the energy of the other person, or even disrupt their balance, depending on their intent and the level of intensity in their attack. The higher the level of incoming energy, the more practice is needed to hold or recover centre.

The same applies in conversation. It's easy to maintain a calm presence in the face of a half-hearted point of view, but much harder if another person is deeply committed to their position and putting a lot of energy into getting their way. In bringing the practices of mindfulness and dialogue to leadership conversations, we aim to cultivate our capacity to hold our own position (or balance, or centre) in a way that enables another person to hold theirs. If we can both be poised and collected, we will retain our human grace and dignity and this will create the best conditions for a good conversation.

Being centred is a mind-body-spirit state sometimes described as being 'in the zone,' being 'in flow,' or being fully present. It is a state in which we are calm, collected and purposeful. When we are centred, our mind is clear and undistracted, we are not caught up in emotions and narratives, and everything feels effortless. It is as if we are connected to something bigger, more universal. This resourceful and relaxed place is a skilful way of being in conversation, especially when an issue is emotionally charged. What might change if we cultivate the habit of bringing ourselves to centre whenever we experience a jolt or a flinch in a conversation, or whenever we find ourselves warming up to a rant? What if we paused and centred whenever we felt the urge to resist or correct the opinion of others? What if we centred as we listen to others, becoming fully present to them as they speak and being fully present to ourselves as we respond?

You have probably experienced being centred, perhaps when you have been completely absorbed in something, such as a competitive event, an engaging piece of work, or making music or art. Can you remember such a time? How would you describe the experience? What characterises this state for you?

The state of flow or centre can be accessed intentionally, through mind, body or spirit practices. Experiencing a sense of physical centre is a straightforward way to begin, and it links to the soothing cycle of the fight/flight/freeze system, in which blood returns to the peripheries, heartbeat slows, breath lengthens, and the mouth moistens again. These physiological changes are all interconnected and one aspect of them can be brought into consciousness and acted on directly. That aspect is breathing.

Breathing is an activity that mostly occurs outside our awareness. In, out, in, out, in, out, from the moment we are born to the moment of our death. Our breath is always with us. What we often forget is that we can influence our breath with our attention.

Try it now. Become aware of your breath for a moment and become curious about this complex physiological process. Each breath enters by the nose or mouth and travels into the lungs, where it enriches blood with oxygen and collects toxic gases to transport outside our bodies. Follow the journey for a couple of breaths. Notice which parts of your ribcage expand and contract as you breathe. Notice whether your abdomen rises and falls. Can you sense your diaphragm contracting and releasing? Is there a gap between the inbreath and the outbreath? Between the outbreath and the inbreath?

Now play with your breath a little, perhaps make the inbreath longer, or make the outbreath a series of short 'puffs,' or lengthen the gap between inbreath and outbreath. You can, with mindful attention, direct your breath. If you lengthen and deepen your breathing, particularly the outbreath, you encourage the soothing cycle of the autonomic nervous system and calm your physiology, beginning to move towards a more centred state.

The calming action of deeper breathing can be reinforced by posture and by visualisation. First of all, refine your posture so you are upright and dignified. If you are sitting, move towards the front of your chair, put your feet flat on the floor and sense your spine lengthening upwards from your pelvis. If you are standing, place your feet approximately hip width apart and stand tall. Whether sitting or standing, imagine a silken thread attached to the crown of your head, drawing your crown towards the sky. The back of your neck will be long, your chin tilted slightly inwards towards your throat. This posture lengthens your upper body and creates more room to breathe.

Now imagine your breath as travelling up and down your body. On an inbreath, imagine it moving upwards, gently lengthening your spine and refining your posture. On an outbreath, imagine it moving downwards, softening your chest and belly whilst remaining upright and tall. After a few breaths, imagine that the inbreath travels up and out of the top of your head, spiralling up the silken thread between your crown and the sky. Next, sense your outbreath moving down through your body, perhaps spiralling, and imagine that it flows out through the soles of your feet, forming roots in the ground below you.

How do you feel after bringing your attention fully to your breathing? Notice any changes in your breath. You can use this breathing practice to pause for breath whenever you want to regain your composure.

There are many practices for using the breath as part of a process to bring you to calmness, and the description above draws on threads common to martial arts, yoga and meditation. You can use your imagination in any way that helps you achieve a sense of connection between sky and ground, passing through your human form.

Tom Crum sets out a foundation breathing practice in *Three Deep Breaths,*[14] which is a parable about a busy executive living life in an uncentred way and the impact this has on those around him. The words I use when guiding Tom's three deep breaths are:

Breath 1: Centre

Breathe in the present moment – sounds, colours, textures, feelings – with balance and energy.

Breathing out, let go of any tension, niggles or irritations you're holding on to.

Breath 2: Possibility

Breathe in your broadest perspective, your highest and most generous intent to offer service.

Breathing out, let go of any limiting thoughts, feelings and beliefs that restrict your options. Let go of any certainties, any should's or ought's, any easy answers or advice.

Breath 3: Discovery

Breathe in the things you don't understand, the freedom to play in the vastness of what is not known, in support of discovering a path through your challenge.

Breathing out, let go of judgement.

143

As you centre, your attention is internal for a few moments. Once centred, turn your attention outwards. You may find you become aware of all that surrounds you in a heightened way, with curiosity, but without attachment.

❚❚

Another centring practice comes from Wendy Palmer.[15] Once we have an upright and dignified posture, Wendy invites us to become aware of the space, or energy field, that we occupy. Our presence does not stop at our skin – we emit heat (and possibly other energies) from our body, reaching several inches into the atmosphere around us. As largely visual creatures, we tend to be more aware of what is in front of us than behind, or above and below. Perhaps we also have more awareness of one side than another. Ask yourself: what if there was a little more balance in the energy all around me, front and back, left and right, above and below? Experience your mind, body and spirit in the centre of your energy field. While our skeleton holds us upright and tall, we can imagine our flesh softening. Let go of any tension in your forehead, your jaw and your shoulders. Imagine being relaxed like a cat, soft and yet completely alert.

As the final part of her centring practice, Wendy Palmer strengthens and supports emotional resilience by cultivating a quality of leadership presence. What quality might enhance your leadership presence and make a material difference to your leadership conversations? Examples are: composure, clarity, confidence, ease, inclusion, groundedness, generosity and respect. Choose a quality and ask yourself: what if there was a little more of my quality in my being right now?

❚❚

If centre is a state we can access from choice, the principal challenge is remembering this when we are caught in the throes of a heated or tricky conversation. Centre is a skilful state and contributes materially to developing our scope for having 'good conversations in bad weather.' If we can commit to developing our capacity for being in this resourceful state, we increase our options in challenging circumstances. To cultivate the ability to recover centre when under pressure we have to practice.

The purpose of practising is to train your body into a centring habit. I have a tip to pass on from my own experience: however skillful I get at bringing myself to centre when I'm on my own, it is much harder to centre when engaged with someone else's energy in a conversation. If you are truly curious about developing the capacity for stability of mind, body and spirit in charged or turbulent circumstances, I invite you to find a group to work with. There is no substitute for working with others in a safe environment to strengthen your capacity for recovering centre.

Practice *18* – developing a centring routine and cultivating a centring habit

Connecting to centre is most powerful if you engage body, mind and spirit. In creating a centring practice, be mindful of practicalities. A practice takes many repetitions to become a habit, and yet more to be accessible under pressure. Develop a practice you can stick with over time.

Body element:
Revisit the basic breathing practice from this chapter. When you attain a sense of centre, what does it feel like? Which parts of the body are you particularly aware of? What phrase or checklist might help you to reproduce this posture?

What works best for you to support your breath lengthening, deepening, slowing? Is there a physical action, such as placing your hand on your abdomen, that might help you breathe more deeply?

Mind element:
A core practice for calming the mind is to follow the breath. You can also calm the mind through visualisation, physical activity or music – something that gives your mind a brief time-out from whatever is currently occupying it.

Spirit element:
What personal quality do you want to embody and cultivate in your leadership conversations? You might ask, 'what would it be like if I could have a little more of my leadership quality in my being right now?' (Wendy Palmer).

Practising your mind, body, spirit elements:
Which situations can you use to practice bringing your body, mind and spirit to rest in centre, becoming completely present to the moment? For example, sitting at traffic lights, waiting for the kettle to boil, etc. How will you remind yourself that these events are opportunities to centre? Plan to practice centring at least ten times a day.

146

Notes and reflections

Chapter *19* Skilful advocacy, inquiry and pause

'Music is the spaces between the notes.'
Claude Debussy

The impact of difference, pressure and the unfamiliar on our physiology is to trigger fight/flight/freeze reactions. In terms of conversation, I equate these three reactions to verbal brawling (spoken conflict), avoidance of conflict (external or internal) and indecision, which can manifest as no decision/choice or as swinging from one view to another. As contributions to conversation, these three approaches represent unskilful advocacy, unskilful inquiry and something I will call unskilful pausing. As conversational reflexes, they are uncentred or reactive and they tend to be enacted outside awareness; we are not making fully conscious choices, we are reacting to the present based on our fears, anxieties, previous experiences and our risk profile. If we can access a centred state, we return to our capacity for skilful advocacy, inquiry and pausing for breath.

I will start with a metaphor. There is a beautiful Zen painting called *Circle, Triangle, Square* by Sengai Gibon, which simply depicts these shapes in brushstrokes. I understand the painting to represent the universe, in that everything is symbolised by one or other of these forms. This concept is used by Aikido practitioners and other martial artists to define the different energies used in martial practice. Circle, triangle and square might also be used as a metaphor for energies engaged in conversation.

In martial arts, a triangular shape can represent something penetrating, such as a punch or other attack. It can also represent a shape that moves sleekly past an incoming energy, the point of a triangle making a small target, and the strong sides offering a shape like the bow of a boat, carving through waves.

In contrast, a circular shape can either spiral inwards or spiral outwards. Incoming energy can be spiralled in on itself, closing it down, or it can be spiralled out, and be redirected out of range. It can also represent a shape that is open and inclusive, ready to receive and ask questions of other energies.

A square shape can stop and neutralise incoming energy, creating a block. It can also represent a shape that is still and stable.

In translating these ideas into conversations, I think of a triangle as, quite literally, making a point. A triangle can be directional and is a strong shape. If I choose one point of a triangle and focus on it, I see two straight sides leading into that point, containing a wedge of space, supported by a third straight line at the back. As a metaphor for advocacy, the point is the position being taken or the opinion being presented, while the strong triangular shape represents clear boundaries around a wedge of information and experience that has been taken into account by an advocator. Somewhere in this triangular shape of advocacy we might imagine a ladder of inference; the strong sides can make it difficult for another perspective, or point, to penetrate. In its triangular nature, advocacy can become too pointed, too excluding, too forceful. It can represent dogmatic thinking or violent opposition to other points of view.

A circular shape is softer and can be inclusive, as represented by the many traditions that sit in a circle to talk. If I think of a spiral, I can imagine it as a metaphor for two aspects of inquiry, spiralling inwards to better understand someone's point of view, and spiralling outwards to get more perspective. A spiral either focuses in on an issue, getting clearer about the nub of it, or it circles out, getting a sense of the bigger context of an issue. A circle can also represent directionless and enclosed thinking, or a diffuse and abstract response to other points of view.

A square shape can represent a stable and steady demeanour; standing one's ground. It can be a shape of stillness and so a shape of centre and presence. A square can represent a receptive wait-and-see stance, a solid place of attending. However, it can also represent stuckness in thinking or be an inflexible block in the face of other points of view.

Up to this point, I have referred to dialogue as a balance of advocacy and inquiry (Argyris). In the metaphor of shapes, dialogue would be a balance of triangular advocating energy, and circular inquiring energy. Drawing on the ancient Zen wisdom of circle, triangle, square, I expand this to include the notion of a square pausing energy – a centred stillness – as an integral part of dialogue. Dialogue is then a conversation in which centred (or skilful) advocating, inquiring and pausing are in balance.

❙❙

In using triangle, circle and square to link martial arts ideas with advocacy, inquiry and pausing, it is apparent that each shape has both beneficial attributes and a shadow side. When we engage from centre, a core place of integrity, we tend to be skilful in our advocacy, inquiry and pausing. When we engage in an uncentred way, we tend to be less skilful and more prone to perpetuating familiar patterns when they no longer serve us.

There are many ways to be uncentred or off-balance. However, if I reflect on my experience with the martial aspects of T'ai Chi, I find I either try too hard, becoming tense, or I am a little bit too relaxed and floppy. This suggests two ways for being off-centre: over-exerting and under-exerting. The energies of too much and too little can be linked to yang and yin which, in Chinese philosophy, represent two fundamental principles of the universe. Yang is active and masculine in nature, whilst yin is receptive and feminine. They are opposites, and are complementary rather than opposing. They demonstrate that difference can be generative, as masculine and feminine combine in so many different circumstances to create new life.

As human beings, in all our living, thinking, talking, acting and being, we can see ourselves as a blend of these two fundamental principles. In an ideal (and idealistic) world, we would be a perfect blend, poised and balanced in yin and yang: we would be centred. In reality, we each have a tendency for either yin or yang to dominate. We generally tend to be off-centre and too yang (for example, too rigid or forceful) or off-centre and too yin (for example, too relaxed or accommodating). My own tendency is to be tilted towards yang, eager to engage, trying too hard, fixing, progressing and over-playing my hand. What is yours?

If we return to circle, triangle and square, how might we make practical use of a sense of shape for advocacy, inquiry and pausing? First of all, consider how you might describe your own tendency in conversational style – is it edgy, sharp or pointed for instance? Is it rounded, encompassing, at ease? Do you tend to be even-handed, stable? Are you most comfortable with making points or with receiving what is said and perhaps turning it around, circling it to see it from different angles and to gain understanding? Or perhaps you are most comfortable waiting and seeing, sitting all-square and considering whether or how to make a point, or how you might look into someone else's perspective.

Taking this sense of your tendency in style, how does it play out when you are centred? How is it different when you are off-balance? The following three tables explore the possibilities for advocacy, inquiry and pause. The columns in each

151

table represent a centred, poised contribution or response, and what might be expressed in an uncentred way (either yang or yin) when faced with conflict, stress, pressure, threat, fear or anxiety. A brief explanation follows each table.

We start with advocacy:

	Centred, poised	Uncentred, over-exerting (too yang)	Uncentred, under-exerting (too yin)
Triangle ▲	Skilful advocacy. Offers position, or approach. Contributes direction or alignment/ performance. I intend to enter, offer a point. I recognise that others will have a different view and I invite their voices into the conversation. Perhaps an equilateral triangle.	Unskilful advocacy. Imposes, exploits, fixes, rescues. Is sure of being 'right.' Is forceful, and this may feel like attack, push-back, perhaps violence. Tends towards finalising, to closure/ settlement. Tends to exclude or discount other voices. Perhaps too 'pointy' – an acute triangle, a spear-head.	Unskilful advocacy. Tends to exclude or discount own voice. Withholds energy, information, time, power, resources. Disagrees through silence and advocates outside a conversation or through actions. Perhaps not pointy enough – slightly flat, an obtuse triangle.

When we make a point, we often reinforce it with a physical movement, such as pointing a finger or making a chopping motion with our hand. These movements introduce a sense of a triangular body shape when we consider that they extend forward into a point, and we can imagine that, with our back as the base of a triangle, our energetic shape is also triangular, with the apex ahead of us. In skilful advocacy, our intent to advocate, our energy and our words will align to give a powerful clarity in speaking our truth.

152

However, we can miscalibrate and be too forceful in making a point, which others may experience as overbearing, or we can lack precision, which others may experience as lack of focus. It is sometimes easier to get an initial sense of this by reflecting on the impact that other people have on you. Begin to listen for skilful advocacy in your friends and colleagues. Do you have someone in your environment who predominately uses advocacy, making statements in the form of answers, directions, fixes? What does this feel like energetically? What happens when someone is overly pointed? What happens when someone is trying to make a point but is diffuse in what they are saying? How do you experience this?

Next we consider inquiry:

	Centred, poised	Uncentred, over-exerting (too yang)	Uncentred, under-exerting (too yin)
Circle ●	Skilful inquiry. Contributes 'making whole,' building on ideas and creating perspective. Offers curiosity, exploration, discovery. Meets other voices and moves side by side. I intend to include all voices. I seek to understand other points of view. A circle, spiralling inwards or outwards.	Unskilful inquiry. Tends to add too much energy and interest to other voices, to almost 'add spin' where in agreement. Tends to defend 'on behalf of' where injustice is perceived. Might rescue or minimise difference, might smooth things over. Can seek to include everyone and everything. Perhaps an ellipse, with two foci rather than one centre.	Unskilful inquiry. Tends to appease and to be passive, wishy-washy, avoiding issues and conflict. Is over-accommodating. Seeks protection and tends to defer to other voices, perhaps with resignation. Drains energy from a situation. Perhaps a dot, a circle with a collapsed boundary.

What physical indications suggest that someone is listening, curious and seeking to understand our position? A first element is that they attend fully to what is being said. What does attending fully look like, physically? It is much harder to describe this than it is to describe advocacy. We certainly know when someone's attention is elsewhere; their face or body is often turned slightly away. We also know the signs of active listening, such as nodding, leaning slightly towards a speaker and making affirmative sounds, but this can be happening at a surface level. When someone is listening profoundly, how do we know?

The question of which physical and energetic indications give a sense of profound listening is particularly important for professional listeners. When, as a coach, I am fully present to my client's story, how do I convey this? How am I sitting? I will be upright, but relaxed. My spine will be long and open, not collapsed forward, squashing my abdomen, or leaning back into the chair. I will have a sense of being centred in my own energy and wisdom, whilst listening to my client's story with compassion and impartiality. My hands will be resting somewhere. My feet will be on the ground. At some level, this posture minimises edges – it is contained and grounded, yet open. I have a sense of my energy being circular and inclusive, emanating out from my centre to include my client. An open attitude of sitting evokes a circular sense of listening and inquiring energy. The balance is delicate because in practice I am listening to my client and also listening lightly for what arises in me, so that my own internal dialogue is available too. How do you sit when you are attending fully, listening profoundly? What is your sense of your energy?

As with advocacy, we can miscalibrate the balance of listening – we can lean in too much, over-listening, smothering the other person's energy and not attending to our own strength and centre. When we inquire or listen too closely, we can close down a conversation just as effectively as someone who advocates loudly and inflexibly. The notion that there can be such a thing as too much listening may feel challenging at first: consider it a hypothesis and test your experience.

When we inquire or listen too loosely, the conversation can lose energy and stutter just as effectively as when someone advocates too generally or with too little commitment to their point of view. Returning to posture and the impact of our shape, if we lean back too far in our seat, it's harder to maintain connected attention and we may look (and possibly feel) disinterested. Slumping back in a chair looks (and feels) casual, and depending on the circumstance, this may convey the impression that the conversation is not important.

Finally, we look at pausing:

	Centred, poised	Uncentred, over-exerting (too yang)	Uncentred, under-exerting (too yin)
Square	Skilful pausing. Waits and sees, is open, attending, receptive. Senses own internal voices, achieving clarity, creating choices. I am present. Perhaps an empty square.	Unskilful pausing. Freezes, endures, blocks, resists. Can be stubborn, defiant, unmoving. Seeks survival. Engaged but rigid. Perhaps a filled-in square or a cube/block.	Unskilful pausing. Is stuck, indecisive. Absents self, avoids people, holds self separate, remote. Is unconnected and untouchable, out of reach. Disengaged. Perhaps a squashed square, a rhomboid.

For pausing, I suggest that the physical manifestation is a centred stillness. The pause is mindfulness, the moment of being aware of our reactions and yet choosing to let them go and be fully present and responsive. We collect ourselves, so we can respond from a generous and abundant place rather than seeking to win, or to help, or some other habitual motivation. Our attention may be inwards for a moment, while we feel for, hear and consider different perspectives internally.

It is possible to over-exert and under-exert with pausing, just as it is with advocacy and inquiry. In under-exerting, I might become too internally focused and disconnect from others in the conversation. I may become self-absorbed. In over-exerting, I may block, and become stubborn and unmoving. I may decide to sit out a conflict in silence, to endure and not offer my position or inquire into anyone else's. Or I may pause, because I notice a reaction to something, but not pause long enough, and so fall into uncentred advocacy or uncentred inquiry. So with pausing too, there is a centred balance; checking internally with sufficient care and depth to offer a considered response, whether that is to state my position or to seek further information or perspective.

In reflecting on this metaphor, I invite you to see if you get a sense of the energetic feeling of conversations – some are too edgy, pointy or hard and some are too diffuse, loose and soft. Similarly our physical being can be tense, rigid, edgy or collapsed, floppy and casual. We find balance in our physical and energetic presence by being centred, and there is an equivalent in terms of conversation, a sense of centred, balanced energy that is poised, natural and effortless.

If we accept that we have an energetic shape when we speak, what happens if our words and our energy are at odds? For example, what happens if we state our position when our energy is organised in an open, inquiring way? Or what happens if we ask for more information when our energy is organised in a pointed, advocating way? What is the likely impact on others? I invite you to begin to explore this as you engage in conversation. What is the impact on you when another person's words, body and energy seem out of alignment?

Aligning and centring ourselves, so that our words, intent and energy are congruent, is a matter of dynamic balance. Moment by moment we are

156

influenced by our environment, circumstances and incoming information. Internally, we wobble, we recover. We react, we pause and centre. This can happen many times in a single conversation. Similarly, any sense of balance of skilful advocacy, inquiry and pausing in dialogue is dynamic, shaped by setting, words, relationships, energy, time, circumstances and many other factors.

I gained insight into the complexity and delicacy of dynamic balance when I sprained my ankle badly. I quickly regained some movement and mobility in my normal walking plane, but if my weight was in any way skewed towards the outside of my foot, I got a sharp reminder that my healing was a work in progress. When I returned to some gentle T'ai Chi practice, all was well until I tried to stand on my injured leg to make a sweeping kick. Until that moment, I had no idea how much movement takes place in a foot when we balance on one leg; the many small bones in my foot and the connecting tissues across the top of my foot and around my ankle were in constant subtle movement which, because of my injury, was sharply painful. The act of balancing on one leg involves many more parts of the body than I was aware of, and is a complex and dynamic process at a subtle level, below everyday awareness.

This offers a metaphor for attending to less-than-obvious aspects of conversations if we want to find balance in advocacy, inquiry and pausing. At an obvious visual level of balancing on one leg, I know that if I try too hard, I contract my energy and wobble. If I am too casual, with dissipated energy or attention, I may not get the sense of alignment required to support myself. I may over-exert or under-exert. If I centre, I align my energy and balance effortlessly. This offers a potent metaphor for offering poised, skilful contributions to conversation.

Finally, if I am balancing on one leg, whether injured or not, my attention tends to be in my body. If a thought comes into my mind, I get distracted by it and tend to wobble. If our body is doing one thing, and our mind another, we are off-balance or uncentred. This is a powerful reason to become more aware of the language of the body and to cultivate the capacity to sense whether body and mind are aligned.

Practice *19* – attending to your energy and physicality in conversation

When you are next in a charged or tense conversation, attend to what is happening in your body. Where, specifically, is any tension situated? What other sensations do you notice?

What is the orientation of your body to others in the conversation? Leaning in, turned away, a bit of both? Do your hands move instinctively to protect a part of your body, for example, your throat? Your heart?

How would you describe your energy at these moments?

You are noticing the impact on your physiology of difficult conversations and the energy of other people. Repeat this inquiry in different situations. Is there a pattern? Now experiment with your sense of personal space and centre.

Choose a conversation with one other person, where you find yourself in a charged dialogue situation with a familiar pattern beginning to manifest. Notice your personal space, the space of the other person and the space connecting you. How appropriate does it feel?

Now practice centre. On an inbreath, refine your posture, slowly exhale and soften your jaw and shoulders. Become aware of the space you occupy and envisage it as a circle, balanced front, back, left, right, above and below. Sense yourself in the centre of your field.

Now expand your energetic field to include the other person while remaining calm and poised in the centre of it. You will need to expand the back and sides, above and below, as well as the front. What impact does centring and adjusting your space have on you, on the other person and on the conversation? Try this several times.

Notes and reflections

Chapter *20* Internal conflict

'Energy organises around what is most articulate in a system.' Wendy Palmer

I've already touched on the principle that, as human beings, we are not coherent in our views about the world we inhabit and about our experiences. We have many voices and can be in two minds about an issue. This is a fairly normal state of affairs. However, when an issue becomes important, or we have to make a decision, our multiple perspectives can be confusing. If we are skilful, we will try to unpick our confusion, examine our ambivalence, and make a settled choice. If we don't do this, we risk confusing others by giving out mixed messages or appearing to change our minds frequently.

A simple example might involve my being invited to take on an additional project. Part of me welcomes the opportunity, but another part of me knows I am already over-committed. Perhaps I am excited by what is on offer and I don't want to risk upsetting someone by saying, 'no.' However, I know in my heart that someone else could lead the project just as well, if not better. My truth is a complex 'both/and' response – yes, I'd love to, and no, it's not good timing. The question is whether to respond 'yes' and possibly feel resentful and pressured, or respond 'no' and regret the missed opportunity and risk the disappointment of the project sponsor. Or is there another option which would allow me to be true to both parts of me? That would depend on many things, such as my relationship with the project sponsor, the nature of the other things I'm juggling and any flexibility in project timelines.

There are some fairly obvious multiple voices within us. We might belong to a profession, and we will have a role or roles in a family. We may also see ourselves as artists, musicians or dancers, or as belonging to a club or community, or as a sportsperson or gardener. What defining roles and identities do you have within? Each of these aspects enables us to see the world in a different way, offering contrasting perspectives and insights. However, they can also generate internal conflict.

In addition, we have more subtle and nuanced shades of voice within us. Some might link to our formative years and experiences, perhaps giving rise to incompatible beliefs and values. Again this is usual, yet it can be challenging to uncover internal inconsistencies when we have choices to make. For example, I recall the internal conflict of a leader who felt she was acting uncharacteristically in a work context, compromising on an important value by not speaking out about something she saw as unethical. Her point of view, had she expressed it, would have been at best unpopular, and at worst career-limiting. In our conversation it became apparent that there was another important value in play; she was supporting her children through university and this influenced her approach to risk. She was full of self-recrimination about her failure to uphold her values at work. I asked some questions to discern the relative importance of her values, and we found that her work-related value was secondary to her family-related value and that this was appropriate for her at the time. She was able to settle her perspective; she had effectively accommodated two different voices within her.

Another way to explore our different voices is to tune into key energy centres in our bodies. The Taoist tradition, often linked with T'ai Chi, recognises three 'tan tiens' (said dun-ti-ens), or energy centres, in our bodies. These are located in the very centre of our heads (behind what is known as the third eye between the eyebrows), the centre of our solar plexus area (which includes the heart), and our centre of gravity, in the middle of the space that is a little below our navel. In this approach, we assume that we have a thinking view, an emotion-oriented perspective and a deeper gut-feel for a predicament, and that they are often different. To be aligned and congruent, we can identify and clarify these voices and, perhaps, be curious about the relationship between them.

For my part, my mind-voice or head-voice is dominant. It is quick to assume that it knows what is needed in any given circumstance. It is loud and righteous, confident in its reasoning and judgement. My solar plexus/heart voice is slower and quieter. Not only is it softly-spoken, I experience it as speaking in a foreign tongue – my mind does not always understand its language and so I have to pay close attention to discern it. My gut voice, in my centre of gravity, is slower again to formulate and articulate a response. However, my gut voice seems louder than my heart voice and its language is easier for my mind to comprehend and take account of, if I remember to listen in the first place. What is the balance within you? Which is your loudest and most persistent voice? Which is the quietest and most difficult to understand? How might you cultivate the capacity to tune into your quieter voice(s)?

Our non-mind voices may speak in images, sounds or sensations. I have found that when I am uncertain, confused or pressured, it pays to listen for them. For example, when I first offered a leadership retreat, my head was completely sure about it. However, in doing some deeper reflection, I found that my heart was fearful and anxious about what people would think of this

162

less-than-mainstream endeavour. I also found that my gut was just plain afraid that I would not be up to the job. I have a history of situations where I've bitten off more than I can chew and found myself out of my depth; these memories reside in my gut, while my head thinks it has reasoned them away. To offer the retreat congruently, whole-heartedly and from centre, I needed to listen to all these voices and to inquire into whether I could find an approach that would accommodate the concerns of my heart and gut. Eventually I remembered that I am not solely responsible for the outcomes of a retreat, meeting the concerns of my gut. I was able to see myself as a host rather than a creator or leader, meeting the concerns of my heart. By acknowledging my anxieties and fears, I was able to be more aligned than I would have been had I simply followed my no-limits head-voice and ignored my heart and gut.

The framework of head, heart and gut voices offers an entry point for tuning into our body-voices. For those who readily access their many voices, there is a third way to explore them, which is to listen more generally, more freely, for the nature and style of each voice. When you are in conversation, notice where in your body you experience sensations and responses. Are there any patterns? Where are the most consistent contributors? If you are skilled in the languages of your body, be curious about the role of your head-voice in your internal conversation – how does your mind respond to contributions from your body? How are you balancing thinking, emotions, sensations and other energetic patterns as you respond to life?

My working hypothesis is that very few of us have equal access to all our voices. We habitually pay more attention to some than to others. If our head-voice is loud and clear, our body-voices may get much less attention. If we are alert to our body-voices, they can sometimes drown out our mind. The inquiry for each of us is to seek to understand the forms, shapes and habits of our internal conversations well enough to find dynamic balance, or centre, in the midst of our personal complexity and conflict.

When conflict in our internal dialogue goes unrecognised, it can lead to conflict with others. If we don't have an opportunity to express any internal unease, irritation or frustration, we risk expressing it (or leaking it) into unrelated external situations. In being clear about the nature of our internal dialogue, we can be skilful in ensuring that underlying beliefs, values, feelings or viewpoints do not unintentionally colour our advocacy or our inquiry. Some of our latent internal positions and agendas may be dark, shadowy, unworthy or shameful, which is one of the reasons we conceal them, even from ourselves. We don't like to acknowledge our more tarnished motives, but if we don't acknowledge these darker aspects, it is my experience that they leak into important conversations in subversive and unhelpful ways.

For example, have you ever taken back a piece of work from someone you initially delegated it to and completed it yourself? Alternatively, you may have been on the receiving end of this kind of behaviour. What is really going on? As delegator, I am probably thinking that the work isn't being done to my standard. I may have tried to give feedback to this effect but, for whatever reason, nothing changed, or I may not have even attempted to give feedback. In either case I have got frustrated by the perceived inadequacy of the person doing the work. My attention has shifted from the quality of the work to generalisations about the person, and since I don't like to think of myself as judgemental, I form another strategy for dealing with the situation. I take over the work rather than investing time in finding a skilful way to talk honestly about the situation and how we are creating it between us. What is the impact when a delegator reclaims work? When this happened to me, I felt my boss didn't trust me and didn't rate my work. I also felt incensed by his explanation because it didn't ring true; his unspoken judgement was manifest in his action.

164

The complexity and subtlety of our internal dialogue means that we need to slow down to elucidate and articulate our true thinking, feeling and sensing about a situation. To do this, I find I need to create time and space, often walking on a beach, or climbing a hill. What circumstances, conditions or activities allow you to tune into your deeper feelings about an issue? How might you cultivate more capacity to sense any unhelpful conflict in your internal dialogue?

Practice *20* – raising awareness of your internal dialogue

When you are next in a dilemma about something, find some quiet space and commit to exploring what you really think, feel and sense in relation to your issue.

Write down the nub of your dilemma. Note the key points of your thinking about it, from any or all perspectives, with any consequences.

Now sit in a comfortable and upright posture and bring your attention to your breath for a moment or two. Just notice the inhale and the exhale, one after another. See if you can let your breath 'breathe you' for a while.

Now bring your attention to your dilemma and see what aspect of it arises first. Give this aspect a name or short description and then ask: where in my body does this arise? Notice any sensations arising in your body.

When you feel you have found the source, you might make a note or two, then return your attention to the breath and your inhale and exhale for a few moments. Adjust your posture to be upright again and let your breath breathe you.

Now place your attention on your dilemma again and notice what aspect of it arises next. Give this aspect a name or short description and then ask: where in my body does this arise? Notice any sensations occurring.

Repeat this cycle of attending to your breath and your dilemma until nothing more arises. Then ask: what is needed in response to this situation? Wait for a settled sense of acceptance. If your mind jumps in with an answer, thank it and say, 'not right now.' Bring your attention back to your breath and ask again, 'what is needed in response to this situation?'

166

What are you learning about the way you approach complex situations
where there is no single 'right' answer?

Notes and reflections

Chapter *21* Why body and conversation matters

'Have your feelings (or they will have you).'
Stone, Patton and Heen

To some extent, I've asked you to take the link between body and conversation on trust. Why might we want to develop our faculties in these matters? How will more awareness of physiology affect our conversations, and our influence? When is it most necessary to bring this heightened awareness into play? This chapter outlines three examples in which being aware of physiology and having the capacity to recover centre might make a difference.

Shrinking logic

A primary reason for paying attention to physiology is the way that our fight/flight/freeze system hijacks our logic and our ability to reason. Have you ever found yourself set on a course of action, and then meeting an immovable obstacle that seems specifically designed to thwart you in getting the result you want? It can be quite a simple thing.

For example, as a young woman, I went to my local supermarket and did the weekly shop, only for something to happen at the till that caused a problem. I had stacked all my shopping on the conveyor, with the exception of a bag of cat litter that was too heavy to lift. To acquire it, I had slid it from a low shelf onto the low rack of the trolley, but I couldn't lift it from there to the conveyor. I cannot now remember the exchange that took place about how to get the cat litter scanned, I just remember it reached an impasse very quickly. Hot, bothered, tired and doing one of my least favourite activities (shopping), I literally became speechless and I simply walked away, leaving my shopping on the conveyor. I was probably smirking slightly – the unhelpful assistant would now have some explaining to do.

Of course, as I calmed down, I realised that I would now have to drive to another supermarket and do the shopping again. Basically, in the heat of my irritation and frustration, my capacity for logic shrank and I made a completely irrational choice. I had been hijacked by my physiology to the extent that I could not reason with the check-out person or myself. I was unable to think. I could only react. Whilst the result in this instance was only some inconvenience, there have been many other occasions when this pattern has had seriously adverse consequences.

On what occasions have you experienced a complete shutdown of logic in the face of frustration, irritation, resentment or anger? What happens to your physiology and your ability to think? What can you learn about your patterns and the triggers for such loss of capacity?

When you are next in a conversation where this happens, see if you can pause, align your posture, take some deep breaths and centre. What happens?

Displacement

Another reason for paying attention to our physiology is to become familiar with the body-sensations of states such as stress, fear, anger, anxiety, disappointment and loss. Sensations such as churning, tension, constriction, heat and pain can give vital early clues to emotions that we are not fully experiencing or taking into account. At one level, ignoring this information might be a helpful containing or coping strategy. However, on other levels, our body may be taking the strain, risking illness, or we may find ourselves displacing these emotions into other unrelated situations.

A personal example of this happened at a time when I was under very great stress both in terms of the viability of my business and the wellbeing of some key relationships in my life. I felt alone, under pressure and anxious. Being a sturdy type, I was just getting on with it, working very hard to keep my business afloat, whilst discounting the impact of some fractured relationships. At this time I was studying to become a coach supervisor. I was genuinely committed to the programme, but I was struggling to find the time, money and energy necessary for it. I found myself resentful of the required group work as my preference for studying is solitary. I was unable to understand or articulate why I was resentful, but I thought I was managing the situation. Eventually emotions blew up in a conference call, resulting in an angry fight and the dissolution of a work group.

Given the context, I reflected deeply on the matter. There were systemic issues at play, and also some unskilful communication and clashes of style, but I couldn't quite understand how a working relationship had unravelled so spectacularly. Help came from Mary Beth O'Neill's book, *Executive Coaching with Backbone and Heart*.[16] In it, she describes how we can displace anxiety from a system where expressing it is perceived to be high risk, into a system that is perceived as lower risk. This described what I had been doing; I couldn't afford to express myself in my local networks so my anxiety popped up (unskilfully) in a more remote system of relative strangers, and in a way that was disproportionate to the actual stressors in that system. If I had been more alert to the tensions that were clearly building in my body over a considerable period of time, I may have been able to be more skilful, authentic and appropriate in each system.

Can you think of a time when you have tried to ignore a stressful situation in one part of your life, only to become irritable, inarticulate or unpredictable in another context? Are there any contexts in which long-standing pressures are building? Where do you displace them?

In a smaller context, have you displaced emotion suppressed from one conversation into another? For example you may have been sharp with your direct report after you have been criticised by your boss. When you suppress your voice, how can you become alert to the impact of this on unrelated situations?

Leakage

A third reason for paying attention to physiology is closely related to displacement, but feels subtly different. By leakage, I mean that the emotions we think we are containing and managing begin to show up in the external world as something like behavioural tics. My personal favourite is the way I find myself making a mess in my living space when I am stressed and anxious. It is as if I want to make things worse for myself, and will keep adding to the mess until it becomes untenable. I now catch myself quite early in this leakage process and acknowledge my stress, then tidy up and have an early night.

Another example of leakage is where the impact of a major life event – such as loss – impacts on working life. I had an experience of this when my marriage broke down. I was on edge generally, with my fight/flight/freeze system on full alert all the time. I had an exaggerated startle reaction, which meant that the smallest surprise caused me to jump out of my skin. I thought I was being normal but I was, quite literally, not myself. I behaved out of character in a number of ways. It was long before I had heard of centring, or being mindful, and long before I understood how my body speaks one language and my mind another. I do remember a colleague taking me aside and gently telling me that in a meeting with a potential client, I covered my mouth every time I spoke. This wasn't how I usually presented myself. Whilst there was nothing I could do about the circumstances that were so affecting my confidence and presence, I might have attended more to their impact on me and taken steps to get more support and more rest through a challenging time.

In general, leakage manifests as incongruence. We think we are managing or coping, but our body shows how we are not aligned. I see examples of this kind of tic all the time. For example, as a rookie coach, I had a client who clenched his jaw subtly whenever he was irritated by something I said. His response was always courteous, but I knew he was displeased. I was not experienced enough to handle this discrepancy in his demeanour at the time; we were both trapped by routines of what was acceptable behaviour in the circumstances. However, it remains with me as a powerful example of how the body speaks.

How does your physiology indicate that there is something you must attend to in your life? Is confusion, unhappiness, stress or pressure showing up in unhelpful ways in your leadership conversations? If so, how can you make sure you are getting appropriate support and how can you develop capacity for being centred, for being in flow, even in challenging situations?

Practice *21* – reflecting on the influence of fight/flight/freeze

Recall a time when your body chemistry hijacked your reason, and then reflect on the following questions:

What form does your 'hijack' take – fight, flight, or freeze?

What was the trigger point for fight, flight or freeze?

Track back to discover any previous events that meant your alarm system was already primed. Was pressure already building?

Does this pattern feel familiar? Can you identify any other situations where a similar pattern has played out?

With the benefit of hindsight (and with kindness and fascination), what are the key stages in the process of 'rising' to a situation – what happens in your body? At what point might you have taken some time out?

What might you learn about your earliest signs of rising tension, pressure and stress? Do you have any tell-tale feelings or behaviours that might signal a need to gain perspective?

How might you handle similar predicaments in the future?

Notes and reflections

Chapter 22 Pause for breath

'Our bodies communicate to us clearly and specifically,
if we are willing to listen to them.' Shakti Gawain

The focus of our inquiry into links between body and conversation has been on the legacy system that has evolved to keep us alive. Our fight/flight/freeze system is a chemical process, designed to flood the body with adrenalin and other agents to maximise the probability of survival. Once underway, this process focuses on the perceived threat and our capacity to reason, and gain perspective, shrinks or contracts.

In modern times, we need to become aware of the impact of this primitive arrangement and to develop the capacity to make a different choice when it begins to kick in. The different choice is centre. Centred, we have a quality of grounded empowerment that supports our ability to operate effectively. We can see the bigger picture, think creatively and hold difference in balance. From this place we can be resourceful and discerning, making mindful choices about our contributions to conversations.

The body has a deeper wisdom to offer us, if we attend to it. This invites us to make good contact with our body, to listen to the different parts of it and to nourish our physical being through this attention. So many of us take our bodies for granted, only paying attention when something goes wrong. How might you bring greater kindness and care-taking to your physical wellbeing? How can you ensure that your physical container is healthy and resilient in supporting your mind, body and spirit in leadership conversations?

My general premise is that the more often we can be centred and present in our conversations, the more we are able to conduct ourselves with grace, dignity and generosity. This leads us into the next inquiry, in which we explore how we can bring the best of ourselves to our leadership conversations, and perhaps tap into a sense of universal wisdom.

Practice 22 – pause for breath

This foundation practice appears at the end of each section of the book.

Sit in a comfortable upright posture, so that your feet are firmly planted on the floor and you are supporting your own back, rather than leaning against a chair. Rest your hands on your thighs, palms down.

Become aware of the contact between your feet/shoes and the floor. Become aware of the contact between your hands and your thighs. Become aware of the contact between your thighs and the chair. Become aware of the sitting bones, the bones at the base of the pelvis, pressing into the chair seat.

Notice your strong base, formed by your feet and sitting bones, and allow your spine to grow to its full length by gently imagining each vertebra lifting slightly from the one below. Sense lightness and spaciousness in your spine. Notice that your neck becomes long at the back, your chin tilted slightly towards your chest.

Now bring your attention to your breath. On each inhale, imagine your breath seeping into the spaces in your spine, allowing it to lengthen just a little bit more. On each exhale, imagine your breath flowing down through your chest and belly, softening any tension. Follow your breath for a few moments.

Now mentally scan your body and notice any places of tension, aching or discomfort. Choose one and, for a few breaths, imagine your inbreath soaking into this place and, on a longer exhale, imagine your outbreath dissolving any discomfort and carrying it out into the air around you, letting you rest.

After a few breaths, become aware of the contact between your sitting bones and the chair, between your hands and thighs, and between your feet and the ground.

Rise gently and stretch. You are ready to re-engage with the world.

Resource list for inquiry into impact of physiology

Journey to Centre, Tom Crum
Magic of Conflict, Tom Crum
Three Deep Breaths, Tom Crum
Focusing, Eugene Gendlin
The Tao of Pooh, Benjamin Hoff
Tai Chi as a Path of Wisdom, Linda Myoki Lehrhaupt
The Tao of Natural Breathing, Dennis Lewis
The Intuitive Body, Wendy Palmer
The Practice of Freedom, Wendy Palmer
Unlikely Teachers, Judy Ringer
From Chaos to Centre, Judy Warner

Part Four

SPIRIT AND CONVERSATION

Chapter 23   **Introduction**

Chapter 24   **Spirit as individual essence**

Chapter 25   **Spirit as collective energy**

Chapter 26   **Spirit in the face of challenging conversations**

Chapter 27   **Cultivating spirit as practice/discipline**

Chapter 28   **Pause for breath**

Resource list for more on cultivating your finest leadership spirit

Chapter 23 Introduction

*'In many traditional cultures, breath is envisioned as
a direct manifestation of spirit.' Dennis Lewis*

What is the relationship between our experience, our spirit and our talk? What does spirit mean in the context of leadership conversations? How does our spirit influence how we respond to circumstances?

My mental model for spirit is two-fold. One aspect relates to individuals and the other acknowledges that there is something beyond the individual, a sense of collective energy that links us all. For individuals, my sense of spirit is connected to the way we experience ourselves and how others experience us; namely, our presence. This is linked to the qualities that we bring into our leadership and the way we live our lives. It's about being in good contact with ourselves and our surroundings. Individual spirit has a sense of transcendence about it, of the kind described by Viktor Frankl when he spoke of spiritual freedom and inner liberty:

'Everything can be taken from a man but one thing: the last of the human freedoms – to choose one's attitude in any given set of circumstances, to choose one's own way.'

In our leadership conversations, individual spirit supports us when we need to say or hear difficult or unwelcome truths.

Beyond the individual, we may experience collective spirit when people come together to share in something that matters deeply to them all. Less tangibly, we may experience collective spirit as a deep sense of connection to our world, perhaps through a powerful feeling of our relationship to others, or a profound link with nature. In collective spirit we are in good contact with all that is possible, and in a way that is beyond our individual concerns. We know, in some way, that we are greater than the sum of individuals. In our leadership conversations we might seek to cultivate collective spirit as we engage with complex or challenging issues.

If these descriptions of individual and collective spirit ring true, how might we cultivate potential for them in our leadership conversations?

Revisiting the four fields of conversation,[6] introduced in Chapter 5, can provide a context. In the first energy field of politeness/routines, individual spirit sustains us in speaking out, despite social norms, and this may catalyse a more challenging conversation. Individual spirit provides courage and resilience so that we can stay with, and hold, the heightened energy in the second field of breaking open/debate. And individual spirit finds the humility, compassion and generosity to lay down the 'weapons' of our fiercely reasoned opinions, creating conditions for inquiry and reflection.

The third field of inquiry/reflection is defined by individual concerns and mindfulness, and this energy emerges when individuals are centred, when they are truly curious about the perspectives of others and are open to new thinking. Being centred brings with it a greater awareness and perspective; we are alive to, and inclusive of, the thinking and feelings of others. In this state, we may begin to open up to the possibility of a greater sense of collective spirit. As this possibility deepens, the collective may again become more important than individual voices and concerns, developing energy through which the fourth energy field of flow/dialogue manifests. In collective presence, it is as if we are a single intelligence, creating the conditions for universal truths to be expressed through us. This collective way of being is, of course, a new suite of social norms: as being part of the collective continues to predominate, we risk establishing a new form of politeness.

In exploring the territory of spirit and conversation, the invitation is to become more aware of our presence. In this endeavour, each of us will have a unique, and deeply personal starting place, and a perspective on what is important. We will each have our own journey to travel. The territory is, broadly, to be in deep contact with our essence, with our individual energy or spirit, and, at the same time, to be in deep contact with universal energy or spirit.

Practice *23* – noticing individual and collective spirit

Recall a conversation in which you felt a sense of shared purpose and connection. How would you describe your presence, your way of being in this conversation? How would you describe the presence of others? What qualities describe the conversation?

Notice if you have any sense of a shared presence, or energetic field, greater than the individuals present.

Now recall a conversation that seemed frustrating or aimless in some way. How would you describe your presence, your way of being, in this conversation? How would you describe the presence of others? In contrast to the purposeful and connected conversation, what was missing?

In reflecting, what can you learn?

Notes and reflections

Chapter 24 Spirit as individual essence

'Each of us must make his own true way, and when we do, that way will express the universal way.' Shunryu Suzuki

If individual spirit is related to our leadership presence and the qualities that we embody, then it is pivotal to our impact in conversations. If we turn up for a conversation short of time, distracted and crabby, how are others likely to respond, whatever we say? If we turn up calm, receptive and measured, what affect will this have, even if we have an unpopular message to share? This is not rocket science, and yet I have certainly done my share of being off-centre when turning up for a conversation significant enough to deserve more presence and attention. What do we need to attend to in order to bring our finest leadership presence to our important conversations?

My T'ai Chi teacher, Ian Cameron, talks about forging the spirit, in the way that metal is worked into artefacts. In *T'ai Chi Magazine* (Spring 2009), he writes about regular practice:

'The spirit to carry on, no matter what, gives you a vitality for life, a resilience and a lifelong interest. True spirit is not for show, it is personal, it lies within.'

185

These words offer a sense of spirit as character, in the same way that Stephen Covey speaks of character in his book *The 7 Habits of Highly Effective People.*[17] Covey's character habits focus on developing a clear sense of your contribution, qualities and intended legacy, and advocate starting with important things rather than urgent, pressing things. For most of us, there is work to be done in developing clarity about our character, gaining a strong sense of our internal core, values and ethics, and then living and working in a way that is congruent with them.

This way of living is part of what I see as spirit. It's about having the courage to live a life that is aligned with whatever we personally believe to be good, true and beautiful, regardless of what other people think. In our day and age, this can feel quite challenging. We live in an era of consuming, of image, of disposable fashion and goods, of pressure to keep up with technology, of 24/7 availability and countless other reasons to keep acquiring stuff or polishing our 'look.' To live in a way that considers legacy, our impact on the environment, for example, means consuming less, perhaps by wearing the same clothes for years. This risks comment, ridicule or even mild persecution.

In choosing our lifestyle, spirit and character can help us to hold our course when others question it. In conversation, depth of character, or spirit, can support us in voicing an unpopular opinion or speaking in contravention of established norms. Spirit helps us gracefully acknowledge when we are wrong. Character strengthens us to be true to our principles, perhaps as a lone voice when others want to take a more expedient path. Individual spirit has resilience, courage and determination. It also has something lighter, perhaps expansiveness and generosity, perhaps happiness, because it is grounded in a rich soil of deep values and purpose. Individual spirit, similar to Covey's character ethic, cannot be manufactured; it is not a technique, it is a way of being, a sense of deep congruence within. It builds on the stability of mind and stability of physiology outlined in earlier chapters, and goes beyond them.

Spirit represents humanity at its best. In his book *Authentic Happiness*,[18] Martin Seligman describes research undertaken to establish whether core human values transcend cultures. He and his team found that almost every tradition and philosophy shared a variation on just six themes in articulating their foundations for good and true living. Seligman named these six themes 'virtues.' They are:

- Wisdom and knowledge
- Courage
- Love and humanity
- Justice
- Temperance
- Spirituality and transcendence

I invite you to read this list again and notice your response to each virtue. Which do you regard as important for your own sense of what is good in our world? Which do you most value in others? For which would you most like to be personally recognised or appreciated?

   In describing your own spirit, what words might you use in addition to those you selected from Seligman's virtues? What qualities and attributes do you embody when you are at your very best? Seligman's premise is that the more opportunities we create to live our values, and to express them in our daily life and work, the happier we will be. This resonates strongly with my sense of individual spirit.

When speaking of individual spirit, I sometimes use the metaphor of spirit in the sense of fortified wines and liquors – these are concentrated liquids, distilled for depth of character, for their complex flavours and notes/nuances. If you consider how you might taste if you were distilled in this way, what is your essence?

Which aromas and flavours powerfully describe your unique character? Which notes nuance them?

As we become clearer about the qualities we embody when we bring our finest leadership spirit to a conversation, we increase our capacity for inhabiting this presence. We are also more likely to notice quickly when we are not embodying our finest presence and we can recover by centring.

In seeking to consistently bring forward our finest leadership spirit or presence, we may need to cultivate resilience. For instance, sometimes you may try practices from this book with great success, and at other times you may be clumsy and feel you have had an adverse impact. You may falter and ask yourself whether you can continue to risk your sense of self, and your reputation, in trying something unfamiliar yet again. If you risk opening to a sense of collective spirit, you may feel that your individual identity has less importance and fear you will be diminished by this. More generally, in changing our conversations, we may need to draw on qualities that are not habitually associated with leadership, such as humility and generosity. Strength and clarity in our individual spirit will help us to navigate these challenges.

What other qualities might we need if we are to refine our leadership spirit and presence? One of Wendy Palmer's practices is to choose a leadership quality and to develop capacity for embodying it over the course of a year. If you were to choose one quality to support you in bringing a different spirit to your leadership conversations, what would it be? Can you commit to mindfully cultivating this quality for a period of time, perhaps a few months, or even a year?

One way to bring our finest leadership presence into conversations is to become physically centred, using our breath and posture to become upright yet relaxed. A metaphor to strengthen the link between spirit and physical centre is to use spine and heart to represent the character and courage of spirit.

Our spine is upright and articulated and so is both strong and flexible within the bounds of its own nature. It is structural and solid (relative to our flesh) and is central to our individual functioning as an organism, playing a part in relaying messages from all over our body to our brain.

Our heart is, at one level, simply a muscle. Yet it has been shown to have 'intelligence' and has many components similar to the cranial brain.[19] In many cultures, heart is associated with emotions such as love and compassion, and it is seen as a centre of connection to other people, to nature and to the universe. Science now confirms traditional narratives, finding the heart to be a complex nervous system separate from, but interconnected with, both brain and central nervous system.

Spirit has the attributes of both heart and spine – a strong, dignified core and a sense of intelligent connection to our universe. Centre shares these attributes.

Heart and spine can also represent the description of dialogue as a balance of advocacy and inquiry. Skilful advocacy requires backbone to speak from a place of deeper truth, whatever the circumstances, and requires heart to take account of, and stay connected to, the truths of others. Skilful inquiry requires backbone to 'not know' or to risk looking a fool in asking a 'daft question,' and requires heart to accept others in all their richness and difference, to connect with them and support them in their uncertainty, fear and doubt. This interplay of strength and gentleness characterises the territory of spirit – can we be both firm and soft,

189

both upright and relaxed, both powerful and connected? Can we be in dynamic balance in all our complexity? Can we be centred?

There is also a connection between mind and spirit. You may remember that, in Taoist thinking, there are three primary energy centres or tan tiens, located in the belly, the heart/solar plexus area and the mind. When we are centred, all these tan tiens are aligned, with the mind focusing on the breath moving up and down through the body. Focusing on breathing is a foundation practice of mindfulness. As the mind becomes centred and calm, it becomes possible to tune into a part of the mind that I call 'wisdom mind,' a connection with universal energy that can bring profound insight. You may recognise this as intuition.

To develop this theme, I recount some introductory teachings on consciousness given by Clive Holmes, at Samye Ling, a Buddhist centre in Scotland. He describes three areas of the brain: the limbic or reptilian brain; the mammalian brain; and the human brain. The reptilian brain is our basic brain and is largely hardwired for survival. It is the seat of impulses such as hunger and the fight/flight/freeze system. This part of the brain was first to evolve and is millennia old; it is unadapted from our most primitive roots. The hardwired nature of this aspect of our brain means we cannot override it; we can, though, become familiar with its workings and moderate any unhelpful impact by centring when we notice our reptilian brain starting to direct our actions.

Our mammalian brain evolved next, memorably characterised by Clive Holmes as our 'meerkat brain:' alert, chattering, nervy, sociable, worrying. As I understand it, this aspect of our brain is where we become conscious of incoming sensations and data, and weigh up our actions. I call it the maximising brain; it is the part of us that likes to re-use past patterns for efficiency. It is the busy mind, sorting, organising, and deciding (or not). It is the seat of our likes and dislikes, of judgements and preferences, and of habits, all based on its vast library of past experiences. It is, largely, the aspect of the brain that runs us. In becoming more aware of its functioning, we increase our opportunities to make choices: do we want to fall in with the apparent efficiency of this highly active mind or do we want to pause and consider other options?

The third stage of brain evolution added the unique mindpower of humankind: the frontal-lobe brain. This is the mind of perspective and reflective thinking. It has the capacity to transcend the earlier evolutions of the brain, but needs quiet attention and mindfulness to do this. In calm conditions, or the conditions of centre, this mind can witness, with discernment, the activities of the reptilian and mammalian aspects of our brain. This faculty requires a sense of spaciousness that tends to be crowded out when our meerkat brain is in overdrive; the busy activity squeezes out any capacity for quieter knowing.

Many people practice meditation to create the space needed to witness the activities of their minds. In time, and with practice, the mind is able to become more settled in meditation. Eventually, it may be possible to access deep insight with this part of the mind: this is wisdom mind. Wisdom mind is open, receptive and clear. In wisdom mind we are deeply centred and connected to a sense of universal energy. This opens us to insight or profound intuition. There are other approaches to accessing wisdom mind and we may also experience it spontaneously, as the following story illustrates.

In March 2002, I was in a car crash. I left my home at about 4.30am to drive to the airport. It was a cold, icy morning. I scraped the windscreen and set off, slightly late. As I drove out of my village on the familiar country road, my mind was busy considering parking options at the airport. I took the first curve of an S-bend slightly too fast and on the second curve I felt the car slide sideways. It didn't correct as it sometimes seems to and I knew immediately that I had hit ice and no longer had control of the car. This 'knowing' arrived fully formed, rather than in words, and was accompanied by a spike of alarm – my reptilian brain in action. My mammalian brain kicked in quickly: what to do? Don't know. Mustn't touch the brakes. What then? Don't know, mustn't touch the brakes. All in a second. Panic.

Then something else happened: a calm assessment. I only know what I mustn't do, so I must go with this. A memory of falling in a faint and landing unhurt flashed through my mind and I thought, 'my best chance is to relax until the car comes to a halt.' My mind was clear, spacious and light. I relaxed back into the seat, closed my eyes, experienced jolts and bumps as the car hit the opposite verge, spun 180 degrees, tipped into a ditch and stopped. I thought, 'I'm alive' and scanned my body. There were no obvious signals of damage. Later I found I had a couple of bumps and bruises and slight whiplash, but basically I was okay.

In this experience, my minds and body co-operated to give me a good chance of survival, thanks also to the fact that the car did what it should and crumpled, protecting me. I attribute my experience to quickly accepting that my analytical, problem-solving brain had run out of options, and in being able to let go, I created space for wisdom mind.

Does any part of this story resonate for you? How do you receive the internal alarm calls that your nervous system and basic brain provide? What activity does this typically spark in your problem-solving mind? How do you recognise when wisdom mind is present? Each of these aspects of brain has utility and purpose. In cultivating mindfulness, we become sensitive to the activities of our mind and so are able to consider which aspect offers a skilful and appropriate response to our current circumstances.

If we seek to grow our capacity to more consistently inhabit our finest leadership spirit, we will support our quest by practice in centring body, energy and mind.

As we become centred, the focus of our attention shifts. We are less interested in task, in what is produced or delivered, and we begin to attend to how things come into being, and the qualities that create the conditions for potential to emerge. In Taoist philosophy, this moment is called wu chi, the moment of stillness and emptiness that is full of potential. Perhaps it is our way of being that creates potential, not what we do or say. How would the quality of our leadership conversations change if we believed this statement to be true?

As we inhabit a different form of presence, we invoke a change in energy in our conversations, prompting a different form of presence in those around us. The quality of our presence influences what is possible, and since this is a factor in which we have some sway, this is fertile ground for changing our leadership conversations.

Practice *24* – cultivating individual spirit

Sit in a comfortable upright posture in a chair. Exhale slowly and lengthen your spine. Imagine a silken thread extending from the crown of your head, drawing you gently upwards towards the sky, lengthening the back of your neck (tucking your chin slightly towards your throat). Relax your shoulders on the next exhale.

Now bring your attention fully to your breath. Imagine breath as up and down rather than in and out. Inhale and imagine your breath rising through belly, ribs and throat, whilst your spine slightly straightens and lengthens. Exhale, and imagine your breath flowing down into the ground, forming a root, as your shoulders and core relax. Do three breaths this way, then simply follow the breath for a while.

Settle into your body. Feel the contact between your feet and the ground. Feel the contact between your thighs and the chair, and between your sitting bones and the chair. Become aware of your body and gently scan upwards – feet, legs, abdomen, solar plexus, ribs and lungs, hands and arms, throat and neck, head. Notice any sensations: heat, cold, tingling, itching, tension, pain, aches, spaciousness, warmth, pleasant feelings. Simply notice. Don't name the sensation. Don't wonder about it. Simply mindfully experience it as it is.

Now bring your attention to your mind. With impartial curiosity, simply notice any thoughts arising (your left hand column). Do not follow the storyline or train of thought, simply witness with kindness and fascination, until the thought dissolves in its own time. If you find yourself getting caught up in a storyline, gently draw your attention back to the breath for a few breaths, then scan your body, noticing sensation.

After a few minutes, bring your attention back to your breath for a few breaths. Bring the practice to a close and notice any effects.

Notes and reflections

Chapter 25 Spirit as collective energy

'We shape clay into a pot,
But it is the emptiness inside
That holds what we want.'
Lao Tzu, translated by Stephen Mitchell

In considering collective spirit, I invite you to notice your current beliefs, judgements and paradigms. How do you feel about the proposition that, when people meet and talk, they generate a collective energy or spirit that is greater than the sum of the individuals? What are you inclined to believe or discount? What might you hold lightly and inquire into?

Collective spirit, a sense of being part of something bigger, is tricky to articulate. One way of approaching it is through narratives from Eastern cultures, many of which reference a universal energy or life-force. In China, this is called ch'i (sometimes written qi), in Japan ki, in India prana. In each of these cultures there is a strong tradition of acknowledging the presence of a universal life-force.

A sense of being part of something bigger can also be described in the language of quantum physics, or in the traditions of faith, belief and religion. Quantum physics describes universal energy in terms of vibrating wave-particles and energy fields, while faith describes it in terms of God, a source, a mystery.

How or whether you relate to any of these possibilities is a personal choice, particularly as the experience of collective spirit is essentially beyond words. My preference is to approach the subject through the lens of universal energy or ch'i. I invite you to hold my narrative in a spirit of inquiry; work with those things that resonate, hold lightly those things that are at the edges of your experience and might become intriguing, and let go of those things that alienate you.

The general principle of universal energy is that all beings and things are created from it, and everything is connected through it. Matter, including flesh, is a more dense manifestation of energy than, for example, air, but both are essentially made of minute energetic wave-particles. As a child I was fascinated by an explanation that the electricity that powered a light or television was generated because particles in the wire nudge those next to them, which nudge those next to them, and so on. Similarly, it seems credible that my personal energetic presence will nudge the energetic presence of others when I enter a room.

What happens when a number of people meet and combine their energy, their life-force? Have you ever been in a room where a conversation has begun to develop a certain quality of attention and purpose, only for that to be unsettled by a latecomer breezing in with apologies and a drama to cover their embarrassment? The energy in the room changes, and may take some time to resettle, if indeed it does.

It seems that when we meet others, we create a sense of collective presence through the combination of our unique individual energies. To envisage this, bring to mind an image of two people engaged in a meaningful conversation. They lean into one another as if they are in a bubble, absorbed and connected. The energy between them is almost palpable. If a third person were to approach, it might be hard to enter their conversation. In recognising the collective energetic presence of two people, we can see that it is possible in a bigger gathering. This begins to link spirit, individual and collective, to the quality of our conversations.

There is a bigger sense of collective spirit to consider. Whether we use the narratives of universal energy, or the science of quantum physics, the universe is understood to be energetic and dynamic. Whether I describe energy in the language of ch'i or in the language of wavelengths and probabilities, the universe is constantly changing. Everything around us is energy in some form or another, unless there is a vacuum.

How we perceive a thing is, to some extent, dependent on the density of energetic particles associated with it. This is self-evident if we consider water and air. Water is denser and we can see it, hold it and experience it pouring through our fingers. Air is less dense and we cannot see it in the palm of our cupped hand, or feel it moving through our fingers. Nevertheless it is there.

The air or space around us consists of particles, atoms and molecules of gases such as oxygen, carbon dioxide, and nitrogen. We know now, thanks to quantum physics, that these particles also have attributes of waves and that they are complex, dynamic energies, and they don't exist all the time. It's somewhat different to the pictures of atoms that I drew in physics lessons in the 1970s, showing electrons as little planets orbiting the sun of a nucleus. A common thread remains though – atoms are more space than matter, so even our apparently solid human body is more space than stuff.

To understand the proportions of space to matter, I recall an illustration from a television programme. In it, the nucleus of an atom was represented by a football, an electron by a tennis ball. On this scale, how far away from the nucleus is an electron? Two miles! This means that each atom consists of thousands of times more space than matter.

Neither the space within us nor that external to us is empty. It is dynamic, full of particle energy that appears and disappears to a rhythm beyond our immediate experience. This energetic space connects everything, and so is potentially available to us as a medium to reach beyond our individual selves.

When I move, my energy perturbs the energy of the space around me, affecting the energy of others in the space. I imagine it as a less dense version of swimming; when I swim, the water both supports me and moves around me in swirls and currents. If I swim close to someone else, the water turbulence from their movement changes my swimming experience, and even my movement, if they are energetic enough. In air, though mostly not visible, the same kinds of swirls and currents are in play. Think of a beam of light cutting across a darker space to show dust motes shimmering and dancing. We move in a light density fluid – air – which responds in a similar way to the heavier density fluid that is water. Just because we can't always see things, it doesn't mean there is nothing there.

My preferred approach for explaining connecting energy is Taoist philosophy, which preceded quantum physics by a few thousand years. As explained earlier, this philosophy proposes two fundamental energies in the universe: yin and yang. These opposite and complementary energies combine to generate universal life-force or ch'i, from which all life is created. In the broadest sense, yin and yang can be imagined as a receptive energy or principle (yin) and an active energy or principle (yang). They may also be characterised, for example, as female and male, silence and speech, darkness (absence of light) and light, soft and hard, inquiry and advocacy.

The concept is more subtle than black and white, because whenever two objects, ideas or states are compared, one will be yang, relative to the yin of the other. For example, for any two shades of grey, one will be slightly lighter than the other and so will be yang relative to the yin of the darker shade. In this approach, yin and yang can only exist together, they are not separate from one another. This means that sound cannot exist without silence, advocacy cannot exist without inquiry; each is defined relative to the other.

In addition, the two elemental energies are understood to be continuously transforming from one to the other. They are in dynamic balance, in both

199

unending movement and eternal equilibrium. This is represented in snapshot form by the familiar T'ai Chi symbol in which we see a blend of yin and yang, creating a whole, whilst maintaining their separate natures.

The symbol shows the seed of yin (the black dot) present in yang (the white half) and the seed of yang (the white dot) present in yin (the black half). The snapshot captures a moment in a process of perpetual change. To imagine a cycle of change, picture the dots increasing in size, the white dot gradually expanding to fill the black space, the black dot simultaneously expanding to fill the white space. Just as each dot reaches the full potential of the space it occupies, a seed of the opposite colour appears in its belly. The implication is that nothing is entirely yin or entirely yang as each contains the seed of the other. Together the energies blend and transform, both male and female, neither male nor female. In wholeness, there is ambiguity.

In the extract from the *Tao Te Ching*[20] at the beginning of this chapter, we see yin and yang in practical terms. The yang clay shape of a pottery bowl is what we can grip and see, but it is the empty space contained within that we use. The yin of the space is defined by the yang of the container. Both must be present to be of value.

To explore the implications of universal energy and collective spirit in our conversations, we can revisit the fourth field of conversation of flow/dialogue.[6] This field is defined by the interests of the collective and by mindfulness of thinking and action.

Fields of conversation

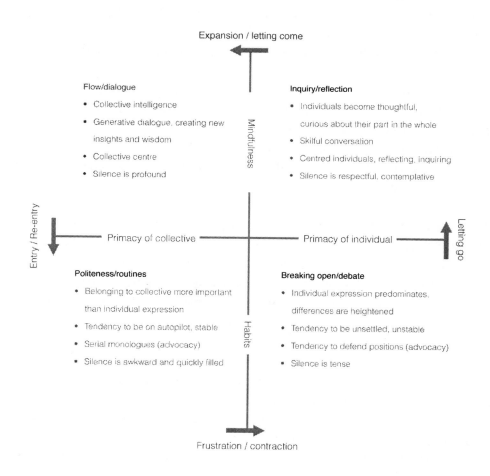

Expansion / letting come

Flow/dialogue
- Collective intelligence
- Generative dialogue, creating new insights and wisdom
- Collective centre
- Silence is profound

Inquiry/reflection
- Individuals become thoughtful, curious about their part in the whole
- Skilful conversation
- Centred individuals, reflecting, inquiring
- Silence is respectful, contemplative

Mindfulness

Entry / Re-entry

Primacy of collective ———— Primacy of individual

Letting go

Politeness/routines
- Belonging to collective more important than individual expression
- Tendency to be on autopilot, stable
- Serial monologues (advocacy)
- Silence is awkward and quickly filled

Breaking open/debate
- Individual expression predominates, differences are heightened
- Tendency to be unsettled, unstable
- Tendency to defend positions (advocacy)
- Silence is tense

Habits

Frustration / contraction

Adapted from C Otto Sharmer et al

201

In the field of flow/dialogue, the boundaries between centred individuals dissolve, and for a time, they become a single system, a whole. It is as if a conversation unfolds through collective spirit, evoked by the alchemy of those present, with their experiences and history representing universal experiences and history. Advocacy seeks to express collective truths; inquiry seeks to explore collective questions. Advocacy contains the seeds of inquiry, and inquiry holds the seeds of truths. In this dynamic balance, silence is profound and full of potential, like wu chi, the moment of stillness and emptiness before creation. The emergence of new insights and new wisdom is possible. Collective truths unfold.

One of the characteristics of dialogue is that we pay attention to spaces, to silence, to pauses. To get a sense of the potential in this, consider the metaphor of a professional double bass player who told me that her playing was transformed when she realised that she needed to relax her fingers off the strings between notes. We habitually pay attention to activity, to words, to things; what if we were to attend to the moments between?

If we do pause, what is the quality of our pause? What is the feeling tone of our silences? Often, silence represents incredulity, approbation, accusation or an exercise of power through withdrawing our voice. These are all examples of unskilful pausing. When we are centred, our pausing is skilful and our silence is evocative: wu chi, a moment of potential. In dialogue, silence is profound.

If we revisit all four conversational fields, we can imagine how we might use the material in this book to develop our capacity to engage in each one. As we develop our awareness of how our mind influences our contribution to conversations, we cultivate our capacity to be skilful in the fields of politeness/ routines and breaking open/debate. To deepen our capacity for handling more heightened energy in breaking open/debate, we cultivate awareness of how our body influences our participation in conversation. We begin to develop the capacity to be centred in the face of unwieldy energy. In becoming clearer about the quality and resilience of our individual leadership spirit, our capacity for inhabiting centre grows. We more quickly realise when we are being reactive and are more able to recover centre under pressure. This, in turn, expands our capacity for mindfulness and inquiry/dialogue. As we more consistently embody our finest leadership presence, our energy influences others, enabling collective spirit to emerge. This creates the conditions in which generative dialogue is possible.

Practice *25* – cultivating collective spirit

As before, sit in a comfortable upright posture in a chair. Inhaling, lengthen your spine and the back of your neck (tucking your chin slightly towards your throat). Exhaling, relax your shoulders and bring your attention fully to your breath.

Inhale and imagine your breath spiralling upwards out of the crown of your head. Exhale and imagine your breath flowing down into the ground, forming a root.

Settle into your body – feel the contact between your feet and the ground, and between your thighs and the chair. Now become aware of your whole body and the space that you occupy. Sense the shape and extent of this space and notice any other qualities it has – perhaps a colour, texture, sound or smell. Is the space even and balanced around you?

Now begin to slowly expand the space that you occupy in the following stages – if you feel uncomfortable at any time, simply allow your space to relax into your centre and rest. Place your attention on your breath for a few moments.

1. *On your inbreath, expand your sense of your space to include the room you are sitting in, and any people within it. On your outbreath, allow this sense of space to relax into your centre. Repeat for a few breaths and then rest.*
2. *On your inbreath, expand your sense of your space to include the building you are in, and any people within it. On your outbreath, allow this sense of space to relax into your centre. Repeat for a few breaths then rest.*
3. *On your inbreath, expand your sense of your space to include the neighbourhood you are in, and any people in it. On your outbreath, allow this sense of space to relax into your centre. Repeat for a few breaths then rest.*

After a few moments, become aware of the space that you occupy. What do you notice?

Notes and reflections

Chapter 26 Spirit in the face of challenging conversations

'The man who never alters his opinion is like standing water and breeds reptiles of the mind.' William Blake

In this chapter we look at how we might use some of the practices of mindfulness and dialogue to tackle everyday challenges in our leadership conversations. In this way, we can begin to bridge the gap between concepts that feel good when sitting in comfort and actually putting them into practice.

The scenarios we will explore are:

- When it is difficult to speak our truth
- When it is difficult to listen
- When we are caught in the energy of others
- When complexity and paradox are present

The common factor in these situations is that our leadership energy is diminished or contracted by fear, judgement or by being blinkered. We are tense, stressed, uncentred and habit-prompted. Our leadership spirit is less than we aspire to and we have lost any sense of connection with bigger perspective and deeper wisdom. Our attention has a particular focus, limiting our creativity and heightening the likelihood that we will operate reactively. If we can centre in these circumstances, we can access both a steadier sense of self and an open and expansive spaciousness that offers the possibility of some currently unimaginable potential emerging.

As we explore some of the challenges of bringing the practices of dialogue and mindfulness to our leadership conversations, the foundation response is:

- To pause and centre;
- To connect to a bigger perspective and our finest leadership spirit;
- To consider options; and then
- To choose mindfully.

This is difficult to do. When caught by surprise, I frequently find myself trying to follow this guidance and being unable to hold a sense of equanimity about my situation. So I rant, sulk, fight or run away until, in time, the initial hurt, anger or fear subsides and I am able to make a mindful choice. Despite these setbacks, I believe that the more I practice this approach in the heat of real situations, the more I develop my capacity for doing it. I periodically revisit this foundation practice, and in this way I develop my tolerance and resilience, raising the threshold at which I succumb to ranting or running.

The focus of this chapter is on finding a way to speak out, from a sense of our deepest truth, regardless of whether it is welcomed by others. It is also about enabling others to speak their truth, even when it may be unwelcome. Both require spirit.

When it is difficult to speak our truth

There are occasions when we are called to speak out with the cards stacked against us, perhaps when there is risk or when elements of power, fear and high stakes are present. For example, perhaps your organisation is implementing an innovative project and your boss and your boss's boss are fully committed to the cause. The future of the organisation depends on the project in some way. The stakes are high and leaders are heavily invested in success, both for the organisation and for their own reputations. What if you are becoming concerned about the viability and the relevance of the project?

In these circumstances it is typically difficult to speak out. And even if you do, no-one with any clout listens. You may grumble to your peers, where there is less risk, and less influence. The project continues but your contribution is half-hearted and perhaps you are even influencing the commitment of your peers. Does this scenario bring a similar experience to mind?

In these situations, the dynamic of the system is that those involved in the project are locked-on in some way, with their fight/flight/freeze system in permanent overdrive with the excitement and pressure of a high-profile, high-stakes endeavour. They might over-identify with a single course of action and have a corresponding tendency for their peripheral vision to shrink.

Aware of this dynamic, of this strong energy in the system, if you try to speak out about your concerns, you are likely to do so with an eye to your own survival and reputation. There are worse things than not being listened to; you might be ridiculed, be sidelined or lose your job. If you do speak, you may not be fully aligned in what you say because parts of you have other motivations. Your mind sees the problem, but your heart wants to stay in relationship with your colleagues, boss and the positive energy that is being generated. You appreciate the pressure they are under and perhaps don't want to add to their stress. In addition, you are not 100% confident that you are right, and your spirit shrinks from the imagined confrontation. Your centre isn't engaged, and so your presence lacks confidence and power. Your voice is not compelling because of your doubts.

The challenge of this situation is how to advocate skilfully, with a balance of pointedness and openness. If you offer your truth as a perspective and invite others to give their point of view, whether they agree with you or not, you may create the conditions in which you can be heard.

To surface the full complexity of your position, including any fears and doubts, you may listen for different voices within you, such as the three energy centres of head, heart and gut. If you are able to find some alignment in your internal dialogue, your energy will be more coherent, whatever course of action you choose.

It is usually most difficult to speak our truth when it matters most, so practising being able to do this under pressure is important. The time and place for making your contribution is also important. If you have choices in these factors and can influence them, be thoughtful about how you might give yourself the best chance of being heard.

To prepare to speak your truth in an important situation, begin by pausing for breath and centring. You might use Practice 20 or Practice 29 to become aware of multiple perspectives within you and become clear about what you want to say. Be thoughtful about the time and place to share your thinking. When an appropriate moment arises, pause, centre and imagine inhabiting your finest leadership spirit. Imagine your energy becoming triangular in shape, streaming to a clear point. Say what you need to say and then recover your centre and imagine your energy becoming circular, open and receptive. Be ready to hear how your thinking sits with others.

When it is difficult to listen

In contrast, we can be on the receiving end of the previous scenario. There are occasions when we simply don't want to hear what we are being told. Perhaps the message is that our course of action is not wise. Perhaps it contravenes a deep belief. Perhaps it hurts us, disgusts us or offends us. We metaphorically put our fingers in our ears and close our eyes.

More subtly, we brush aside the words as foolish or uninformed, or we claim to be too busy for this now. We assume we know best. We justify ourselves. Perhaps we discount the value of the person speaking and label them stupid or resistant to change. Or perhaps we try to reason away the unwanted perspectives, either internally in our thoughts, or externally by debating them, setting up an advocatory-based exchange.

These responses are all energy patterns of contraction, and are tactics that seek to control or to limit the possibilities that we might be judged wrong or be wounded, or that our limited energy might be taken away from what we believe to be crucial/imperative. We might ask ourselves which part of us is so determined not to hear this news? What are we protecting ourselves from?

Are any of these patterns familiar? Do you have examples of situations in which it is habitually difficult to listen? Are there individuals whose contribution you routinely discount? In teams, it is common to find someone who takes on a dissenting habit and who is routinely ignored. They tend to gradually contribute less and less, perhaps even becoming silent. Their dissent will, however, be expressed somewhere, and it might be useful to reflect on where.

The challenge in situations when it is difficult to listen, is to embody skilful inquiry. How can we organise ourselves to hear such things, difficult though they are? How can we truly hear them, find some value in them and respond with our finest leadership spirit?

The basic practice is to centre, inhabiting our finest leadership spirit, and becoming aware of the space that we occupy. We envisage our energy field as balanced and circular. Our field can form a neutral space, or buffer, into which words can land. We can then imagine that what is being said is landing in the space between the speaker and ourselves. This allows us to hear what is said impartially, perhaps enabling us to hold the message lightly and examine it with curiosity. What is the essential truth in what is being said?

A specific example of a situation where it is difficult to listen, is when our history with a person makes it difficult to respect them. Perhaps they have undermined, harmed or threatened us in the past, or perhaps we have seen them fail at something, or perhaps they simply fall short of our standards in some way. In other words, we have an assumption about someone (ladder of inference) or carry a template of them with an emotional tag. In these cases, we have an advocatory stance about another person – we have a point of view, a judgement about them, and it is emotionally charged. These thoughts and feelings do not represent our finest leadership spirit and so we need to balance this certainty with inquiry.

In organisations, a common occurrence is that a view of a person gets frozen at a point in time, perhaps how they appeared when they first joined the organisation, or perhaps tied to an error of judgement, for which they carry a badge in perpetuity. When I worked in the National Health Service, I often heard a newly promoted manager being diminished by remarks such as, 'I remember her when she was an orderly on Ward Two,' as if nothing had changed in the intervening twenty years.

Whenever we limit others through our judgements, we devalue our leadership spirit. In trapping others in our past perceptions of them, we also constrain ourselves and narrow our options. In dealing with these circumstances, we need to first notice our pattern. When, where and how did our opinion form? Was it triggered by particular events, or is it just a feeling? Perhaps we are simply reminded of someone we don't like, or who caused trouble for us. Next time you encounter such a person, commit to hearing what they have to say. Be curious; how does this human being perceive the world?

To prepare to encounter someone you don't rate or respect, or someone with a message you don't want to hear, begin by acknowledging this tendency to dismiss or avoid. Commit to making a change and, when you next meet them, pause for breath, centre yourself, and inhabit your finest leadership spirit. Imagine your field as circular, extending to include the other person. When centred, take the lead and ask them something about themselves, or invite their message. Listen with kindness and fascination. Ask yourself, 'what is it that I don't yet understand about how they are seeing this situation?' or, 'what am I not yet giving them credit for?' Ask a question to discover more. Be ready to receive their response.

When we are caught in the energy of others
What happens when we get caught in the energy of others who are stuck, anxious, frustrated or otherwise under pressure? I might go into a conversation open, receptive, clear, confident and centred, but what I find is another person working from an old story, under deadline or focused on their own priorities. Perhaps their emotions are also heightened. Perhaps they are attached to a very clear view of the rights and wrongs of a situation, or of my role in it. Before I know it, I am operating from a similarly unhelpful place. It is as if I have been infected by a virus of uncentred energy. Our conversation gets into trouble fairly quickly.

The challenge with this type of situation is that it is quite hard to spot when you're in it. For no apparent reason, you find yourself meeting lack of respect with lack of respect, meeting judgement with judgement, or matching raised emotions with charged feelings of your own. It's only in reflecting afterwards that you might notice that the feelings, judgements or behaviours weren't truly your own – it was as if you were hijacked by the other person's energy.

This circumstance explains why the practices in this book are so important – we can be infected by the energy of others and we need to be alert enough to centre and rebalance when this happens. The good news is that the opposite is also true – the energy and spirit that we cultivate in our own presence can affect others. A place where I experience this phenomenon in a positive way is in my local swimming pool in the morning. There is a team of four female swimmers who train together for master's events (for which read 'old' in terms of competitive racing). They train hard but with such pleasure. When I walk through the showers at the end of a session, or if I am near them in the changing rooms, I am infected by their joy in their swimming and by their camaraderie. Simply by their presence and chat, I get a boost that lightens the start of my day.

In the context of leadership conversations, we might reflect on the impact of our emotions being fully engaged, whether potentially positive emotions such as a passionate belief in something, or more obviously unhelpful emotions such as anger or fear. When emotions are engaged, we tend to lose perspective. Our attention contracts to focus on the topic or issue at the heart of our emotional engagement, making it prominent in our thinking. We tend to lose our peripheral vision. Passionate belief in a single 'right' course of action is just as potent as resistance to proposed change. Each is a form of fight, and can blinker us to other possibilities. All highly-charged emotions shrink our perspective, our sense of space, and induce a form of weapon focus, where we don't notice anything outside our immediate purpose. In this state, we may push for something we believe in, to the detriment of a bigger picture. Or we may become locked-on to winning (or revenge, or justice), determined to get our way at almost any cost.

The deep challenge is that this emotional charge can then subtly affect others. My premise is that we are more susceptible to the moods and energy of others than we commonly acknowledge. So, when we are not having the conversation we expected, this is one place to look. We can ask ourselves, 'has my mood,

213

demeanour or energy changed significantly since I engaged in this conversation?' If so, we can reflect on whether that change is due to significant new information, or a response to something we heard. If we have changed our mood for no clear reason, we may have been affected by the mood of others. If we notice this, we can recover centre and become present. Our energy will change, and we will be less influenced by the disposition of another. As a bonus, our energy may begin to positively affect theirs.

In creating the conditions for others to be present and centred around us, we need to lead by example in our own leadership presence, and be a model of how we want others to be. I invite you to experiment with this a bit – explore whether you can virally affect the energy of others. If you speak with calmness, integrity, respect and congruence, how do others respond? If you handle criticism, challenge, or opposition lightly, then how do those around you respond? If you trust others, how do they respond? How can you truly embody your finest leadership spirit and thereby encourage others to raise their own game?

To prepare for situations where emotions 'catch' and spread virally, begin by noticing symptoms: voices get louder and speed up, people interrupt one another, energy gathers momentum. When you are next in one of these conversations, pause, centre, and inhabit your finest leadership spirit. Become aware of your personal space or field and imagine it becoming circular, receptive and expansive, filling the whole room. Sit with a sense of calmness and openness. Be curious about the impact.

When complexity and paradox are present
When the actions that flow from a conversation are not those that we thought were agreed, it may be a clue that a situation is complex, or a 'wicked issue.' Setting aside the possibility that incongruent actions arise from negative intent,

214

this may indicate that there was no genuine shared understanding of the presenting issue. It is likely that those involved are operating from fundamental differences in their assumptions, beliefs, values, perspectives or paradigms.

This is a situation in which a different kind of conversation is needed; a conversation where ambiguity, uncertainty and 'not knowing' can be accommodated. If we can bring forward our finest leadership presence, we can influence the leadership spirit of others and the tone of the conversation. We can seek to surface and hold differences to enable inquiry into them. This way of being in conversation is crucial to approaching the dynamic complexity of wicked issues, because for these issues everything is connected, and an action 'here' may trigger an unintended response 'there.' In these circumstances, as Einstein noted, the issues can't be solved at the level of the mind that created them in the first place. We must look beyond individual intelligence to the power of collective thinking.

There is a profound need for deeper collective wisdom when we approach wicked issues, because paradox is an inevitable aspect of complexity. If we move to action too quickly, paradoxical and unintended consequences tend to arise. The basis of moving quickly to action can be fear – we are afraid to do nothing, to not know, because, as leaders, we are expected to have answers. We tense into knee jerk activity (albeit informed and intelligent) rather than sit with the discomfort of not having answers. In complexity there is often much we do not yet know or understand. How can we develop the leadership spirit to sit with this unfamiliar situation, and then inquire and see what emerges? How can we become adept at noticing the energetic contraction that precedes an impulse to action, then pause for breath and make different choices?

This is territory beyond conflict. When we hear conflicting views (or experience conflicting views in our internal dialogue), how might we hold the paradox that both might be true? How do we hold and understand the bigger whole, in which my truth and your truth sit legitimately side-by-side and generate a deeper truth? How do we find dynamic balance within complexity?

215

The systemic response to this kind of predicament is to cultivate collective spirit, to think together. For an individual leader this may seem impossible, certainly when faced with an immediate need for a response to an issue. A first step might be to cultivate and strengthen your own leadership presence, to model the qualities we wish to evoke in others, and to nurture a profound sense of curiosity and inquiry; how did things come to be this way?

Summary

In speaking our deepest truth, we tend to offer more of our thinking than is customary. Not only is our truth complex, we may also harbour doubts. It requires spirit to risk sharing uncertainties, feelings and ambiguities.

In offering our truth skilfully, we do not impose on others. This helps create the conditions in which they can also speak authentically and honestly. This too requires spirit. When we hear what others have to say, we may need to adjust our thinking and perhaps even change our mind.

Practice *26* – encountering complexity

Next time you feel a sense of unease that an expedient 'compromise' may have been reached or a single voice has led to 'agreement' on an issue you feel is complex, then try the following steps:

1. Identify two (or more) aspects of the issue that do not sit comfortably with one another, perhaps conflicting perspectives, or perhaps a discrepancy between ways and means, or between what is espoused and what is being suggested.

2. Pause for breath, centring yourself, and inhabit your finest leadership spirit.

3. Become aware of your personal space or field and imagine it becoming circular, receptive, calm, expansive.

4. Look around the room you are in and ask yourself what it would be like if your field expanded to include the whole room and all the people in it.

5. Remain aware of this sense of bigger space and inclusion and calmly and impartially offer your perspective of any aspects of the situation that do not sit comfortably with each other.

6. Express any concern you have about ignoring the apparent incongruity and invite your colleagues to consider how this inconsistency sits with them. How do they feel about it?

Notice what happens to the conversation. In particular notice contributions that seek to discount your invitation or to distract attention from it. Gently draw the conversation back to this line of inquiry as often as you feel able.

Notes and reflections

Chapter 27 Cultivating spirit as practice/discipline

*'When the structure of attention moves deeper,
so does the ensuing change process.'* Peter Senge

What happens when I am centred? What is my impact on others when I embody this depth of presence? When I am with others who are centred, what is their impact on me?

I can recall, sometimes years later, a small handful of people who have left an indelible impression on me, simply by the manner of their greeting. As they said 'hello,' or 'welcome,' their warmth, invitation and connectedness was palpable. In their presence I felt accepted, loved even, though we were meeting for the first time. I had a sense that each of these people had an open mind and an open heart. Have you ever felt this depth of presence? You will surely remember if you have. Cultivating centre and our capacity for this quality of presence, attention and connection is really at the core of bringing the practices of mindfulness and dialogue to leadership.

One of my favourite books is *After the Ecstasy, the Laundry,*[22] by Jack Kornfield, in which he describes how spiritual experiences go hand-in-hand with day-to-day engagement in the less-than-sexy parts of life. So having waxed lyrical about the potential of true presence, I will mention the laundry of practice. When we are used to mastering ideas quickly, it can be hard to accept the need for practice when what we aspire to master goes beyond an idea. If we want to have more capacity for accessing centre and an authentic quality of presence, we need to practice: thinking about it won't change anything.

To truly open our mind, we must first see our mind clearly, which is to develop a practice in mindfulness. To truly open our heart, in a way that is healthy and includes self as well as others, we must foster a leadership presence that embodies values such as generosity and inclusiveness. To be readily able to come to centre, we need to repeatedly experience a balanced, expansive, energetic presence in everyday situations. Only then will the experience be familiar enough to use in tough circumstances. None of the qualities of open mind, open heart or centre can happen overnight. They tend to take many years to cultivate, and even then can be challenged by unexpected and unwelcome circumstances.

A gentle place to begin to cultivate our practice is to ask how we might nourish and nurture our spirit. What activities, places, experiences or connections bring us into good contact with our finest selves? Under what circumstances is our spirit naturally present? How do we feel when this happens? What do we need to bring into our lives to strengthen our experience of being centred and connected, so that we can more easily access it when we choose? Nature, music, art, quality time with family and friends, spiritual practices, gardening, walking, kayaking, snowboarding or riding are just a few of the ways we might find connection to spirit. What awakens your spirit? When do you feel happiest? How can you set aside time and energy to invest in this, as a foundation for developing contact with your finest leadership spirit?

In my coaching work I often encounter resistance to any suggestion that my client might take time out to do something for themselves, something that nurtures them. The reason they give is that they don't have time, with their responsibilities at work, at home and in the community. I gently suggest that they are short-changing others if they don't invest in themselves.

I once saw a demonstration of what happens when we give energy to others, without replenishing our own. The metaphor was a jug of water representing a leader, with some glasses representing team members. The water was the leader's energy. When team members requested help, water was poured into the glasses. As the jug became emptier, cling film was placed over the top, representing the leader growing a protective skin. If someone now tries to help the leader, offering energy, pouring water into the jug, it just splashes away. I see many leaders in this state of exhaustion, without energy to accept help. It is a false economy of spirit if we don't create space and time to nurture our own wellbeing and happiness. It is essential that we nourish ourselves if we aspire to support others.

The purpose of making a commitment to regularly and mindfully participate in activities that foster your connection with your finest self, is that practice leads to awareness. For example, a central tenet of Gestalt Theory is that full awareness of current reality evokes change.[23] Bringing mindful awareness to practice leads, in itself, to change. I know this most powerfully through my T'ai Chi practice. We are taught a form, a long sequence of flowing movements, and then we practice it again and again.

Each time I repeat the form it becomes more familiar. I will be learning new things alongside my practice of the form, perhaps through other T'ai Chi experiences such as pushing hands, perhaps through life events, or perhaps through my coaching or dialogue work. As I go about my work and living, I grow. And the form, as I continue to simply practice it, grows with me. I described this some years ago when I wrote about learning the sword form:

'Martial arts in general, and mastery of the sword in particular, require practice, practice, practice. My experience of the learning process over ten years is that I start by copying my teacher and my attention is mainly outward. I get the movements so they more-or-less imitate my teacher, then I spend time becoming familiar with the sequence of those movements. At this stage, my attention is mainly on myself, but in the context of what my form looks like to the teacher. I get bored with the sequence, and on the face of it there is nothing more to learn. I keep repeating the form, asking questions of clarification from time to time, noticing what others are doing when we do the form together. Gradually the sequence becomes automatic and then I start to get curious about different expressions of the same movements. I find a movement changes subtly if I concentrate on my breathing, or on my feet, or on my centre. The quality of my movement begins to change. In the sword form, this shift corresponded with a sudden realisation, after several years, that I don't need to look at the sword all the time. This simple realisation liberated my attention and I began to feel my movements more deeply. With this change, the sword becomes part of me and I become part of the ground and the air. I am never bored again. Each time I express the form it is different, and I am endlessly engaged, endlessly curious.'

You can perhaps discern my level of commitment to practice in the context of T'ai Chi, the slow, dedicated refining of movement, even though I'm not always sure what I'm doing. This is what my teacher refers to when he speaks of forging the spirit. Part of my mission in life is to bring practice into leadership development, liberating leaders from feeling they have to be good at everything, immediately.

In terms of forging leadership spirit, I am inviting you to cultivate practices in mindfulness, centre and dialogue. As you practice some of the approaches set out in this book, you will gradually notice changes in your presence and your conversations. You will increase your awareness of the things that knock you off-balance and into old habits, or into a place of impoverished spirit.

This brings me to probably the most important point in the book: it is recovering centre that is crucial to developing leadership spirit. I practice so that I am able to recover, so that I am familiar enough with a centred state that I can return to it under pressure or stress. This is resilience; if I am knocked off-balance and react, but I am mindful, then I notice, pause for breath, and am able to recover by refining my posture, breathing, centring and accessing my finest leadership spirit. Like a Japanese Daruma Doll, I return to the upright when tilted.

What I also notice as I practice, is that I raise the threshold for the situations that knock me off-balance. I become more able to remain balanced in the face of pressure, surprises, challenges or stress. However, I also notice that while it is pretty easy to centre alone, or in the company of one other person, the more people that are around me, the more difficult it is. More people mean more energy to handle. In addition, recovery is harder in proportion to the level of charge or turbulence in someone else's energy, for example if they are ranting at me or displaying aggression. These are examples of my learning edge, the limits of my current capacity for centre. What are yours?

In my dialogue-related work, I am often asked, 'but what if I'm the only person that knows/does this stuff? What if no-one else is using dialogue practices?' My experience is that it is possible to change a conversation when the other parties seem unaware of the challenges, or seem unwilling or unable to change. I base my explanation on systems theory. If I am in conversation with another person, our relationship, of whatever quality, is a system. If there is a change in the behaviour of one element in the system – me – the system will change in response. The challenge is that I don't know how the system will change, how the other person will respond.

My more general experience is that if I am centred and present, I create the conditions for others to be centred and present, regardless of whether they know about dialogue practices. I recently experienced the impact of this. In the midst

223

of travel chaos, caused by a volcanic ash cloud in UK airspace, I had changed my travel plans at the last minute, along with many other people. I booked a train online and collected my ticket from a machine. I stood in a long queue, and when I got to the barrier, I was stopped by a train official; I had a seat reservation and a credit card slip, but no ticket. Somehow I had failed to pick it up from the machine. There was less than ten minutes until the train departed and the official was rude and unhelpful. Having been composed in quite testing circumstances, I was now in a panic. I pushed back through the crowds trying to remember which ticket machine I'd used. The ticket wasn't there so I went to the information centre, with my anxiety about getting home now in full flow.

I cornered a customer services man who was crossing the room, and gave a good impression of an hysterical woman. The customer services man was calm, despite the fact that the whole rail system was in upheaval as a result of the flight cancellations. He was courteous. He remained calm, despite my distress. He quietly told me there was probably nothing he could do and that I would have to buy a new ticket but he would go and check.

In the time he was away I realised I had become calmer myself. I could now recover my centre. As I did so I knew I would respond reasonably to whatever he came back to tell me. If I had to buy a new ticket, I would do it gracefully. His demeanour and courtesy had affected me and I came to my senses.

I believe this level of influence is always possible, and so if we cultivate our own leadership spirit and presence, it will have a beneficial impact on our conversations with others. A challenge is that making these changes can be unsettling for your colleagues, your family, your friends and yourself. Again, we can't anticipate how a system will respond to changes we make, we can only predict unsettlement. This, in itself, brings an opportunity to practice. How comfortable are you with unsettled energy around you? What is your capacity to sit calmly in it? How can you support those around you to adapt to any changes as you develop?

Practice *27* – attending to, and nourishing your spirit, based on an approach by Tom Crum

Take some time out to reflect on your wellbeing in the following realms:

1. Physical wellbeing including sleep, weight, exercise, diet, energy levels.

2. Environmental wellbeing including mindful consumption, energy use, transport habits, recycling, using local products.

3. Mental wellbeing including optimism, mindfulness, creativity, goal-setting, concentration, work-life balance.

4. Emotional wellbeing including expressing emotions, dealing with negative emotions, tuning into others, handling stress and pressure, experiencing happiness.

5. Social wellbeing including quality of close relationships, time spent with loved ones, receiving support and challenge, handling conflict, loving and being loved.

6. Spiritual wellbeing including gratitude, sense of purpose, living your values, giving service, offering compassion, trusting, a sense of belonging.

Choose one area where you feel depleted, and imagine how you might nurture this aspect of your wellbeing. In your mind and heart, set a clear intent to nourish this part of yourself and create three practices:

• *A regular physical/environmental practice, such as going for a walk.*

• *A regular mental/emotional practice, such as doing something creative.*

• *A regular social/spiritual practice, such as quality time with yourself or a loved one.*

The practices don't need to be huge commitments. It will be better if you can fit them naturally into your day, for example, a mindful walk to the bus stop. Aim to commit twenty minutes a day to replenishing your spirit.

Commit to doing your practices for six weeks. Then reflect on the effects.

Notes and reflections

Chapter 28 Pause for breath

'Awareness is not a giver of solace – it is just the opposite. It is a disturber and an awakener. Able leaders are usually sharply awake and reasonably disturbed. They are not seekers after solace. They have their own inner serenity.' R K Greenleaf

The focus of spirit and conversation has been on cultivating our sense of leadership presence through forging our character or spirit, and through practising centre and connecting with a bigger space and perspective. The potential is that in developing the capacity for profound leadership presence, we influence the presence of others, thereby enabling deeper conversations to unfold.

In developing centre, presence and the capacity to live, and lead, in a way that is true to our values, we become more attuned to what connects us to others and to our world. Whether we think of it in narrative terms such as ch'i or faith, or in scientific terms through the lens of quantum physics, this connectivity enables us to tune into the energy of the collective. In doing this, we open to the possibility that we may be able to access wisdom and insight that is beyond that of an individual.

Both individual spirit/centre and collective spirit/centre are flow states; they are not separate, but are interdependent. Good contact with individual spirit creates the conditions in which collective spirit is possible. The presence of collective spirit brings out the best in us individually.

This good contact can be described in different ways: being present, being centred or being in flow. It is a state of relaxed focus or soft concentration. Taoists describe it as a state of effortless effort, and, paradoxically, it is hard to attain and maintain because much of the time we are either distracted or trying too hard. Either our attention becomes flighty and we lose focus, or our attention becomes forced and we lock-on to a particular focus. Sometimes we are both distracted and trying too hard. One way or another, we are mostly off-centre and so we need to practice recovering centre, returning our attention to being in deep contact with ourselves and with our surroundings.

It is at an individual level that we create the possibilities for collective spirit, and we do this through cultivating our presence and our capacity for centre. Herein lies a paradox. If we practice to achieve something, we will not be centred; a centred state is in some way indifferent to outcome as it is simply alive to the moment. This invites us to cultivate an attitude to practice that means we do it for its own sake, bringing an inquiring approach to developing our leadership presence and our capacity for centre. The spirit of this might be that we practice centring in a conversation and notice the impact, and that we do this repeatedly until we get a sense of what is possible. What do we discover if we practice centre? What changes? What possibilities unfold?

In spirit and conversation, much of the focus has been internal, and on influences on our presence that are difficult to articulate. Our attention has also been more on leadership presence than on conversations, because our presence is a foundation for dialogue practices. Next we return to the practical territory of conversations and explore frameworks that will enable us to inquire into our habits of speech and will provide reference points for expanding our conversational versatility.

Practice *28* – pause for breath

This foundation practice appears at the end of each section of the book.

Sit in a comfortable upright posture, so that your feet are firmly planted on the floor and you are supporting your own back, rather than leaning against a chair. Rest your hands on your thighs, palms down.

Become aware of the contact between your feet/shoes and the floor. Become aware of the contact between your hands and your thighs. Become aware of the contact between your thighs and the chair. Become aware of the sitting bones, the bones at the base of the pelvis, pressing into the chair seat.

Notice your strong base, formed by your feet and sitting bones, and allow your spine to grow to its full length by gently imagining each vertebra lifting slightly from the one below. Sense lightness and spaciousness in your spine. Notice that your neck becomes long at the back, your chin tilted slightly towards your chest.

Now bring your attention to your breath. On each inhale, imagine your breath seeping into the spaces in your spine, allowing it to lengthen just a little bit more. On each exhale, imagine your breath flowing down through your chest and belly, softening any tension. Follow your breath for a few moments.

Now mentally scan your body and notice any places of tension, aching or discomfort. Choose one and, for a few breaths, imagine your inbreath soaking into this place, and on a longer exhale, imagine your outbreath dissolving any discomfort and carrying it out into the air around you, letting you rest.

After a few breaths, become aware of the contact between your sitting bones and the chair, between your hands and thighs, and between your feet and the ground.

Rise gently and stretch. You are ready to re-engage with the world.

Resource list for more on cultivating your finest leadership spirit

Radical Acceptance, Tara Brach
The Manual of the Warrior of Light, Paulo Coelho
The 7 Habits of Highly Effective People, Stephen Covey
The Universe in a Single Atom, The Dalai Lama
The Invitation, Oriah Mountain Dreamer
The Art of Being, Erich Fromm
The Art of Loving, Erich Fromm
The Prophet, Kahlil Gibran
Working with Emotional Intelligence, Daniel Goleman
10 Poems to Change your Life, Roger Housden
Synchronicity and the Inner Path of Leadership, Joseph Jaworksi
A Path with Heart, Jack Kornfield
After the Ecstasy, the Laundry, Jack Kornfield
Let your Life Speak, Parker Palmer
Authentic Happiness, Martyn Seligman
The Courage to Lead, Transform Self, Transform Society, R Brian Stanfield
Zen Mind, Beginners Mind, Shunryu Suzuki
Little Book of Practice, for Authentic Leadership in Action, Susan Szpakowski
The Tao Te Ching, Lao Tsu, various translations

Part Five

VERSATILITY IN CONVERSATIONS

Chapter 29   **Introduction**

Chapter 30   **Kantor's four players and linked frameworks**

Chapter 31   **Moves, direction and authentic voicing**

Chapter 32   **Opposes, integrity and respecting**

Chapter 33   **Follows, service and listening**

Chapter 34   **Bystands, perspective and suspending judgement**

Chapter 35   **Silences, mindful presence and pausing for breath – a speculation**

Chapter 36   **Pause for breath**

Resources list for more on the principles and practices of dialogue

Chapter 29 Introduction

'Choice of attention – to pay attention to this and to ignore that – is to the inner life what choice of action is to the outer. In both cases a man is responsible for his choice and must accept the consequences.' W H Auden

What part do we tend to play in conversations? To what extent are we aware of the ways in which we tend to hold patterns of conversation in place? How versatile are we when a conversation seems to veer off-track?

David Kantor and other dialogue practitioners offer frameworks that enable us to engage with these questions and to develop flexibility in the way in which we contribute to conversations. As a family therapist, Kantor[24] undertook research into effective communication and showed that members of a family system had a favoured way of contributing to conversations. They tended to be movers, opposers, followers or bystanders. In productive conversations these four 'players' are present.

Over time, the model evolved to reference speech actions and intentions and was enriched by others such as Peter Garrett, William Isaacs and Michael Jones. There are now up to six frameworks that can be linked to the original four-player model. In bringing the practices of mindfulness and dialogue to leadership conversations, I focus principally on four frameworks:

- the speech actions of move, oppose, follow and bystand, developed by David Kantor;
- the internal intentions that are associated with skilful speech actions, developed by David Kantor;
- the practices in which skilful speech actions are rooted, developed by Peter Garrett, William Isaacs and Michael Jones; and
- leadership energies that may reflect qualities of presence in conversations, initially based on Jungian archetypes and further developed by other practitioners.

Kantor's original model of speech actions and intents offers support in identifying conversational habits, and provides potential for increasing conversational versatility. The practices developed by Garrett, Isaacs, and Jones add depth to making speech actions skilfully. If the practices are embodied, there is a firm foundation for what is said, even if the speaker feels awkward or clumsy. The leadership energies can represent our spirit or personal presence in conversations.

Together, the frameworks of speech actions, intents, practices and leadership energies offer languages to describe patterns in conversation and to help us articulate and expand the contributions we make. In the following chapters, I invite you to explore interplays between different voices. What is the music they make and how does each voice, including your own, serve the whole?

Practice 29 – authentic voice, based on a practice from Wendy Palmer

Think of a situation where you have something important to say. Perhaps you want to ask for something, or give feedback, or challenge someone.

Sit or stand in a comfortable upright posture. Bring your attention fully to your breath, imagining it flowing up and down. Inhale, lengthening and straightening your spine. Exhale and imagine your breath flowing down into the ground, forming a root, as your shoulders and core relax. Take two or three breaths this way.

Now bring your attention to your mind. Inhale a sense of space and good intent into the centre of your mind and relax as you exhale. Ask yourself, 'what does my head want to say in this situation?' Find a sentence that expresses this and say it out loud.

Now bring your attention to your heart and solar plexus. Inhale a sense of space and good intent into the centre of your heart and/or solar plexus and relax as you exhale. Ask yourself, 'what does my heart/solar plexus want to say in this situation?' Find a sentence that expresses this and say it out loud.

Now bring your attention to your belly, deep down. Inhale a sense of space and good intent into the centre of your lower abdomen and relax as you exhale. Ask yourself, 'what does my gut want to say in this situation?' Find a sentence that expresses this and say it out loud.

Now let your attention flow through your mind, your heart/solar plexus and your belly. Inhale a sense of space and good intent into these places and relax as you exhale. Ask yourself, 'if my mind, heart and gut are aligned, what do I want to say in this situation? What is my truth?' Find a sentence that expresses this and say it out loud.

Take a few moments to rest and reflect on the effects of this practice.

Notes and reflections

Chapter *30* Kantor's four players and linked frameworks

'And in much of your talking, thinking is half-murdered.
For thought is a bird of space,
that in a cage of words may indeed
unfold its wings but cannot fly.'
Kahlil Gibran

This chapter introduces six frameworks that are sometimes shown as linked.[6] The frameworks have been developed by different practitioners in the field and there are varying perspectives on how, or even whether, the layers fit together. What follows is my own interpretation.

In a system linking six frameworks, the reach and complexity is potentially daunting. The following table summarises the frameworks in single words or short phrases. The summary is offered as an aide to navigating the territory that lies ahead.

Frameworks	Dimensions			
Speech actions (Kantor[24])	Move	Oppose	Follow	Bystand
Intents (Kantor[24])	Direction	Integrity	Service	Perspective
Practices (Garrett, Isaacs, Jones)	Authentic voicing	Respecting	Listening	Suspending judgement
Leadership energy archetypes	Sovereign	Warrior	Lover	Magician
Habits of thinking alone (Isaacs[1])	Recycling the past	Imposing	Fragmenting	Being certain
Principles for thinking together (Isaacs[1])	Unfolding	Coherence	Participation	Awareness

This chapter briefly describes the six frameworks, and subsequent chapters explore more fully each of the four dimensions, focusing on speech actions, intents, practices and leadership energies.

Introducing speech actions and intents

Kantor's model is often depicted as a diamond-like shape, with two advocacy speech actions on the vertical axis and two inquiry speech actions on the horizontal axis, offering a link between the work of Kantor and Agyris. Kantor describes a productive conversation as balancing the four speech actions and Argyris defines dialogue as a balance of advocacy and inquiry.

Kantor's four speech actions are:

- Move (an aspect of advocacy)
- Oppose (an aspect of advocacy)

- Follow (an aspect of inquiry)
- Bystand (an aspect of inquiry)

Speech actions

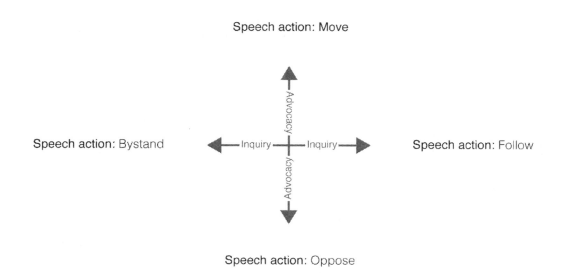

From work by David Kantor

The first three speech actions are fairly self-explanatory. To make a move is to offer a proposal, an opinion, a suggestion, an initiative. This is clearly an aspect of advocacy, of making a point. To make an oppose is to challenge all or part of what has been said, probing, scrutinising or clarifying. Making an oppose offers a counter-point, speaking with a different perspective or tone. This is also an aspect of advocacy.

To make a follow is to support and build on what has been said by another, perhaps by asking a question to elicit more information, context or understanding. A follow may also be a statement of acknowledgement and/or affirmation or a possibility offered as suggestion, without attachment to

238

outcome. When done skilfully, a follow is an aspect of inquiry; it is not an empty agreement, but adds to meaning or expands the potential for discovery, contributing to shared understanding.

The fourth speech action, making a bystand, is a little trickier to interpret. A bystand is impartial and curious. A bystand might seek to clarify what is happening in a conversation, or might explore whether a conversation remains collectively relevant and of service. A bystand offers those present an opportunity to step back, to gain perspective and to reflect on how they are conducting their conversation, rather than staying in the thick of a topic. Making a bystand is active and spoken; bystanding is not 'standing by.' When skilfully made, a bystand is an aspect of inquiry, in that it seeks to surface how a conversation is unfolding. There is a witnessing or observing quality to active bystanding. It seeks to reflect what is happening and to act as a mirror. Skilful bystanding looks beyond what is being said in a conversation and sheds light on how and why something is said (or not said) and who is speaking (or not speaking).

In deliberately using the phrase, 'to make …' in this description, I aim to emphasise the creative act of speaking. I am evoking the way an artist finds expression through making work, a deliberate inventive, expressive act. Adding our voice to a conversation is a key form of expression. If we view our words as a creative act, does this influence the way we contribute them?

One use of speech actions is to provide a language to describe patterns in conversation. A widespread pattern is that of move-oppose, move-oppose, essentially the structure of debate, which is a cultural norm in the UK. We are immersed in debate from our earliest days at school, being asked to compare and contrast two ideas, or to make a case for a position. Our parliament is based on debate or advocacy, as is our legal system. Our universities require the defence of a thesis. Debate is valuable and yet, as a cultural norm, we can

239

become immune to its presence and effects. We may need to heighten our awareness of its prevalence and notice when it is no longer fit-for-purpose.

Other patterns include move-move-move-move, sometimes described as serial monologue, and move-follow-follow-follow, which can indicate compliance. A sequence of bystands might suggest a collective unwillingness to tackle an issue. The language of move, follow, oppose and bystand means we can begin to articulate patterns, raising awareness of them and creating the potential for change.

The apparent simplicity of Kantor's speech actions is seductive. In practice, a speech action is often not clear-cut. A move can be made in a confused way if the 'mover' expects resistance and second-guesses this, or if they lack self-confidence in voicing their true opinion. A move may be veiled, or otherwise moderated, in circumstances where power or safety issues limit what seems possible. An oppose might be fashioned to look like a follow, but have a sting in its tail; it might also be made to look like a move or even a bystand, feigning neutrality whilst using an 'observation' to mask a challenge. A follow might be made as a compliant action of agreeing with perceived leadership power rather than as genuine support for something that has been said. The neutral perspective of a bystand might be unknowingly caught up in emotions, leaning towards one or other of the perspectives in play. A bystand might be distorted inadvertently by power differentials in the room. True impartiality (whilst participating, being engaged) is a subtle art, an exacting contribution based on the practices of mindfulness and centre.

When we are speaking, we can refine and clarify a speech action by being mindful of our intent. When someone's words impact on us in an unexpected or charged way, we can inquire into their intent. Being clear about our own intent and supporting others to reflect on their intent can help to avoid confusion and unintended consequences in conversations.

Kantor[24] describes a range of intents for each speech action as follows:

- A skilful move intends: direction, discipline, commitment, clarity
- A skilful follow intends: completion, compassion, loyalty, service, continuity
- A skilful oppose intends: correction, courage, protection, integrity
- A skilful bystand intends: perspective, patience, preservation, moderation.

In what follows, I have selected a single intent for each speech action, choosing a word that most resonates for me.

Intents

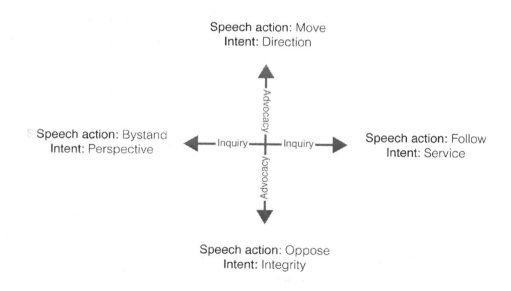

From work by David Kantor

The implication of Kantor's work is that effective communication includes:

- direction (move)
- integrity/internal consistency (oppose)
- service (follow)
- perspective (bystand)

In seeking to understand a contribution to a conversation it can be helpful to ask about intent. For instance, when we're not sure why a suggestion has been made, we might ask the speaker about their intent – are they offering a new direction, a challenge, an addition? When a group is silent in response to a proposal, what is their intent – agreement or opposition? When a question or statement evokes an unexpected response, we might inquire into the speaker's intent.

My experience is that many people speak without clear intent and when asked about their purpose, feel some confusion. A simple dialogue practice might be to reflect on intent before speaking – what do I mean to provide through my contribution?

An aspiring dialogue practitioner will cultivate the capacity to contribute each speech action with clear intent and in service to the collective purpose. This increases versatility in conversations and specifically means that we can contribute any missing elements to bring balance in move, follow, oppose and bystand. Initially, however, we generally favour one or two of Kantor's speech actions while being less at ease with the others. In developing our impact in conversations, there are essentially two challenges:

- to build on our strengths by ensuring that the contributions we make more naturally and frequently are made with awareness, skill and clear intent; and

- to add new capability by expanding our repertoire to include more often the speech actions we don't use or use rarely.

To consider your own versatility, I invite you to reflect on which speech actions you tend to favour. How can you use intent to hone your effectiveness? Which speech actions or intents feel unfamiliar to you and how might you begin to introduce these into your conversations?

Introducing practices or core conditions

As you know, practices lie close to my heart. By a practice, I mean a quality or attribute that, with attention and mindful repetition, becomes embodied, giving depth and congruence to whatever we do. In what follows, each practice is a quality or core condition that, if we inhabit it fully, provides a sound foundation for what we say.

The following practices were developed by Peter Garrett, William Isaacs, and Michael Jones. They propose that dialogue is supported when these core conditions are present:

- Speaking with authentic voice (authentic voicing)
- Respecting
- Listening to understand
- Suspending judgement

Each practice might support any of Kantor's speech actions, bringing body and weight to what is being said. When introducing the practices, I take the view that each plays a primary role in supporting a particular speech action, shown in the following diagram.

Practices

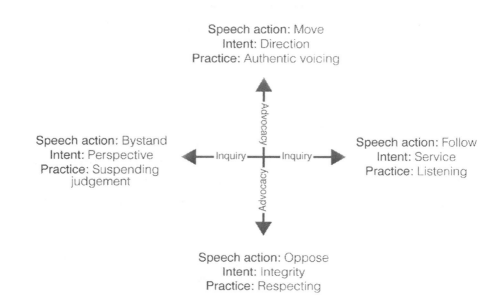

Adapted from work by Kantor, Garrett, Isaacs and others

Each practice applies to both self and others. If I practice suspending judgement, I suspend judgement about my own thinking and feeling as well as about what is being said and done by others. In suspending judgement, I hold a judgement lightly; I am not without judgement but I do not regard my judgement as a truth. If I practice listening to understand, I listen internally for my own voices as well as listening for the voices of others. In practising respect, I regard my own truth as legitimate alongside the truths of others. In speaking with authentic voice, I create space for the voices of others whilst committing to sharing the complexity of my deeper truth.

Together, these practices offer robust core conditions for deeper and richer conversations. They are not separate and one engenders another. For example, if I listen deeply to another, seeking to understand, I increase the possibility that they will speak their deepest truth. If I practice respect for another and their views, I am more likely to listen and to suspend judgement.

Inhabiting these qualities consistently, and well, requires discipline of mind, body and spirit. We may be able to practice them in favourable circumstances, but it is harder to bring them to situations in which we're not getting what we want or where the stakes are high. A significant element of developing capacity for dialogue is to cultivate these practices so that we are able to embody them more frequently and in charged circumstances, increasing our resilience in conversations and in relationships.

This is important because the quality of our energy influences those around us. For example, if I practice respect for others, and for myself, I will communicate the energy of this quality to those around me, affecting the tone of collective presence. If we intend to change our leadership conversations, these four core conditions represent key qualities to embody in our leadership presence so that we evoke them in others. If we were able to inhabit these practices, it's easy to imagine that our conversations would be transformed.

Which practices are important to you in the way you currently engage in your leadership conversations? How consistently do you embody them? What, if anything, needs to change?

Introducing archetypes for leadership spirit
A fourth framework outlines four archetypes for leadership energy or spirit, reflecting a quality of presence that supports skilful speech actions, deliberate intent and congruent practice.

The original framing of leadership spirit drew on classical archetypes from the work of Carl Jung. These representations of leadership presence, with associated speech actions, intents and practices, are:

- sovereign/statesman (move, direction, authentic voice)
- lover (follow, service, listening)
- warrior (oppose, integrity, respecting)
- magician (bystand, perspective, suspending judgement)

Leadership

Speech action: Move
Intent: Direction
Practice: Authentic voicing
Leadership: Sovereign

Advocacy

Speech action: Bystand
Intent: Perspective
Practice: Suspending judgement
Leadership: Magician

Inquiry ← → Inquiry

Speech action: Follow
Intent: Service
Practice: Listening
Leadership: Lover

Advocacy

Speech action: Oppose
Intent: Integrity
Practice: Respecting
Leadership: Warrior

Adapted from work by Kantor, Garrett, Isaacs and others

As we look at each aspect of Kantor's model in more depth, I encourage you to find your own references for your varying experiences of leadership spirit.

Habits of thinking alone and principles for thinking together

In *Dialogue and the Art of Thinking Together*,[1] Isaacs outlines a theory of thought. He describes the impact of our human tendency to think alone, and offers potential remedies for these habits of thought, which get in the way of our capacity to think together. The remedies represent profound responses to habitual thought patterns, and Isaacs calls them principles for dialogue. I call them principles for thinking together.

The framing of both the habits of thinking alone and the principles for thinking together is highly conceptual and complex, and the details are beyond the scope of this book. For completeness, and at the risk of over-simplifying and misrepresenting them, I offer a brief outline of them.

The four habits of thinking alone and the corresponding principles for thinking together are:

- recycling the past because we place too much store by its veracity, remedied by being present and responding to the potential of an unfolding future (move, direction, authentic voice)
- imposing our view on others and defending ourselves from the views of others, remedied by recalling that everything is connected; there is a natural coherence in the universe (oppose, integrity, respecting)
- fragmenting and separating matters that are fundamentally connected at a deeper level, remedied by fully participating in our experience and bringing a beginner's mind to it (follow, service, listening)
- being certain of our beliefs, values and experience and believing them to be unchanging in the face of a changing world, remedied by awareness that everything is in motion, is impermanent, and will pass (bystand, perspective, suspending judgement)

247

Our tendency to recycle past experiences in response to current predicaments is labelled idolatry by Isaacs. It includes the propensity to believe our 'own press.' The way to transcend this tendency is to create space, both individually and together, in which a bigger truth can unfold through us, as described in the chapter on collective spirit.

Our tendency to impose our own view on others, or to defend our position vehemently is labelled violence by Isaacs. In verbal violence, we deny the legitimacy of others. The remedy is to recognise the experience of each person, making an assumption of coherence and asking how different truths fit together.

Our tendency to fragment things that are connected at a more profound level or to take a partial view out of context, is labelled abstraction by Isaacs. To heal fragmentation, we can participate fully in the world and be present to our experience, seeing ourselves as reflected in the world and the world as reflected in us.

Being certain refers to our tendency to believe that we are right, and to fix our stories, even as the world changes around us. An antidote is to cultivate an impartial awareness, based on the principle that awareness of something changes it (see, for example, *The Paradoxical Theory of Change*[23]).

In summary, habits of thinking alone describe human patterns so fundamental that it is difficult for us to genuinely think together. We must bring profound mindfulness and presence to our conversations if we are to transcend these tendencies. We must experience and acknowledge our connectedness and our frailties; we must be ready to change our minds. If you wish to explore these matters in more depth, I invite you to read the work of Isaacs[1] or Bohm.[25]

Summary
Writing about these frameworks has changed my understanding and perception of them; I find them infinitely rich and yet incomplete. After exploring each

framework in more depth, I speculate that there may be a fifth speech action, with associated intent, practice and leadership spirit. This fifth speech action is to deliberately make a silence. The following chapters explore in more depth the speech actions of move, oppose, follow and bystand before considering the case for making a silence.

Practice *30* – cultivating dialogue practices

Choose one practice:

> *Respecting (self and others)*
> *Listening to understand*
> *Speaking with authentic voice*
> *Suspending judgement (self and others)*

Firstly, reflect on your current experience of the practice you have chosen:

- *how do you extend this quality to others?*
- *how do you experience it when it is offered to you?*

Pay particular attention to your internal dialogue. How does the practice you have chosen, or it's opposite, show up? For example, if you choose suspending judgement, how much and how often do you judge others in your mind and feelings? How often are you able to suspend judgement and be curious? How accepting are you of yourself and others?

On the receiving end, how do you respond when you feel judged? How do you respond when you feel acknowledged and accepted?

As you develop your understanding, consider how you might more fully inhabit the practice you have chosen. Set a clear intent to do this. How can you remember to pause, centre and extend the quality of your chosen practice into your conversation? What is the impact on others? What do you notice about yourself? What changes in your conversations?

Notes and reflections

Chapter 31 Moves, direction and authentic voicing

'He is quick, thinking in clear images;
I am slow, thinking in broken images.
He becomes dull, trusting to his clear images;
I become sharp, mistrusting my broken images.'
Robert Graves

This chapter explores making a move more fully, with the intent of offering a deeper sense of how this contribution to a conversation might be made skilfully. After a description that connects speech action, intent, practice and leadership energy, there are some practice notes to ground this model in experience. The elements considered in the description are:

- Speech action: move
- Intent: direction
- Practice: authentic voicing
- Leadership energy: sovereign

Description
The leadership spirit of sovereign and the speech action of moving encompass a statesman-like perspective with the potential for providing vision and inspiring commitment. When embodying sovereign energy, a skilful move suggests what

is possible and may speak on behalf of collective concerns. Sovereign leadership spirit risks being patrician, but this risk is mitigated if what is said is supported by the practice of authentic voicing.

The practice of authentic voicing has depth, requiring us to set aside our roles, our conditioning and our masks, and to speak of our experience in the present moment. In speaking with authenticity, we will pay close attention to what is real within us and what we truly think and feel in response to what is taking place around us.

What does this mean in practice? When we offer an opinion, it's often a mish-mash of reactions to the ideas of others, things we've been taught and whatever currently interests us. It comes from our mindshelf. If we seek to attribute what we say to source material, we might find that the views of our parents feature, and perhaps aspects of our education and professional training, along with other significant influences on our lives, such as the views of our friends or our spirituality, faith (or lack of it). We may also be influenced by current events and recent experiences. These factors may, or may not, represent our own deeply held truth, our authentic voice. The issue is that we tend not to reflect on this until an accessible, recycled point of view has given rise to unintended consequences.

When you are next offering an opinion, reflect for a moment. How did you form this opinion? Where did it come from? Is it truly your authentic voice, reflecting the complexity of what you think and feel?

Revisiting my cooking metaphor for mindshelf responses – that they are like ready meals, prepared, packaged and ready to heat through – confirms that authentic voicing is the opposite. In practising authentic voice, we search within for the ingredients of what we want to say, selecting the freshest, then combining them and cooking them to create a response that reflects what we truly think and feel, in the moment. Just as a chef tastes their food, balances flavours, responds to the vagaries of the oven, and fine-tunes presentation, so a skilful mover feels for what they truly want to say, balancing the complexity of their internal dialogue with the energy and interests that are present in the external environment. In seeking to practice authentic voicing, we notice the impulse to pop out a mindshelf contribution and pause for breath, taking the time to consider what's needed in *this* conversation, at *this* time.

To put it another way, David Bohm makes the distinction between thoughts and thinking. He describes thoughts as pre-prepared products of our minds which are stored in our memory banks for (often useful) recycling. In contrast, thinking is a current, fresh process that takes place as we become present to this conversation, these perspectives, in this moment. Our authentic voice expresses our thinking, not our thoughts. Peter Garrett makes a similar distinction between feelings and 'felts.' I will add a distinction between speaking and 'spokes.'

Voicing our current (and changing) feelings and thinking, is often challenging. As our brains follow their programming and trawl efficiently for past experiences that seem relevant to a current conversation, these are often 'spoke,' without awareness. In developing the capacity to bring the practices of dialogue into our conversations, we must discern when this retrieval process is helpful and when it's not. Do you know the saying, 'that'll put a spoke in their wheel?' When we speak on autopilot and offer spokes, we may thwart feelings, thinking or speaking that, given more space, might emerge to make a greater contribution than our spoke. In practising speaking with authentic voice, we work with current emerging experience and seek to minimise the impact of recalled or recycled memory.

The intent associated with skilful moving is to provide direction and clarity. Moving is an initiating energy, expressed through positions, proposals, suggestions, ideas, potential and vision. It offers commitment and can inspire commitment in others. A skilful move provides something to follow, oppose or bystand, providing momentum or traction or grist. The challenge of moving is to bring clarity as well as direction, as depicted earlier by triangular, or wedge-shaped, advocating energy. This energetic shape has a point, but also clear, bounded sides. It's not a warm, fuzzy shape, it's strong and incisive. In offering a skilful move, we will include the key thinking and feeling that informs the point we are making. Sharing some of the information, experience, values and steps offers an opportunity for others to engage more fully with what is being said.

In returning to leadership spirit, what qualities or energy might support making a skilful move with authentic voice? At its best, sovereign spirit is wise and speaks in service to the collective. At less than its best, sovereign energy risks imposing a view, being rigidly attached to a particular way forward or becoming overly knowing and forceful. In making a skilful, authentic move we may need to acknowledge that we are uncertain about consequences, or that we don't understand something, or that we don't have an answer. Humility and generosity are two qualities that may temper a tendency to omnipotence in sovereign leadership and, if cultivated, may enable true statesmanship.

Another risk of sovereign leadership spirit is coming to believe our own press, perhaps thinking that only we can see what is possible. This may blind us to alternative storylines and to our own human frailties. To balance this risk, we might ask ourselves how we can stay grounded and present to the realities and perceptions of others.

When I invite others to explore their sense of the leadership spirit associated with skilfully offering direction from a place of authenticity, they offer words such as pioneer, captain and enabler alongside statesman. What form does your own initiating style of leadership take?

In summary, speaking our truth with authentic voice is the practice in which skilfully making a move can be fruitfully rooted; we offer our truth lightly, as a gift, pooling it with the truths of others. In other words, we are centred and present. If we attach too much importance to our own truth, we risk believing that our recycled thoughts equate to current reality; we lose our centre, our sense of presence and our sense of being part of collective spirit.

Practice notes
1. Making a move 'out there' (external dialogue)
In many conversations, moves are either very obvious (edging towards the overbearing), or surprisingly hard to spot because an attempt to offer a direction of travel is delivered in a passive, stifled, or deferent voice. Alternatively, a move is expressed as contingent on other things, or is offered abstractly or as a generalisation that isn't recognised as a clear proposal. These are all examples of uncentred moves, where the delivery is too hard, risking too forceful a use of power, or too soft, risking fuzziness and undefined direction. To respond skilfully to an uncentred move, we might make a follow to open out an overly-focused move, or to clarify the intent of an indistinct move.

When contributing a centred move to a conversation, we balance clarity in our own point of view with openness to the perspectives of others. In using authentic voice, we acknowledge that our contribution is based on a partial perspective and we speak in a way that reflects this. We all have blind spots and deaf spots, and as we invite others to offer alternative points of view or to ask questions, we embrace the power of collective wisdom.

What do you notice about how you make moves? What do you notice about how others make moves? What can you learn?

2. Making a move 'in here' (internal dialogue)
I experience internal moves as my judgements, opinions, prejudices and impulses: all the advocatory elements of my left hand column (what I am

256

thinking and feeling but not saying). These internal moves are largely pre-programmed and unskilful; they are reactions to immediate circumstances and, if I express them, it is likely that I will be uncentred and off-balance. Internal moves respond well to pausing for breath and centring. We can then exercise discernment about whether to act on our impulse to speak or simply notice what is arising with curiosity.

What do you notice about moves in your internal dialogue? What is the quality of voice in any thoughts that arise? How do you discern whether to act on an impulse to speak?

3. When a move is met with a move

When a move is met with a move, the first move is often reiterated, prompting a repetition of the second move, prompting another cycle of the same. Positions rapidly solidify and moves quickly become pitted against one another, escalating in pointedness, when this may not have been anyone's original intent.

I work with small groups of people to explore dialogic practices, and in an early session with one of these groups, a participant made a statement about the link between emotions and thinking. Another participant said that his experience was different to the view being described. There was an opening for a follow at this point, for someone to inquire into the personal experience of others. Instead, the first voice expanded on her (very well informed) perspective, drawing on theory and expertise. An unintended consequence of this further move was that the truth of the other person's experience went unacknowledged. Feeling unheard, the second voice said again that his experience was different. Everyone else remained silent and there was an air of genuine curiosity and inquiry. However, the first voice moved again, with more facts and references, and I felt the energy of the listeners draining away.

The conversation continued for a while between two voices, becoming more generalised because the second speaker started to invoke evidence to legitimise

257

their perspective. One or two new voices tried valiantly to join the conversation, by making more moves. The conversation had now become an exchange of theories, and felt less relevant and accessible to those without knowledge. If we had taken the route of speaking about our individual experience of the connection between thinking and emotions, we would all have had relevant perspectives to contribute and so could have remained connected to the conversation.

The key to unlocking move-to-move patterns is to acknowledge that each person's opinion is legitimate, and then to explore how they have come to their view. It is also helpful to encourage inquiry into perceived truths of gurus and authorities; erudite concepts and theories may be being misapplied, or whilst being true in general, may not be a good fit with the particulars of a current situation.

4. The consequences of not making moves
Without moves there is no direction. There is nothing to follow, nothing to test for resonance or dissonance, no landmarks from which to gain perspective. The direction of any particular move may or may not be relevant to the eventual horizons of a conversation, but it is human nature to react internally to a statement of position and that generates reference points that support participation.

For example, in facilitating a three-day programme to support dialogue practice, I misjudged the need to make a move on the second day. My co-facilitator and I had different perspectives of the interest and capacity of the group and whether we should stay with the programme we had designed (the move, or proposal, for the day). He felt constrained by the plan and silenced by me, and I, typically the mover in our partnership, felt silenced in turn. We decided that we should check-in with the group and choose a way forward with their participation.

I took the lead in facilitating a check-in with the group and sought some guidance on the direction we should take. In response to a question, I outlined the original plan for the day. The eventual decision was to engage with all the proposed elements of the day, but in a different order. The result was an unintended and unanticipated implosion just before lunchtime, with disturbance for most of the rest of the day. On reflection, we saw that without providing (enough) direction, we asked a newly formed (and temporary) group to navigate across some tricky terrain without a map or a compass. With not-quite-enough-of-a-move, we wandered somewhat aimlessly, with unhappy consequences.

Practice 31 – moves, direction and authentic voicing

Out there: *listen for a sense of direction in a conversation and notice if, how, and when it changes. Become curious about how a collective sense of direction develops – how is it initiated? What helps? What hinders? What changes it?*

Listen for a sense of authentic voice in others. When you experience it, how do you know? What is the impact of authentic voice?

Notice when, where and under what circumstances you speak with authentic voice. What is your impact? How do others respond?

In here: *develop your awareness of how and when an intent to influence the direction of a conversation arises in you. Do you choose to speak? What impact do you have? If you don't speak, does someone else suggest a similar direction?*

Pay attention to your (recalled) thoughts and 'felts.' How are they influencing/colouring your current experience? Can you set them aside? What thinking and feeling is immediately relevant? What authentic voices rise within you? How do you move amongst them and choose what to say?

Notes and reflections

Chapter *32* Opposes, integrity and respecting

'The moment we want to believe something, we suddenly see all the arguments for it, and become blind to the arguments against it.' George Bernard Shaw

This chapter explores making an oppose more fully, with the intent of offering a deeper sense of how this contribution to a conversation might be made skilfully. After a description that connects speech action, intent, practice and leadership energy, there are some practice notes to ground this model in experience. The elements considered in the description are:

- Speech action: oppose
- Intent: integrity
- Practice: respecting
- Leadership energy: warrior

Description

The leadership spirit of warrior can be easily misunderstood. From a martial arts perspective, I see warrior spirit as passion for the ethical, the 'right' in some framework, tempered by discipline. For a skilled warrior faced with conflict, the best outcome is not to fight. Fighting risks damage, injury or death. A warrior therefore considers carefully what is worth fighting for, and is respectful of the power and position of others. In choosing to fight, a warrior is strategic, incisive and spare in effort, seeking to align a wrong with minimum collateral damage. True warrior spirit is a noble force for good, whereas shadow warrior energy may be a violent mercenary using skill and power to overcome or exploit others.

At its best, warrior leadership spirit has integrity, courage and discipline. It also challenges incongruent or incomplete proposals. At less than its best, warrior leadership risks wielding force, correcting things for the sake of perfection, or crusading. When I invite others to explore their sense of this leadership spirit, they offer words such as challenger, craftsperson/artisan and optimiser alongside warrior. What form does your own aligning style of leadership take?

The intent for skilful opposing is integrity. At its most obvious, to oppose is to provide a counter-view, to disagree, or to correct. However, this can suggest negativity, seeing only errors or mistakes. Skilful opposing intends alignment and integrity, the internal consistency of means being congruent with ends. Those who oppose are often trying to improve things, to bring rigour to thinking, or to help. In this context, skilful opposing can be seen as testing the robustness of a strategy, or bringing coherence to it. If our intent is to enhance the integrity of a proposal, then we are opposing, whether we ask a question, make a statement or, indeed, are silent.

Making a skilful oppose is grounded in the practice of respecting, a quality that mitigates the risk of using disproportionate force. Opposing without respect disregards the legitimacy of another person's point of view; it potentially silences their voice. Without respect, opposing belittles another's perspective and often triggers a trial of strength, through skilful argument or use of power. However, it's difficult to oppose with respect. It requires that an opposer voluntarily legitimises the point of view that they are challenging. Opposing with respect puts both opinions on an equal footing and may leave an opposer's position vulnerable to change or rejection. Opposing with respect requires courage.

If we do not practice respect, we risk imposing our view on others. In imposing, we deny the legitimacy of another, we discount their perspective, we cut it down. In denying a person's voice, we risk holding their experience to be less relevant or valid than our own. We risk rejecting or excluding them, challenging their very identity. However, if we attach too much importance to respecting others, we risk denying our own legitimacy and so deny others our contribution.

Opposing is an aspect of the triangular energy of advocacy, potentially cutting through inconsistency or generalities. Skilful opposing reveals and respects differences. If overdone, the sharp edge of opposing can be destructive. If too tentative, an oppose can be easily brushed aside.

In her book *The Invitation,*[26] Oriah Mountain Dreamer writes that on her fortieth birthday she decided that she was only going to make 'real mistakes' in future. She describes real mistakes as:

'Genuine errors in judgement, choices that can be seen, with the wisdom of hindsight, not to have been the best.'

She wants to avoid mistakes where she discounts her initial judgement about a situation and explains away her reservations. She illustrates what she means by recounting a time when she failed to express her doubts about a course of action proposed by some co-workers. She didn't oppose when she foresaw some difficulties. Unchallenged, her co-workers implemented their approach, which

264

proved disastrous and her misgivings came to pass. If she had shared her concerns when they arose, she might have influenced the outcome.

In summary, respecting is the practice in which skilfully making an oppose can be fruitfully rooted; we offer our opposition with care for the truths of others. We are centred, and secure enough in that calm resilient place that we can hold our truth and the truths of others in parity. If we are attached to correcting the views of others, we risk imposing our own position. We become forceful and lose our centre, our sense of presence, and we separate ourselves from collective spirit.

Practice notes
1. Making an oppose 'out there' (external dialogue)
Opposing is the speech action most often disguised or dressed up in a conversation. Opposing tends not to be socially acceptable or polite, and so we find ways of hinting at it; we ask for more information or we stay silent. Opposing shows up as debate, as argument, as conflict, often accompanied by feelings of discomfort. A skilful oppose might take the form of a show-stopping question, a question from left field that no-one else has considered.

When opposing is present, there are necessarily at least two positions in play. Some people respond by taking sides, others seek to minimise difference in points of view by smoothing them over, and yet others disengage, particularly if they recognise a familiar pattern. In these circumstances, it can be helpful to make a bystand to offer an impartial sense of what is taking place, and to hold all opinions with equal legitimacy. This creates an opportunity for people to pause, reflect, and reconnect to the purpose of the conversation.

We don't tend to offer our opinions and ideas to have them opposed, challenged or tested. Sometimes we say that this is what we want, but inviting challenge can be a way of paying lip-service to participation or consultation. An opposer, therefore, needs to be courageous, thick-skinned or both. An oppose might be dispatched quickly by being discounted, shouted down or simply ignored. Yet opposition is needed if proposals, decisions and choices are to be robust and are to take account of all relevant facets of a situation.

Oppose is frequently present in formal meetings of organisations. If the culture is not conducive to including difference, then a move from a person with perceived power (whether positional, personal or another form) will be met with silence. This silence can be an oppose. After the meeting, participants may make their real views known to one another, often overtly disagreeing with what was said during the meeting. A rule of thumb is that oppose will be present in a conversation, whether spoken or not, so it's best to seek it out. After all, when we think rationally, it is obvious that no two people will precisely agree in their thinking.

Habitual opposers often become caricatured as 'the pessimist,' 'the party-pooper' or 'the grumbler.' This enables a system to increasingly discount their voices. If this is your experience, how can you develop your practice in respecting, and find a way to oppose which interrupts this pattern and fully engages the attention of others?

It's easy to imagine an oppose beginning with good intent and moving subtly to imposing a view, through passion or strength of opinion. If disregarded, an oppose might escalate into a forceful opinion, becoming excessive. Some opposes begin as playful sparring, but harden to argument, and then to a conviction that, for one opinion to prevail, the opinions of others must be defeated. It's a small step from defeating the argument to defeating the person.

What do you notice about how you make opposes? What do you notice about how others make opposes? What can you learn?

2. Making an oppose 'in here' (internal dialogue)

Becoming aware of internal conflict can be important to contributing effectively to dialogue. Where we are muddled in our thinking, feeling and values, our internal conflict will be reflected in unclear moves, ambiguous opposes, biased bystands and half-hearted follows. Personally, my first awareness of an internal conflict often comes when I find myself changing my mind frequently on something – I think, 'I'll accept that piece of work' and draft an email, only to find myself not sending it because I'm thinking, 'I'd rather not do that piece of work.' Then I'll find myself editing the email, a sign that I am considering the work again. The email remains unsent – because I am doubtful again.

When I notice a swing to and from positions, I now know that I need to pause and think through what is drawing me towards each position. What is motivating my impulse to accept the piece of work? What are my concerns? If I understand this, I can then say to my client, 'in principle I'd like to accept the work, but I have some concerns I'd like to explore first.' This is a clean statement of my current thinking and creates an opportunity for greater understanding between us.

Sometimes our internal opposes are silent or go unnoticed because we often can't afford to hear our doubts. Yet we must listen for them and attend to them if we want to bring integrity to our speech, actions and energy.

What do you notice about opposes in your internal dialogue? Do you discount them and gloss over them? Do you put too much reliance on them, allowing them to limit what you think and do? How can you be respectful of your internal opposes and include them in your thinking?

3. When an oppose is met with an oppose

When oppose meets oppose we may have a stand-off, with two opposers circling one another warily, trying to establish their relative power or the relative weight of their reasoning. How is oppose-to-oppose different from move-to-move? I have a sense of move-to-move being like a game of chess, where two players essentially out-reason one another. A mover is speaking for a point of view and perhaps promoting a point of view. In contrast, I have a sense of oppose-to-oppose being a determination to speak against the other person's point of view, whatever it is and however it develops, and so is attacking another point of view. The aim of oppose-to-oppose feels more like overcoming another, rather than out-reasoning their argument.

Oppose meeting oppose can also be a fight, where the scrap itself has become more important than the positions that began it. If you are witnessing this pattern, there is power in offering a bystand, in the form of a perspective on the dynamic that's playing out. Those engaged in the confrontation have the opportunity to gain insight into their actions. Drawing attention to the dynamic is often enough to create the space for those involved to pause for breath, come to awareness, and make different choices. When oppose meets oppose, another option is to ask a question to clarify the purpose or intent of the conversation (a move), supported by an inquiry into what needs to happen for others to participate (a follow).

4. The consequences of not making opposes
Without opposes, the opportunity for checking integrity is lost. It can be deeply challenging to oppose in a system that provides you with something of value, such as security, status, support, income, regard or friendship. The system might be your organisation, your family or your community.

In *Harry Potter and the Philosopher's Stone*,[27] Professor Dumbledore says:

> *'It takes a great deal of bravery to stand up to our enemies, but just as much to stand up to our friends.'*

The effect is somewhat lessened when he awards ten house-points for standing up to your friends, and fifty or sixty to each person who stood up to their enemies. There were mitigating factors, but let me indulge my opposing nature! I think it takes more courage to stand up to your friends than your enemies as there is so much more to lose. In countering a prevailing paradigm, we risk the pain of rejection or ridicule, or find ourselves being ostracised. If our opposition is on target, it can generate a strong defensive response. Why would we take these risks in a system that provides us with something we value?

In my work, I meet many reluctant opposers who associate opposing with conflict and, as they don't like conflict, they don't oppose. However, ideas which go unopposed can become parodies of themselves, almost inbred. Skilful opposing brings rigour to thinking and improves the quality of decisions. By preferring not to rock the boat, we may lay the foundations for far-reaching consequences. We see this where professionals don't challenge colleagues who sidestep regulations or good practice, with the result that a business fails or someone is harmed.

Speaking in opposition may not be heard, particularly if an oppose is discounted by people with more power or who think they know better. However, in not speaking out, an opposer may be left feeling that they could have done more to deflect problems, if they subsequently arise.

If you are a reluctant opposer, I encourage you to add opposing to your repertoire, and risk rejection or conflict in order to add a further perspective into the mix. Skilful opposing brings the possibility of increasing the robustness and coherence of decisions.

Practice *32* – opposes, integrity and respecting

Out there: *listen for contributions that raise problems with, or otherwise challenge, an emerging direction or process. Become curious about the intent of those 'interruptions' in a growing theme – which are helpful? Which are not? Listen also for silence and inquire into the intent of it.*

Listen for the times when you sense others practising respect. When you experience it, how do you know? What is the impact of respecting?

Notice when, where and under what circumstances you practice respecting. What form does it take? How do others respond?

In here: *develop your awareness of how and when opposition, challenge or disagreement arises within you. Do you choose to speak? What impact do you have? If you don't speak, what stops you? What might you be missing by discounting an internal dissenting voice?*

Pay attention to how you are regarding others in relation to each other and to yourself. In your mind and heart, are you valuing the contribution of some more than others? What can you learn from this? How can you accept each contribution as legitimate?

Notes and reflections

Chapter 33 Follows, service and listening

'He listened in the way that we dream of others listening, his face seeming to reflect on everything said. He did not start forward to seize on my slightest pause, to assert an understanding of something before the thought was finished, or to argue with a swift, irresistible impulse – the things which often make dialogue impossible.' Anne Rice

This chapter explores making a follow more fully, with the intent of offering a deeper sense of how this contribution to a conversation might be made skilfully. After a description that connects speech action, intent, practice and leadership energy, there are some practice notes to ground this model in experience. The elements considered in the description are:

- Speech action: follow
- Intent: service
- Practice: listening
- Leadership energy: lover

Description

When I was first introduced to the leadership energy of lover I simply didn't get it. This one word alienated me for some time, and yet I know that I listen well and am able to support and follow. I offer this as an example of how some aspects of these frameworks can spark confusion and uncertainty. I invite you to reflect on which aspects of these frameworks you instinctively understand and which puzzle or challenge you? There is potential learning in each experience. For the bits we quickly grasp, we can begin to build on that strength, which may be supported by some experience and confidence. For the perplexing bits, we can open up to uncertainty and develop our curiosity to deepen our understanding.

For the archetype of lover leadership spirit, the essence is community, shared purpose, service and relationship. In my early working life, as someone of fierce independence and high logic, it took me some time to figure out why, once I'd set out my leadership vision, my team just didn't get on with it. In their article *Bringing Life to Organisational Change*,[28] Margaret Wheatley and Myron Kellner-Rogers offer a clear perspective on my experience:

> *'People only support what they create. Life insists on its freedom to participate and can never be sold on or bossed into accepting someone else's plans.'*

At its best, lover spirit is nourishing and just, seeking equity and wellbeing for all. At less than its best, this energy risks undiscriminating inclusion, being all things to all men. When I invite others to explore their sense of this leadership spirit they offer words such as supporter, servant and mother, alongside lover. What form does your own inclusive and nourishing style of leadership take?

The practice for skilful following is listening, meaning to attend in a profound way, that enables us to participate in the full richness of a conversation, our individual and shared experience, and our world. We are invited to work directly with our sensory experiences rather than to rely on the shorthand of words. The practice of deep listening gathers in sensory data and asks, 'what am I really seeing, actually hearing, currently sensing and feeling?' We bring a

273

beginners mind to our experiences rather than giving them ready-made labels, with their associated assumptions and meaning. In listening skilfully, attention moves fluidly between inner and outer experiences, balancing these two worlds. In deep listening, we open to experiences that may be beyond words.

In making a follow, we offer service to those present, grounded in profound listening. A skilful follow responds to a move, oppose, or bystand in a way that builds shared understanding. Follow is not given lightly, it's not hollow agreement. In making a follow, we might provide a nuanced perspective of a situation that others are struggling to comprehend, or we might provide words that add colour or texture to what others are saying. A follow enriches, builds, augments.

The intent for a skilful follow is service, embracing all relevant elements, be that people, ideas or tasks. This inclusive energy is inquiring in nature, or circular, if we recall the energetic shapes. If we overdo inclusion, we risk losing depth and relevance to too much breadth. With insufficient inclusion, we may forget our connection with others, even though we participate fully as an individual. In participating fully, we may want to belong too much and so remove our unique voice from a conversation.

How do we balance self with others in full participation? In attending to the whole, we embrace justice, respecting the rights and responsibilities of being part of a collective.

In summary, listening is the practice in which making a skilful follow can be fruitfully rooted and centred. Listening includes attending internally for our own heartfelt responses to an unfolding conversation. If we attach too much importance to listening to others, we risk excluding our voice. If we listen too

274

much to ourselves, we risk excluding others. The challenge is to listen on different levels simultaneously, to words, to intent, to emotion, to musicality, and to feel for meaning, beyond the limitation of words. This takes practice.

Practice notes
1. Following 'out there' (external dialogue)
External following is participating fully, risking our unique perspective in service to others, regardless of sanction or reward. Following adds to meaning and to shared understanding. Following invites, includes, makes connections and builds. A follow uses a question to surface more information, to enable or develop shared perspectives or to offer links. I have a sense that following nourishes relationships and conversations.

In organisations, it may be customary for follows to be unspoken; we agree with a perspective being offered but we don't declare that support. This leaves a lot to chance. Silence can as easily be an oppose as a follow. What stops us from supporting, from building, from declaring allegiance? If we do not follow, how do we generate shared purpose?

What do you notice about how you make follows? What do you notice about how others follow? What can you learn?

2. Following 'in here' (internal dialogue)
The internal aspect of follow honours our right to fully participate, including all our internal voices. It feels closely linked to authentic voice, listening for what is arising within, and discerning what has personal importance. In addition, a deep commitment to participating, for both self and others, may enable us to overcome any self-consciousness or doubt about our legitimacy.

Following is important in our internal dialogue, ensuring we don't discount or devalue our truth. An internal follow might appreciate and affirm our thinking and feeling, thereby enabling us to gather the resources to make a unique contribution externally, however it might be received. Internally, as externally, our follows may be missing or silent. How can we bring more attention to our supporting voices?

What do you notice about how you choose what to include or exclude in your internal dialogue? How do you acknowledge or affirm your own truth?

3. When a follow is met with a follow

When a follow meets a follow, energy builds around a theme or idea. This risks excluding other perspectives. There may be an early sense of completion, albeit illusory. I liken this to a 'false top' in climbing a mountain, where you think you can see the summit only to find, when you get there, that it just looked like the top from your earlier perspective. You may find that a conversation reignites in a richer vein if you pause and sit for a while with any sense of completion, internally checking for perspective. You might collectively ask, 'is there anything we've missed?' When apparent agreement is quickly signed off and people leave a room to take action, there is a risk that time, energy and resources will be wasted because crucial factors haven't been considered.

I've been in many meetings which have started with good intent for inclusion, and then a follow-follow-follow sequence locks a conversation into just a few people. Momentum grows and others find it hard to join in, or to challenge, the building energy. An effective intervention is to bystand, to offer an impartial description of the pattern (the conversation is located in only a few voices) and to invite wider participation. Left unnoticed, this kind of pattern can become group-think, or can favour a vociferous minority, missing a wider constituency.

4. The consequences of not following

Without follows there is no sense of inclusion, of joining together in a shared endeavour. For example, a management team surfaced a pattern of serial

276

monologues (moves or opposes) with the occasional hollow agreement. The resulting conversation stayed in generalities and seemed to go round and round without ever becoming concrete or coming to any shared sense of understanding, let alone action. After meetings, the managers would carry on acting individually. No-one ever picked up on anyone else's contribution and added to it. In the absence of follows, there was no chance of coming to a collective perspective. The pattern was described as being like planes in the stack above Heathrow airport, with none landing. The group began to experiment with following and, slowly, developed some capacity to build shared ownership and approaches.

Another consequence of not following is that a conversation remains in advocacy, in debate, and positions become polarised. Following adds further perspectives and information and makes relational connections.

Practice 33 – follows, service and listening

Out there: *listen for contributions that include, build, expand, affirm and invite participation. What is the impact of them? Become curious about what may be missing in a conversation and experiment with how you might draw fresh perspectives and voices into play.*

Attend to the quality of listening in others. When you experience profound listening, how do you know? What is the impact of profound listening?

Notice when, where and under what circumstances you listen deeply and profoundly. What do you listen for? How do others respond?

In here: *develop your awareness of how and when appreciative connecting energy arises in you. Do you choose to speak? What impact do you have? If you don't speak, what stops you?*

Pay attention to how you are listening to your internal dialogue and notice whether you are appreciative of your own narrative and ideas. How do you approach your internal dialogue to ensure that each part of you can participate?

Notes and reflections

Chapter 34 Bystands, perspective and suspending judgement

'When we pay attention, it becomes possible to become more aware of our intentions and the state of our heart as they arise in conjunction with the actions and speech that are our responses. Usually we are unconscious of them.' Jack Kornfield

This chapter explores making a bystand more fully, with the intent of offering a deeper sense of how this contribution to a conversation might be made skilfully. After a description that connects speech action, intent, practice and leadership energy, there are some practice notes to ground this model in experience. The elements considered in the description are:

- Speech action: bystand
- Intent: perspective
- Practice: suspending judgement
- Leadership energy: magician

Description
The leadership spirit of magician is an archetype for wisdom, or the sage. In Eastern traditions, this would be the master (in the sense of mastery of an art) or the adept.

At its best, magician leadership spirit is unattached to outcome, alive to not knowing and able to hold multiple perspectives in parity, all in service to collective inquiry. At less than its best, magician energy leadership risks appearing all-seeing and infallible, blinding others to gaps or distortions. When I invite others to explore their sense of this leadership spirit they offer words such as facilitating, holding and adaptive alongside magician and sage. What form does your own perceiving style of leadership take?

The speech action of bystanding is an active contribution to conversation. It is not standing by and observing without comment. A bystand notices what is happening in a conversation, without attributing judgement, and narrates this storyline neutrally. This offers the potential to bring to light things that might otherwise remain unseen, unheard or unspoken. Making a bystand supports a conversation to become self-aware, offering a choice point in the midst of patterns, habits or other routines that are manifesting. A bystand invites participants to step back, or step aside, from the lure of an engaging topic.

To illustrate the impact of this kind of awareness on a personal basis, think of a time when you have been in a queue that isn't moving quickly enough for you. If you notice your frustration, you can centre and choose to either wait patiently or leave the errand for another time. If you don't notice the frustration, you become more and more tense, and may end up taking it out on someone else. Internally, bystanding our emotions can limit the extent to which we become entangled in them.

Externally, a bystand offers the possibility of staying in the moment, rather than being caught up in, and led by, any topical energy that is building. A bystand might reflect that a conversation seems stuck, and ask, 'what is needed?' A bystand might describe a pattern such as serial moves and ask, 'what is happening?' A bystand might also reflect a personal position; if we bystand our emotions and responses and share them with others, we may encourage them to reveal their own experiences.

I witnessed a powerful bystand in a conversation that took place between frustrated middle managers and their senior managers, who they perceived to be standing in the way of progress. A senior manager spoke eloquently about what she thought was required to make progress, and a middle manager articulated a contrary view. Each spoke with passion, and the attention in the room was highly engaged. There was a silence, and then a union representative spoke. He said, 'I am confused. When each person spoke, I found myself agreeing wholeheartedly with them, and yet they are disagreeing with each other. How can this be?' This bystand enabled others to become aware of their responses and to connect those responses through time. The conversation shifted in this moment and moved into an inquiry space.

The practice of suspending judgements, assumptions and certainties supports skilful bystanding. If we don't set aside our agenda when we attempt to make a bystand, we will instead make a move, an oppose or a follow. The hard part of making a bystand is the moment beforehand: the moment of noticing the presence and influence of habitual biases and truths. In suspending judgement, there is no support or challenge for any particular line of thought – we simply notice a line of thought and are curious about the impact of it.

The intent of a skilful bystand is to provide perspective in terms of time, space, process and any other appropriate frame. Suspending judgments and certainties enables greater perspective, and making a bystand widens the scope of a conversation. This enables new connections to be made, or allows an issue to be reframed which, in turn, may release stuck patterns or fixed points of view.

We become stuck because our attention fixes on something. We start to marshal our reasoning to support the ideas we favour. We get drawn into argument or debate, stuck at the level of the presenting issue. We lack perspective. If someone bystands and draws our attention to what is happening, they enable us to pause. We then have the opportunity to create space for a spirit of curiosity, discovery, creativity and learning. We can ask, 'what really matters here?' and this invariably enables us to generate more options.

Bystanding is an aspect of the circular energy of inquiry, making space for new thinking and insights, for new possibilities. If overdone, the non-attachment of suspending judgement can become detached and uninterested, as if the circular energy of inquiry is stretched too far. If we don't hold our judgements lightly enough, our attempt to bystand will contain our position or agenda and become advocacy.

In summary, suspending our judgements, beliefs and assumptions is the practice in which making a skilful bystand can be fruitfully rooted and centred. Suspending judgement requires acuity in identifying what happens within us as we listen to others. We remember that we are each a living, complex adaptive system and that our conversation is a living system too. If we are mindful of this, we can relax our grip on certainty, expanding our view and seeing the world from a broader perspective. In suspending judgement, we are able to hold multiple points of view in parity and with curiosity – what might each offer to collective sense-making?

Practice notes
1. Making a bystand 'out there' (external dialogue)
With intent to provide perspective, a bystand is the contribution that explicitly pays attention to the process of a conversation and inquires as to how patterns are playing out or unfolding. A bystand offers the perspective of an observer or witness, and in doing so, might invite reflection on direction of travel, the qualities present, or the focus or breadth of what is being said. A bystand might

sense that something is being missed and ask a question to expand awareness. A bystand might identify and hold differences so that they can be explored generously, without attachment to position. The simplest bystand is often to invite those present to pause and reflect for a moment.

Bystanding is the speech action most often missing in conversations grounded in Western culture. If added, it can significantly change the course, shape and outcome of a conversation. When a skilful bystand catalyses a change of energy in a conversation, it can seem magical to those involved.

What do you notice about how you make bystands? What can you learn?

2. Making a bystand 'in here' (internal dialogue)

Making a bystand in internal dialogue goes hand-in-hand with becoming aware of, and witnessing, our internal processes, rather than becoming involved in them. If I am anxious and I get caught up in my anxiety, then I feed it and make it more real. If, instead, I notice anxiety as part of a larger experience, I can hold it in perspective and, probably, watch my attention turn to something more interesting. In making an internal bystand, I see the partial nature of each feeling and thought and let them go.

I find it helpful to think of my internal dialogue in the language of Kantor. What are my internal moves, follows and opposes, and how are these generated and expressed? I can also inquire into how my internal and external dialogue relate to each other. For example, if I am uncertain of my voice internally, I may become passive externally, devoid of energy, and make myself small.

How does your internal dialogue relate to your external dialogue?

3. When a bystand is met with a bystand

When a bystand is met with a bystand, there is a risk that a conversation becomes conceptual and loses contact with people, becoming less relevant for

284

those present. In becoming overly absorbed in process, it is possible to forget what a conversation is about.

A further risk is that holding an increasing number of different points of view in the neutrality of suspended judgement leads to an escalation in complexity and confusion. This is not problematic in itself, because overwhelming complexity can lead to letting go, enabling new insights and understanding to emerge. However, the energy of increasing complexity and uncertainty needs to be safely held for new potential to emerge, as responses to conceptual complexity include frustration (with ourselves and others) and impatience.

An antidote to a sequence of bystands is to ground the conversation in concrete observation and examples, perhaps by making a clear move.

4. The consequences of not bystanding

Without bystands there is no perspective, and without perspective we risk getting stuck on an issue (weapon focus), or stuck in time, space, process or personalities. Bystanding draws our attention to what is happening and raises awareness of the conversational field itself. Bystanding attends to the topic, perhaps the surface of a pool of conversation, and to the different currents, flows and activities underneath. Bystanding checks the health of the whole conversation, balancing direction, integrity and service with perspective. Without perspective a conversation can become stifled or constrained as voices remain unspoken or unheard, as challenges run out of energy and are dropped, or as a topic loses relevance and people disengage.

The biggest risk in lack of bystanding is that the words and topic seem like the whole conversation. If this happens, little or no attention is given to what is below the surface. How are things said? What kind of non-verbal behaviour is expressed? What emotions are in play? The impact of this is that established routines and patterns go unnoticed, and are perpetuated regardless of whether they are fit for a current purpose.

Practice *34* – bystands, perspective and suspending judgement

Out there: *listen for contributions that inquire into what is happening right now in a conversation, and that exhibit genuine curiosity and impartiality. What is the impact of them? Become curious about process and patterns within conversations, and experiment with how you might draw attention to them.*

Attend to the quality of suspending judgement in others. When you experience profound acceptance, what is it like? What is the impact of it?

Notice when, where and under what circumstances you suspend judgement. What is your impact? How do others respond?

In here: *what most often provokes judgement or certainty in you? Notice when, where and under what circumstances you are most able to suspend judgements and certainties, and so inquire into any assumptions you are making.*

Develop your awareness of what is arising in you – thinking, feeling or sensation, for example, and what stories or memories these prompt in you. Notice your relationship to these stories and how well you hold them in perspective. How do you use your awareness? Do you choose to speak? What impact do you have? If you don't speak, what stops you?

Notes and reflections

Chapter 35 Silences, mindful presence and pausing for breath – a speculation

'See how nature – trees, flowers, grass – grows in silence; see the stars, the moon and the sun, how they move in silence...we need silence to be able to touch souls.' Mother Theresa

In recent times, my understanding of advocacy and inquiry, and of Kantor's speech actions, has been increasingly informed by martial arts and the concepts of entering, (a triangular energy) and blending, (a circular energy). In martial arts, the stillness of square energy can also be a centred response to a situation. In wondering how to bring this option into dialogue work, I began to locate it in Kantor's model, where move and oppose are advocatory, yang or triangular in nature, and follow and bystand are inquiring, yin or circular. What if there is a speech action that is central to bringing balance to advocacy and inquiry? In Taoist philosophy, this might be represented by wu chi, the moment of emptiness before action.

One of my personal inquiries in dialogue practice has been into the quality of silence. Silence is often experienced as uncomfortable, and tends to be quickly filled with a comment or a joke. I draw attention to this in my practice groups and invite inquiry into silence. How might we perceive silence differently?

288

Personally I value silence, and as I coach, I calibrate the quality of my questions by the length of the silence that follows them. A conventional question will evoke a quick response from the mindshelf, a recycled thought or 'felt.' A probing question will evoke silence, in which a search is being made; a response will come slowly, perhaps hesitantly, as new awareness or insight is voiced for the first time.

Silence is often interpreted as assent, even though the intent of it may more often be dissent or oppose. Silence can be tense, it can be relaxed, it can be accusatory, it can be potent and rich with wonder, it can be withdrawn. Silence can convey many qualities and can be eloquent if attended to.

In early 2009, in a coaching supervision seminar, my interests in silence and in the missing square energy came together. Edna Murdoch, founder of The Coaching Supervision Academy, suggested that to 'make silence' is an option for intervention in coaching supervision. I immediately associated this with deliberately making silence as a powerful choice in healthy and purposeful conversations. I saw it as a potential fifth speech action, perhaps internal to Kantor's model, a crux or fulcrum for the choice to speak aloud. Silence could take account of the other four speech actions, whilst not replacing them.

Silence is therefore skilful if our intent is mindful presence: the opportunity to experience things as they are, without preference. This supports us to be discerning in our choice of speech action and to communicate with clear intent. With mindful presence we are deliberate in bringing direction, perspective, service or integrity to a conversation.

A fifth speech action

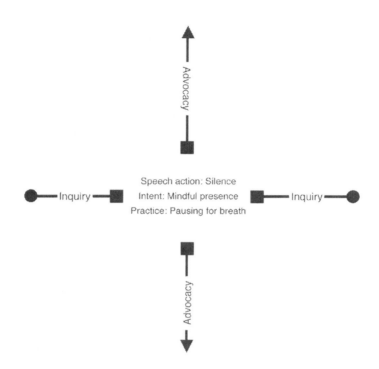

My sense of making a silence is that as a considered and skilful act, it is grounded in the practice of pausing and centring. This ensures that the quality of a silence is open and connected to others and so cannot be mistaken for oppose or follow. Pausing for breath and centring support the other practices. Centred, I will listen to understand, suspend judgement, respect myself and others and speak in my authentic voice. In making centred moves, opposes, follows and bystands, my contribution is more likely to be poised and in balance, and so is less likely to involve over-exertion (off-centre, too yang) or under-exertion (off-centre, too yin).

Energetically, making silence creates space for awareness, individually and collectively. This allows us to reach for, and surface, our deeper wisdom. Embodying skilful silence creates the potential for collective spirit to manifest and for deeper insights to unfold. There is always a risk that silence, as an absence of talk, goes unnoticed, which is why the quality of our presence matters so much. Leaders tell me that when they speak less whilst in a centred, open and curious state, their silence is acknowledged by a remark, an inquiry or a change in energy as colleagues become more thoughtful. Where might you more often make silence? How will you calibrate any impact?

When I witness deliberate and skilful silence, my sense of the leadership energy that is present is that it is almost spiritual or transcendent; it embodies hope, generosity, gratitude and an appreciation of all that is good, true and beautiful. Leadership spirit of this nature supports what is currently manifesting, and is open and receptive, yet discerning and wise. Silence, centre, and the spirit of transcendence create the conditions in which the principles of thinking together (unfolding, coherence, participation and awareness) flourish.

What are the deeper foundations of my case for making silences? In unskilful uses of silence, such as judgement, withdrawal, accusation and self-protection, I perceive a habit of self-interest. Self-interest can be individual in nature or collective to a culture, a nation or a class; a particular form puts humankind as central to the universe. We have moved on from the days when we believed the sun revolved around the Earth and yet there is something in most of us (including me) that believes humans are entitled to our inheritance on this planet. This deep sense of self-interest and entitlement pervades much of our thinking: it is a habit of thinking alone

In self-interest and entitlement, we separate ourselves from others and from our environment and perhaps an appropriate remedy is compassion, or love. It may seem strange to suggest love as a principle for thinking together, which is why I include the word compassion. In Buddhist traditions, where mind and heart are not seen as separate, compassion encompasses both love and reason; it is clear and fearless and is certainly not warm and fuzzy.

To offer a Western perspective on clear and fearless love, I draw on the work of Erich Fromm. In his book *The Art of Loving,*[2] he sees the embodiment of love as based on four practices: care, responsibility, respect and knowledge. Care means active concern for the life and growth of others and self. Responsibility reflects ability to respond appropriately to others and for self. Respect encompasses the practice of seeing others (and self) as they are and accepting each in their uniqueness. Knowledge is both active curiosity to learn about and to truly know others, and willingness to share information about ourselves.

Fromm's four practices seem to align with the dialogic practices developed by Garret, Isaacs and Jones. Respect is present in both frames. Care might reflect listening to understand other perspectives or other lives. Responsibility could relate to speaking our truth and hearing clearly the truth of others. And knowledge could be suspending judgement, being curious and alive to experiencing others and ourselves on a moment-by-moment basis. If this proposal is sound, then the principle of love, or compassion, embraces all four dialogic practices and is central to them.

To summarise, I am proposing a speech action of making a silence, which intends mindful presence. The practice in which a skilful silence can be fruitfully rooted is pausing for breath and centring. Unskilful silence risks separating self from others and prioritising self-interest in preference to offering our voice in service to

292

others. A remedy for self-interest is love, or compassion, of the kind that sees clearly and encompasses reason.

Making a silence creates roominess and a space for truly listening to self and to others. It slows down a conversation, enabling thinking to emerge and interrupting any tendency to perpetually recycle mindshelf thoughts. Skilful silence creates the conditions for collective centre, which has a spiritual quality or presence. This, in turn, conceives the energy of flow/dialogue, the fourth field of conversation.

I offer this speech action. You decide.

Practice 35 – silences, mindful presence and pausing for breath

Out there: *listen for silences. How are they handled? Are they quickly filled or allowed to develop? What quality does any silence have? What is the impact?*

Notice whether and when others pause for breath. What is the impact? Notice when others become off-centre. What is the impact?

When you experience profound presence, how do you know? What is the impact of it? How do others respond to it?

In here: *what most often causes self-interest to arise in you? Notice when, where and under what circumstances you are most able to suspend self-interest and contribute in a way that genuinely serves the whole. What conditions are present when this is possible?*

What is the impact when you pause and centre/become present? What distracts you or knocks you off-balance? How quickly do you notice you are off-centre? How often do you choose to re-centre? What is the impact?

Notes and reflections

Chapter *36* Pause for breath

*'Every journey of a thousand miles begins
with a single step.' Chinese proverb*

The beauty of the Kantor speech actions and intents is that they can be used in conversations with one other person, or with many. They can also be used in witnessing our internal dialogue. Kantor's model offers a practical place to start a deeper inquiry into all our leadership conversations, without an assumption that we will embrace the discipline of dialogue in its entirety. The Kantor model also enables us to notice what is missing in our conversational style and to increase our versatility.

The richness of the dialogic practices is that they begin to place our attention on the way we make our contributions to conversations, on the quality of our presence. If we embody respecting, authentic voice, listening and suspending judgement, our presence and input will be congruent and so will have greater impact.

Where might you start your own deeper inquiry? You might choose to use the speech actions of move, oppose, follow and bystand to begin to understand patterns in conversation. You might start to clarify your intent as you enter into, and contribute to, a conversation. You might decide to cultivate one of the dialogic practices and notice the impact of that. You might begin to inquire into silence.

My intent in sharing these frameworks is to draw you deeper into your curiosity about conversations and to prompt you to commit to taking some steps towards changing your practice. The next part of the journey will begin to lead you to encourage others into deeper, roomier conversations, by considering how to create the conditions for dialogue.

Practice *36* – **pause for breath**

This foundation practice appears at the end of each section of the book.

Sit in a comfortable upright posture, so that your feet are firmly planted on the floor and you are supporting your own back, rather than leaning against a chair. Rest your hands on your thighs, palms down.

Become aware of the contact between your feet/shoes and the floor. Become aware of the contact between your hands and your thighs. Become aware of the contact between your thighs and the chair. Become aware of the sitting bones, the bones at the base of the pelvis, pressing into the chair seat.

Notice your strong base, formed by your feet and sitting bones, and allow your spine to grow to its full length by gently imagining each vertebra lifting slightly from the one below. Sense lightness and spaciousness in your spine. Notice that your neck becomes long at the back, your chin tilted slightly towards your chest.

Now bring your attention to your breath. On each inhale, imagine your breath seeping into the spaces in your spine, allowing it to lengthen just a little bit more. On each exhale, imagine your breath flowing down through your chest and belly, softening any tension. Follow your breath for a few moments.

Now mentally scan your body and notice any places of tension, aching or discomfort. Choose one and, for a few breaths, imagine your inbreath soaking into this place and, on a longer exhale, imagine your outbreath dissolving any discomfort and carrying it out into the air around you, letting you rest.

After a few breaths, become aware of the contact between your sitting bones and the chair, between your hands and thighs, and between your feet and the ground.

Rise gently and stretch. You are ready to re-engage with the world.

Resource list for more on the principles and practices of dialogue

On Dialogue, David Bohm
Manual of the Warrior of Light, Paulo Coelho
The Universe in a Single Atom, The Dalai Lama
The Invitation, Oriah Mountain Dreamer
The Art of Loving, Erich Fromm
My Lover, Myself, David Kantor
Dialogue and the Art of Thinking Together, William Isaacs
Dialogos Fieldguide, William Isaacs and others
The Fifth Discipline Field Book, Peter Senge et al
Bringing Life to Organisational Change, Margaret Wheatley and Myron Kellner-Rogers

Part Six

TOWARDS DIALOGUE

Chapter 37   **Introduction**

Chapter 38   **Preparing for important leadership conversations**

Chapter 39   **Leading others into a different kind of conversation**

Chapter 40   **Arriving, beginning, connecting**

Chapter 41   **Sharing responsibility for cultivating a container**

Chapter 42   **What now? Building your practice**

Chapter 43   **Last touch**

Chapter *37* Introduction

'The work has been given to the sea, as a gift, and the sea has taken the work and made more of it than I could ever have hoped for.' Andy Goldsworthy

How do I draw this book to a close? What else will enable you to move towards bringing the practices of mindfulness and dialogue to your leadership conversations? What guidelines will support you to lead others into deeper conversations?

In the following chapters, we will look beyond our own practice and consider how, as leaders, we might create the conditions for colleagues to engage in different kinds of conversation. As a leader, how can you nudge colleagues to engage with each other differently? What might you need to attend to? These questions set the scene for what William Isaacs describes as the art of building a container for a conversation.

My premise is that, as your interest in conversations grows, you will want to introduce some of the frameworks of mindfulness and dialogue to others. In doing this, it is helpful to first unsettle established routines by making changes to signal that you are setting the scene for a different kind of conversation. This means attending to things we know, but often disregard, such as the way the quality of the space we occupy affects our energy. We can influence many tangible and relational factors to shape the tone of a conversation.

Later, we will return to building individual practice, revisiting Peter Garrett's learning containers to provide a framework to guide you in this. As you deepen your own practice, this will affect your presence in conversations which will, in turn, influence others and affect the qualitative feel of a conversation. My intent is that you will finish this book inspired to change fundamentally both the attention you pay to conversations and the quality of your presence in them.

Practice is so important that I've described the power of it a number of times over the course of the book. Jack Kornfield writes:

'What great art is ever learned quickly? Any deep training opens in direct proportion to how much we give ourselves to it.'

In everyday skills such as conversation, it is very easy to have unrealistic expectations of our ability to add in new approaches. If we were learning a musical instrument, we wouldn't expect to be able to play complex music immediately, especially not in public. If we are learning a new instrument in conversation, such as making a bystand, why would we expect to be skilful in this instantly? Instead we might reflect on, and practice, things that will support making a skilful bystand, such as becoming aware of, and holding lightly, our judgements.

How do we truly internalise a new practice? Wendy Palmer writes about an Aikido teacher who uses the body as a metaphor for different stages in developing the art of Japanese sword drawing and cutting:[15]

'The first level is like bone, hard and solid. The second level is like flesh, still solid but more moveable. The next level is like blood, fluid and liquid. The next level is like nerves, tiny electrical impulses that fire the message. Finally there is breath; you can't see it but you can feel it and the effects of it.'

Embodying a new skill, to the extent that we can readily draw on it in charged and challenging situations, takes time. We may feel self-conscious, awkward or uncertain as we begin. Repetition brings a little more familiarity and ease. We become more confident in using our new approach in different contexts, perhaps feeling able to take more risks. Over time, the skill becomes part of our repertoire. We reach for it automatically when it is the most appropriate response. Eventually, at some stage, we no longer even notice that we are using it; it is as natural as breathing.

In the following chapters, I offer you more concepts and models from the field of dialogue practice. I encourage you to consider creating a development path to embed and embody the things that have caught your attention in this book. I invite you to do this even though you know that there will be few miracles. Over time, however, your way of being in, and your contributions, to conversation will change.

Practice *37* – awareness of attitude to learning and practice

Reflect for a moment on how you have acquired new skills, qualities, behaviours and knowledge over your lifetime. What kind of learning and development has been most effective for you? What most engages you?

What new approaches or activities have you persevered with, and why? Which have you abandoned, and why?

Now, imagine for a moment setting out on a new path of learning, catalysed by a concept or a practice in this book. What will motivate and inspire you to commit to cultivating new approaches? What will it take to stick with it? How can you bring kindness and fascination to the times when you falter?

What have you learned about yourself through this reflection?

Notes and reflections

Chapter *38* Preparing for important leadership conversations

'Space is the breath of art.' Frank Lloyd Wright

One of the most common approaches to a conversation is just to turn up and see how it goes. Many of us think we don't have time for anything else, but experiences in my dialogue practice development groups suggest that preparing for a leadership conversation appropriately can materially influence the shape and tone of that conversation. How much thought do you give to the climate for an important conversation?

In this chapter we look at factors that influence the tenor and outcome of a conversation. What follows is important for conversations between two or three people, but becomes essential when we want to cultivate the practices of dialogue in a larger gathering. As leaders, how do we shape the way a conversation unfolds?

Fashioning conditions for a conversation is a highly nuanced activity. For example, in some circumstances, a physical setting for a conversation may matter little, whilst on other occasions it may be crucial. Being thoughtful about finding and moulding space for a conversation – whether physical, mental or energetic – is key to supporting the practices of both mindfulness and dialogue. Shaping the setting for a conversation is an energetic and creative undertaking, an art, in which 'place' becomes something we actively fashion rather than something that pre-exists, that we simply walk into and use.

William Isaacs calls the process of creating the conditions for dialogue, 'building a container.' The form and feel of a container will influence, and possibly determine, the kind of conversations we have. Revisiting the first two fields of conversation may illuminate this. What conditions encourage the conversations of politeness/routines? What might support a conversation with the energy of breaking open/debate? If we want to enable people to suspend current routines and habits, what do we need to attend to? As a first step, we might change some practical things such as the setting, the time and the layout of the room. We might also be thoughtful about our approach to starting a conversation and the congruence between our intent and our actions. These factors are facets of a container but are not the whole; they provide a tangible starting place to interrupt established patterns, so that the tide of habit and routine might turn.

In unsettling established routines through changing some of the tangible aspects of a container, we create the possibility that a different conversation will unfold. We then need to support this with our leadership, encouraging expression of fresh perspectives and enabling some reflection on the process of a conversation as well as the topic. The impact of making changes will be uncertain – how will people react to the unfamiliar? What else do we need to attend to in order to support people to risk speaking out when they are uncertain? These are some of the questions that invite deeper inquiry into the nature of containers for conversations.

In *Dialogue and the Art of Thinking Together,*[1] Isaacs describes the term 'container' as a setting in which deep and transformative listening becomes possible. Fundamentally, a container is a holding space in which the potential for shared understanding can manifest. This holding space is key to accommodating the disparate energies of a conversation.

To set the scene for the art of forming and fashioning containers, I draw on the energies of yang and yin and some lines from the Tao Te Ching:[20]

> *'We hammer wood for a house*
> *But it is the inner space*
> *That makes it livable.'*

In this metaphor, we see that attending to tangible things can shape an intangible emptiness, or potential, that is purposeful or fruitful. In forming a container, we attend to some practical and relational aspects of coming together, with the intent of influencing the energetic tone of our space in such a way that more profound listening and talking is possible.

I use the term container in my own practice, even though I have reservations about it. I use it partly because it is becoming accepted and understood, and partly because it more-or-less does the job. My reservations centre on a sense that the image evoked by the word 'container' is rather too solid to describe what is created as a conversation deepens. If I use the image of a cup or bowl, a receptacle with durable sides and bottom into which things can be poured or placed, then creating a container is a one-off act, like throwing a pot or blowing a glass. Once made, this kind of container is mostly fixed in size and shape.

In contrast, my experience of containers for conversation is that they are made and re-made many times, and may change in feel, shape, texture and size. My sense of container is that it is dynamic, and I think of it being woven by, and through, the conversation that it holds. In my mind, then, a container is more web-like or net-like than vessel-like. The mesh may be of varying gauges for different kinds of conversation (or different parts of a conversation) and it is constantly being made and unmade. Another metaphor might be that of skin. In and through our conversation we are making a skin to hold us and our talk, safe and yet porous, giving a boundaried shape that is able to grow with our exchanges. In some sense, the conversation is itself the container.

For me then, a container is a living thing which needs nurturing throughout a conversation. This perspective influences what I believe to be in the mix when cultivating the conditions for dialogue. Anything that influences the atmosphere and feeling tone, or energy, of a gathering, and how it changes over time, is a factor in fashioning a container.

My current sense is that there are two key aspects to the art of shaping containers. One encompasses environment and practicalities, and the other encompasses human factors such as the readiness of the people involved, how they come together, and how the conversation begins.

The most tangible aspect of a container is the space that will be used. Space is inextricably interwoven with time, and a first step in creating a container is often to establish a space-time setting. We do this routinely; when arranging any kind of conversation, we identify who needs to be there and agree a date and timeframe, perhaps booking a room. In the simplest sense, a booked room for an allotted time is a space-time container for a conversation. When you next participate in a meeting, reflect on how the room and other facets of the space-time setting impact on the conversation. How do they support the stated intent for the meeting? How not?

The quality of space matters. If you want to create a 'roomier' conversation, it seems logical that a roomier space would support that intent. Light and airy are the words that come to mind, a space that evokes room to breathe. Despite this,

I have participated in good conversations in rooms that are neither light nor airy, but they usually have some other qualities that create a good atmosphere.

Comfort matters too, particularly in the early stages of a conversation. If I want to develop the conditions for mindfulness in a conversation, then those present need to be able to give as much of their attention as is humanly possible to the beginnings of the conversation. Distractions caused by uncomfortable seating, or thirst, or hunger, can interfere with ability to contribute fully. This applies to other sensory distractions too; noises, draughts, uncomfortable temperatures and visual diversions such as activity going on through a window. Our minds will find plenty of opportunities for digression without the sensory stimuli of interesting sights and sounds.

At one level, this is all common sense and well known. In that very familiarity lies a potential trap, as hotels and other conference venues compete to sell us their version of a good venue and a good ambience. It's very easy to fall in with what's on offer. However, whenever we walk into a space that someone else has set up, we inherit a system of assumptions that may or may not support what follows. My proposition is that the layout of a room and how people move into it and claim it have a material impact on what follows.

To illustrate this, have you ever had a party and spent ages setting up various rooms for people to sit in or dance in, choosing music, lighting candles and laying out snacks, only to find that everyone gravitates to the kitchen, or sits on the stairs? What does the self-organisation of an informal gathering like that tell us about meetings? It seems to suggest that it matters how and where refreshments are provided. It also invites reflection about the flow of people as they arrive to participate in a conversation. As with a party, they'll tend to arrive in one's and two's, and will orientate themselves within the location in their own way. How do you support and enable this form of comfort? What is the impact of the layout of a room and facilities on how people gather together?

◫

A venue and time slot – a space-time container – creates boundaries within which people and conversations move about. We tend to think of a meeting starting once everyone is sitting down (around a table, or in rows, or in a circle). But what if the meeting starts much earlier, and people are already in motion as they arrive, bringing their histories and habits with them as they move towards the conversation? As a leader, how might this inform your thinking about establishing a space-time container for an important conversation?

In selecting a location for a conversation, we might also consider whether those present have been in the space before, and for what purpose. Does the venue have a history, a legacy? Consciously or not, if someone is returning to a room where they have been part of an unpleasant or challenging experience, the idea, or sight of the room may trigger memories of that previous experience. Without awareness, they then bring the associated energy and emotional tag into the current experience. It may not even be as dramatic as this. If the room is one in which someone's habitual behaviour is to 'keep their head down,' or, 'get out of the meeting with no actions to my name,' then that pattern will influence the energy they bring into the space. The influence may be faint and/or fleeting, especially if the welcome they are given is warm, open, engaging and enabling, but it may materially impact the way a conversation unfolds.

A general rule is if, as a leader, you wish to host a different kind of conversation, yet you hold it in the usual room, with the usual set-up, you are stacking the odds against an unusual outcome. There are no hard-and-fast rules about what will work and what won't, but every space-choice and time-choice will have consequences for the conversation that takes place in it, and so it is as well to try to consider these variables before you make the booking.

Practice 38 – fieldwork on the impact of setting on conversations

Over the next few days, start to notice the impact of setting on conversations. In particular, look for ways in which the setting gets in the way of a good conversation. Pay attention to the quality, shape, size and feel of the space you are in.

Pay attention to the layout of tables and chair. What is the impact on personal space, lines of eye contact and ability to hear?

Pay attention to the impact of laptops, mobile phones/organisers and any presentations that are made.

Pay attention to any refreshments, the quality and appropriateness of them, and how and when they are set up and consumed.

What do you notice?

Now speculate about the factors that support good conversations. How might you try introducing more of them to your regular meetings?

Take steps to test any conclusions you draw.

Do you participate in a regular meeting that might benefit from attention to setting? How might you engage your colleagues in undertaking some action research to examine the influence of setting on your conversations?

What changes might you make? How will you evaluate the impact of them?

Notes and reflections

Chapter 39 Leading others into a different kind of conversation

*'When we get too caught up in the busyness of the world,
we lose connection with one another
– and ourselves.' Jack Kornfield*

An appropriate space-time container is a first step in creating conditions for bringing the practices of mindfulness and dialogue into conversations. A less tangible aspect of fashioning a container is the human, relational aspect of it. As you prepare for an important conversation and reflect on who will be present, you might consider their (and your own) readiness to engage in a different kind of conversation.

What do I mean by readiness? Whether they are aware of it or not, people come to every gathering with assumptions and expectations about its purpose, and with their own agenda and motivations. That this happens cannot be changed, but with awareness and mindfulness, we can include this reality in the process of shaping a container. There isn't a standard of preparedness without which you can't move towards dialogue; it's simply that your approach to the container will depend on the readiness of those called to the conversation.

How can we assess readiness and what might we do to draw others towards

315

dialogue? Firstly, we can refrain from making too many assumptions. I find that even when I've set up a conversation quite carefully, telling people about the history and purpose of a gathering, some will still arrive unsure of the purpose of the conversation or why they're there. This doesn't mean that the energy I've put into set-up is wasted, but it does mean that I can't assume any particular starting point.

I often use the image of a river system for the energetic human flows that move towards, and are woven into, a container for a conversation. I see each person as a tributary, flowing towards the space-time setting that we have agreed. Some of the tributaries join each other on the journey, by literally travelling together or talking beforehand. Eventually we all arrive and begin to flow together, creating one channel for the duration of our time together. At the end of that time, the process reverses as we separate in two's or three's and leave, eventually returning to our individual systems.

The process of gathering people together for a purpose is an art that is often underestimated in organisations. Energetically, a container starts to form as soon as the need for a conversation is identified. A conversation begins with the 'first touch,' the moment of inviting people to attend, rather than with the first words spoken together. This means that from first contact with those involved, we might seek to model the dialogic practices outlined in Part Five: listening, respecting, suspending judgement and speaking with authentic voice.

I can illustrate what might be required by describing how I build the container for my Pause for Breath leadership retreats. Firstly, I send out emails with dates, information and an invitation to consider participating. This is the potential opening of my conversation with participants. When they read it, they need to hear my voice and connect with it at some level. Quite often a potential participant will then call me, because it's a big commitment, with lots of unknowns. Our phone call begins to weave the connections, the threads of a container, between me, the individual and the entity that will become the retreat. The quality of my presence in that phone call is crucial for the embryonic container.

The next stage in the gathering energy of a retreat, is that a potential participant makes up their mind to be there. Filling in a booking form invites them to think about why they want to come and how they hope to benefit. This orientates them to the collective experience, and energetically engages them in being there. In time, a cohort develops through these steps.

About six weeks before a retreat, I send out joining information comprising a very full description of the physical setting (which is somewhat quirky) and some suggestions about the things they need to bring with them. This email goes out collectively, and so the individuals now have a sense of other people, other energies, moving towards the retreat. Questions arise from the joining information, giving me further opportunity to connect with participants.

Finally, about a week before a retreat, I send a short reminder about the things that are essential to the work we will do together. This moves us all towards being there together within a tangible timeframe. As people arrive at the venue, they are somewhat ready, in that they have some sense of what they're coming to and why they've chosen to be there.

Whilst this example is based on a group whose members have elected to participate, indicating their openness to the experience on offer, I believe this depth of container-building is vital for our ability to be together. If you are leading an important conversation, perhaps where people have little or no choice in their participation, it may be even more crucial to pay attention to how energy is oriented towards that conversation and how the container is built.

Practice *39* – first touch in leading a conversation

In this fieldwork, find a situation where you are taking the lead in bringing people together to talk.

Choose a situation that is not (yet) habitual. Approach it as if this is the first time people have come together for the purpose you have in mind.

For example, you might use:

- *a situation where you are drawing together a new group of people to talk about a joint endeavour; or*

- *an away-day for your team or colleagues.*

Use what you have gleaned from Chapter 38 to attend to the space-time setting.

In preparing the invitation to come and talk, imagine what your invitees might need to know. What assumptions and preconceptions might they have? Are these helpful or unhelpful? What do you need to tell them to support them in arriving in the right frame of mind, body and spirit? What questions might they have, and how will you surface these and respond to them? How will you set the tone for your gathering through this initial contact?

If an assistant is helping you with this process, how will you ensure that they fully understand what you are seeking to cultivate?

On the day, how will you greet them, welcome them, include them? How will you continue to set the tone through your initial face-to-face contact?

At some stage in the proceedings, ask for feedback on how you gathered people together. What can you learn?

Notes and reflections

Chapter 40 Arriving, beginning, connecting

'Trust is the glue of life. It's the most essential ingredient in effective communication. It's the foundational principle that holds all relationships.' Stephen Covey

Once gathered, how might we lead others to arrive fully and to open to revealing more of their thinking and feeling than is usual? How do we support everyone present to be mindful of themselves, each other and the reason for coming together? How do we generate a safe enough space for people to feel able to take risks with trying out new ways of contributing? Safety is an interesting quality; too little of it and we can be too anxious or fearful to reveal ourselves, too much of it and we can feel too comfortable to take risks, perhaps fearing we will risk the comfort itself.

As people gather to talk, they have already started the conversation in their individual minds. They probably have a view on the subject matter and have an idea of what they want to say. They may also have preconceptions about others present and about their agendas. There may have been 'off-line' conversations in preparation for this gathering. Perhaps the current encounter flows from an earlier one. In this case, the earlier conversation will not have stopped when people left the room; they will have continued to process what took place and perhaps spoken to others in the interim. Even if people are coming together for the first time, they may have researched the purpose of the meeting, or the other people present.

The point is that no-one arrives completely fresh, completely open and completely without attachment, and so the first moments of a gathering are important. The way a conversation starts sets the tone for what follows, and in bringing the practices of dialogue to a conversation, it is customary to begin with a check-in. In a check-in, we reconnect with ourselves, with each other and with our topic or subject matter. In doing so we discover and reveal our current perspectives.

A skilful check-in enables people to arrive, to become present. It is a process in which each person speaks, sometimes in response to a question posed by the convenor of a conversation. My practice is to keep my check-in questions simple and focused on the purpose of the gathering. In a dialogue group, I might invite people to consider the question, 'who am I as a dialogue practitioner today?' In a group of coaches a check-in question might be, 'who am I as a coach today?' or, 'how am I as a coach today?'

A skilful check-in question enables individuals to connect in with themselves and become present, perhaps by speaking about, and letting go of, something that is occupying them. In checking-in, we each acknowledge who we are and how we are, in this setting. In hearing others speak, we get a contextual sense of who they are and how they are. Checking-in enables us to connect to each other as human beings, and so encourages a fuller, richer contribution to what follows.

For example, as people arrive for my Pause for Breath leadership retreat, they are met, welcomed, offered a cup of tea and given a quick orientation of the building. They then find a room and get settled. Some come back to the kitchen for tea, and some wander around trying (unsuccessfully) to find a mobile phone signal. Our first collective activity is to have lunch together. Through these

321

interactions, people gain a sense of our location and meet one another in an informal and relatively natural way.

After lunch, we head for the group room and a formal check-in. One approach to check-in is to invite people to select a visual image from a big pile of diverse cards. We just choose something we are drawn to. To check-in, we give our first name and talk about how the image reflects our presence in conversations. This locates us in the work of the week, and circumvents any pre-prepared scripts. It's often quite hard to connect a chosen image to conversational practice, but the approach means we start with a fresh attitude to introducing ourselves, rather than following any automatic habits.

Another aspect of checking-in is that it begins to create the conditions for how we want to relate to each other and to talk together. If we intend to create the conditions for dialogue, we design a check-in that is congruent with the four practices or core conditions of speaking with authentic voice, respecting, suspending judgement and listening to understand. Evoking these four qualities offers a sound foundation for developing trust and creating a safe-enough space for people to talk more openly and freely.

If we are leading a conversation and inviting others to contribute differently, how do we bring the four core conditions to life? Our presence, or the way we show up, sets a tone. We can seek to model and embody the practices in the way we formulate a check-in question, and also in the way we offer our own check-in. We can pause and centre frequently. Our internal stance and the way we think, speak and act enables others to tune into, and resonate with, a quality of being. The impact of our energy and presence reflects that cultivating our capacity for the work of dialogue is a deep practice of aligning mind, body and spirit.

In modelling the four dialogic practices, or core conditions, we aim to ensure our means are aligned with our ends. For example, if you want to invoke more listening in a conversation, it's best to start by listening, rather than asking people to listen while you speak. If you want to invoke respect, you can demonstrate respect by acknowledging a view that opposes yours, holding both as legitimate and inviting further perspectives. If the way we show up is congruent with the practices, then we embed them in the energy of the container we are establishing, and begin to create an environment in which trust develops.

In moving towards dialogue, the quality of trust becomes important. For me, trust and safety are closely linked, and at some level, are indistinguishable. If we are to offer more personal and intimate parts of ourselves to others, such as our beliefs and values and even aspects of our identity, we need to form a safe container in which we collectively place, and hold, our trust. In developing capacity for trust, I draw on a simple model by Jack Gibb, who worked with, researched, and wrote about these issues.[29] Gibb's model offers an explanation for the value of checking-in, and I use it as a guide when I am preparing for a conversation, whether with one person or many.

Gibb's premise is that whenever people convene to work or learn together, four phases unfold. These are:

- a period of settling in and connecting with a sense of self;
- a period of meeting, or getting up to date with each other;
- a period of clarifying why you have gathered together; and
- a period of becoming clear about the tone you want to set collectively.

Working together

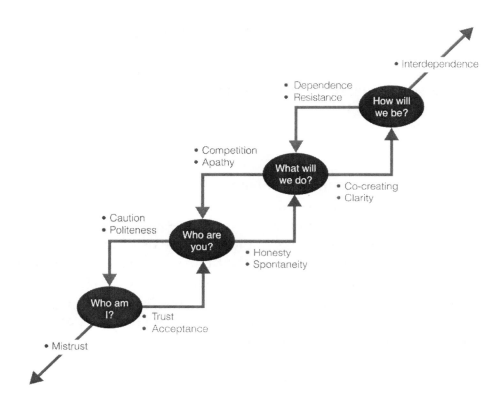

Adapted from the work of Jack Gibb

If the first two phases of Gibb's model are skimped or skipped because a group moves quickly to address a task, there is a risk that individuals don't connect, or reconnect, deeply enough to establish, or re-establish, trust. If trust is lacking, both people and task suffer.

324

We can reference the model to conversations, using it to help fashion an initial container, or to re-shape a container when someone joins a conversation.

At the beginning of a conversation, or if you join one part-way through, you may be wondering about your place in the scheme of things, and about how you fit in. You may be silently asking, 'am I up to this?' If you experience a sense of being accepted and included, you can turn your attention from yourself and begin to consider your relationship with others. If you do not feel included, you may be distrustful and cautious of others.

As you become more comfortable in yourself and your legitimacy, you may become curious about others, perhaps silently asking, 'who are they? How do they fit in? What do they have to contribute?' If you feel comfortable with their authenticity and intentions, you may feel able to relax and engage more spontaneously and openly. If you are uneasy with others, you may remain cautious and polite, and feel unable to express yourself fully.

In the third phase, those present become ready to explore honestly what they are jointly there to do and are open to navigating challenges collaboratively. As trust develops, difference is appreciated and utilised for collective endeavour. This process can be derailed by voices not being heard, or by the conversation not seeming relevant or appropriate. Individuals may then become competitive, jockeying for recognition, or may sink into apathy, feeling undervalued or unappreciated.

As collective presence grows in resilience, clarity and shared purpose, a group may now focus on how they intend to engage with each other. How will we be? What qualities will our conduct embody? In establishing satisfactory responses to these questions, a container becomes more transparent, and developing and nurturing it becomes a shared responsibility. It becomes safer to learn together. The quality of a conversation depends on the qualities in the container, and if these questions remain unanswered, or if the answers feel unsatisfactory, individuals can be resistant to truly engaging in a deeper conversation.

In effective group working, and in good conversations, the phases of this model are cycled through again and again. As a conversation develops, an individual may again become unsure of their identity and legitimacy and so may need to re-establish a sense of themselves and others in order to contribute fully.

Gibb's model is also valuable when a conversation takes place over time, perhaps in a series of meetings. A conversation doesn't stop when you leave a room. As a space-time container comes to a close and people disperse, they continue to think about the conversation, they talk to others outside the container, and their perspective continues to develop, harden or change. In reconvening, the conversation never picks up where it was left, and yet we rarely recognise this or take account of it. Using Gibb's model and the practice of checking-in enables us to reconnect to ourselves, each other and our current stance in relation to our collective endeavour.

I am often asked whether the process of coming together and fashioning a container requires a guide or facilitator. It's a question that can rouse strong feelings, usually towards the view that facilitation is not part of dialogue. In practice, when people are new to these different ways of being in conversation, there is often benefit in providing some support. When I initiate an important conversation that might need to venture beyond conventional talk, I think of myself as a guide or a host, depending on what is needed. If I've been invited to offer a path through the territories of dialogue, I am a guide. If I've been asked to create and hold space for a mindful conversation, I am a host. These two words give me a sense of my responsibilities whilst reminding me of the boundaries of my contribution. Each role is only legitimate if it's in service to collective endeavour, and the need for each role lessens as those present engage with the conversation and jointly shape the space that is needed.

In organisations, a conversation, or meeting is often 'owned' by the person who has called for it and made practical arrangements. This person has a leadership role in the conversation (or arranges for someone else to take this role). The notion of guiding or hosting the conversation can be helpful in this context; what do you need to attend to if you want to ensure that the conversation will be fit for purpose? How will you begin?

Practice 40 – the impact of check-in

Try a process of 'check-in' in some of your regular meetings. Choose a variety of meetings – some could be one-to-one, some informal, some more formal.

Before a selected meeting, reflect on the check-in question or questions you might ask to enable other people (and yourself) to arrive, to become present to the task at hand and to each other.

As a guide, what question might enable you to get a sense of how people are placed today, in the context of the conversation you are about to have? In a conversation to review progress in a project, for instance, you might ask, genuinely, curiously, kindly: 'How does it feel to be a project manager today?'

Over time, what do you notice about the conversations where you invite people to check-in?

Notes and reflections

Chapter *41* Sharing responsibility for cultivating a container

'Begin with the end in mind.' Stephen Covey

Having arrived and checked-in, a leader who intends to create conditions that support a deeper conversation or dialogue will begin a process of clarifying collective intent and agreeing how a conversation will be conducted. In checking-in, we gain a sense of who is present and how they see themselves in the context of the conversation. The next leadership step is to start to surface the issues that matter to those present and to inquire into the qualities that, if embodied, will demonstrate commitment to engaging in a different kind of conversation.

The concept of contract, in the way it is used between a coach and coaching client, is a helpful guide in this aspect of forming a container. A coach will seek to understand their client's context and to clarify what they need from the coaching process. Together, coach and client will clarify some practical points, such as how much time and energy they can invest in the process, how they will contact each other between sessions and where they will meet. They will also talk about how each prefers to work and clarify their respective responsibilities. Balancing challenge and support is crucial in a coaching relationship, and my own practice is to ask how a client prefers to be challenged, and how they know when they are supported.

A similar process seems relevant to creating conditions that will support dialogue, at least in the early stages of talking together. In beginning to make explicit both our purpose and the way we want to conduct ourselves, we signal our intent to engage in a different kind of conversation.

For example, in my dialogue practice development groups, my intent is to co-create a compelling learning experience in which we can explore the practices of dialogue. The group commits to meeting six times over nine months. A week before the first session, I email to ask participants to recall their most compelling learning experience and to reflect on what made it so gripping. After our check-in, I invite people to talk about what they hope to gain from the series of sessions and then ask them to talk about their most compelling learning experience.

As we explore our purpose and what makes it possible to learn, I ask, 'what qualities do we need to bring to these sessions?' We explore the words and phrases that come up so that we begin to share a collective understanding of them. If the four dialogic practices (speaking with authentic voice, listening, respecting, suspending judgement) don't emerge naturally as qualities for the container, I introduce them, thus evoking core conditions for dialogue.

As the qualities for our container emerge, we explore whether everyone can live with them and whether anything is missing. These qualities then form a foundation for describing the type of presence we commit to bringing to the conversation, and how we will relate to one another. At the beginning of later sessions, we may revisit our container qualities and link them to our intent for the day, asking which will be most important to manifest on this occasion.

This process encourages all those present to share in creating and holding the container. Together we shape the energetic tone of our conversation through our individual presence. The qualities we bring to our conversation determine how we connect and interact. Making this explicit supports us to embody our finest leadership presence.

One quality or practice that often comes up as an important aspect of building trust and safety is confidentiality. In my mind, confidentiality is essentially about respecting another person's story and the collective thinking that unfolds in conversation. Respecting in this sense is being clear about the ownership of a story. If I respect your story as yours, only you may tell it. I may only tell the parts of it you have explicitly authorised me to share, and only with those people you have explicitly named. This may sound demanding, even austere, but in a culture where it is acceptable to chat about details of people you haven't even met as if they are absolute and unchanging truths, I feel a high level of integrity is called for in hearing, holding and transmitting the story of another.

Sometimes aspects of a conversation do need to be communicated to, or shared with, people who are not present. If it is collectively agreed that this will be done, I invite you to be deeply thoughtful about what will be said, how it will be said, what the impact might be, and what the intent in sharing is. Too often we disseminate too little, too much, or the wrong things. Just as a container for dialogue begins to be created long before people gather together, so it reaches beyond the gathering. How do you weave a container for what emerges from a dialogue, and extend the reach of it to include those who are not present? The practice of respecting, and the other dialogic practices, can guide and inform your contribution beyond the dialogue itself.

In continuing to cultivate the qualities that support a container for a deeper, more authentic conversation, we will pay attention to less tangible aspects of a conversation.

Less tangible aspects of conversation

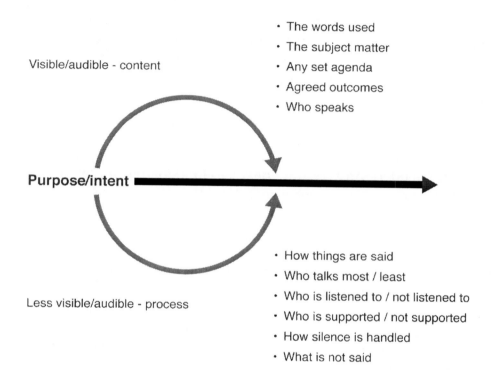

Visible/audible - content

- The words used
- The subject matter
- Any set agenda
- Agreed outcomes
- Who speaks

Purpose/intent

Less visible/audible - process

- How things are said
- Who talks most / least
- Who is listened to / not listened to
- Who is supported / not supported
- How silence is handled
- What is not said

The visible/audible parts of a conversation are subject matters or task, the words used, who speaks and in what sequence and agreed outcomes. Less tangible aspects include: what is not said; the tone in which things are said; the quality of listening; how silence manifests and is broken; the quality of laughter; how people relate to perceived power, whether of hierarchy, age or time-served; the existence of established patterns; and history. In attending to these factors, we sense how they influence and shape the energy of a container.

An individual may choose to comment on one of these less visible/audible energies, perhaps by offering a bystand. This allows collective consideration of the impact of something that would often go unnoticed. Sometimes, simply making one of these factors explicit changes a container in a way that supports collective intent. Sometimes, such a contribution reveals a pattern that enables a collective insight. Sometimes, noticing a discrepancy between the way we have agreed to approach our conversation and what is actually taking place signals the need to re-contract.

This raises an important point – you may agree a contract at the beginning of an important leadership conversation, but at that stage you may not know what will actually be needed. Any contract needs to be dynamic and must be changed if it no longer serves collective purpose or intent.

Finally, the four dialogic practices contribute profoundly to cultivating and maintaining a resilient container. If, as leaders, we model respecting, suspending judgement, listening to understand and speaking with authentic voice, we will influence significantly the qualitative tone of a conversation. Embodying these practices is powerful because each invokes the others. When I feel listened to, really listened to, I am more likely to offer my authentic voice. In addition, I am more likely to accord respect to someone who has listened to me and to suspend judgement when they speak.

When I feel my perspective is acknowledged and respected, I am more likely to listen. In addition, I am more likely to suspend judgement when others speak and to risk more of my authentic voice.

When I feel my contribution is not being judged, I will speak more genuinely and will not use energy in explaining or justifying. I will have more energy to listen to, and respect, the perspectives of others.

334

When I hear the authentic voice of another, I recognise this and instinctively suspend judgement and listen with respect.

Essentially, in embodying these practices, we cultivate capacity to trust and be trusted and so increase the potential for safely holding whatever energies unfold. We enable intimacy, audacious contributions and generative collective thinking.

Practice *41* – contracting

I invite you to use this fieldwork to explore what happens in a regular meeting when you set aside a formal agenda and contract for a different energy in the meeting. Choose a meeting that feels a bit stuck, or one that you know some participants find frustrating.

Try the following:

- *Change the physical setting to signal a different approach*
- *Attend to how people are invited into the fresh approach*
- *Attend to how people arrive*
- *Lead a check-in*

Then clarify the time container that you have, and ask, 'what is most important for each of us to talk about or address in this time together?' Plan to use at least half your available time to listen to, and clarify, what is important and what is needed.

Do not address any issues as they arise – listen and take note, as if you are mentally preparing to write an agenda as a result of the unfolding conversation. Trust that some of the matters raised will automatically find responses in what others say.

As you host the conversation, practice listening, suspending judgement, respecting and speaking with authentic voice.

As you sense that all issues have been aired, summarise what seems to be important. Agree an order in which these matters will be addressed. For each issue ask, 'what outcome is needed?' Follow this agenda.

Collectively reflect on what happened in the meeting. What can be learned?

Notes and reflections

Chapter *42* What now? Building your practice

'We learn by practice. Whether it means to learn to dance by practicing dancing or to learn to live by practicing living, the principles are the same.' Martha Graham

As I have emphasised, many of the approaches in this book require practice to bring them into daily life and to build capacity for accessing them in challenging situations. Practice is necessary because we all have deeply preferred habitual reactions to all kinds of situations, and these automatic attitudes and behaviours are ingrained. If we want to have choices, we need to make our new options enough of a habit that they are available when we most need them, which is often when we are under pressure.

To cultivate new habits, we usually need to have a compelling reason. Imagine taking up exercise when you haven't been in the habit of it, or giving up smoking when you have. What is your compelling reason for committing to bringing the practices of mindfulness and dialogue to your leadership conversations? What have you learned so far that might suggest there is real benefit in cultivating these approaches, both for you and for those around you? What will be your fundamental intent, as you deepen your first person inquiry, your sense of curiosity about how others experience the world, and your understanding of the dynamics and patterns in conversational fields?

⏸

Very early in this book, I briefly introduced three of Peter Garrett's learning containers: realising yourself; showing up; and occupying the ground. We'll now revisit these in more depth and introduce a fourth container. I invite you to take stock of what you have learned in engaging with the theories and practices of this book. How might you continue your learning journey?

One of the challenges with learning is that it often implies we need to correct something we are currently getting wrong. My frame for learning is one of growth and expansion. We are adding new capacity and capability to our repertoire, which will give us more choices. In addition, we can also become more skilful with our current repertoire. For example, if you are a natural advocator (whether mover or opposer), celebrate this and learn to use your aptitude skilfully when it serves your leadership, whilst adopting other practices when advocacy hinders you. If you are an intrinsic inquirer, curious about what is going on around you, honour this quality and become discerning about where it enhances your leadership and where other approaches may be more fruitful.

With this approach in mind, and in a climate of growing our repertoire and versatility, let's revisit Garrett's learning containers.

Learning containers

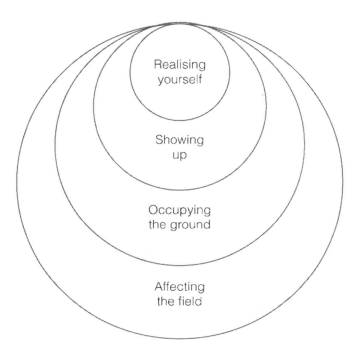

Realising
yourself

Showing
up

Occupying
the ground

Affecting
the field

From work by Peter Garrett

Realising yourself

In the first learning container, something catches your attention, perhaps prompted by an external stimulus or by some reflection on your situation and surroundings. You are inspired in some way, and realise that there are possibilities for new learning, or potential for more depth in something you have already begun to study or practice. You have energy to find out more in your preferred learning style – perhaps reading, perhaps talking ideas through with others, perhaps participating in a course.

For example, my journey with T'ai Chi was sparked by an introductory session at a health farm in the early 1990s. I really liked the sensations that I experienced in that hour, and made a mental note to take up T'ai Chi. There was a lot going on in my life at that time, so I didn't immediately act on my intent. However, when I went to Lancaster University for a year some time later, I had an opportunity to begin classes. Thirteen years later, I remain engaged and still have 'realising' moments as my practice develops. The path through these containers is not linear and new facets of realising yourself arise over time.

This first learning container is important – when the impulse to learn or discover touches you, what do you do with it? Are you swept up in the excitement and enthusiasm of new possibilities, engaging easily with opportunities to further your curiosity? Or are you cautious about finding out more and acting on your interest?

Exploring further can be a difficult time. As I began T'ai Chi, I had to come to terms with being an absolute beginner, aware of my shortcomings and limitations. For example, after six months, I suddenly realised that almost all my habitual movements were counter to what was needed for T'ai Chi. At this point I had a choice – give up something that was just too difficult, or persevere knowing that I was going to be awkward and clunky for a long time. As someone who generally picks things up quickly, this latter choice was hard to make; I was used to being good at things.

On the other hand, with a light approach, exploring within this learning container can be a relatively safe stage. We are simply experimenting with something new and there are no expectations. A few close friends or colleagues may know about it but it is essentially a private adventure. This can mean we are free to play, to make mistakes, to discover.

As energy builds for our intent to learn, we approach a threshold, a gateway into the second container of showing up. We start using our new approaches or practices more publicly. For example, we may start to use an approach from dialogue practices in our workplace or at home.

At this threshold, we may encounter two energies: excitement, curiosity and anticipation provide impetus to cross the threshold and be seen to try out something new, while fear or self-consciousness hold us in the safer place of the familiar and keeping our learning private. The balance may be tipped by the level of importance we attach to the new material or approaches.

My personal way of crossing this first threshold is usually to start talking about my excitement and enthusiasm for the new interest, and to see how it sounds to me. If I remain engaged, I might step into the second container and show up, perhaps trying a new approach in a workshop. For example, with dialogue practices, I started to use some of the models with coaching clients, finding my own language for sharing what I was beginning to understand.

Showing up
The second learning container, showing up, does what it says on the tin: we begin to put new material into practice with others, trying out different approaches, noticing the impact, experimenting, playing and experiencing what happens. We are being seen and heard as we try something new and witness other people's reactions to it.

This is perhaps a fledgling stage of growth; your flying feathers are growing in and you are flexing your wing muscles to strengthen them. This is the stage of beginning to learn through practice, of testing your conceptual understanding and refining and deepening it through real experiences.

For example, in T'ai Chi, my showing up was initially quite literally continuing to make it to classes. My first teacher was in Lancaster and when I came home to

Scotland, I had to find a new class. I tried three before settling with Ian Cameron and Five Winds School, even though choosing this school meant I had to begin again because they practiced a different style of T'ai Chi. Several years later I had another major experience of showing up when I started to explore how I could share some of the potential learning from T'ai Chi with leaders.

As we continue to trial new material with others, we approach another threshold, a gateway into the third container of occupying the ground. As we find that something is working for us, we may want to adopt it more consistently. We may want to declare ourselves as being committed to a particular path. It is becoming part of who we are and how we do things.

For example, we may want to say, 'I am cultivating dialogue practices and intend to bring them into my leadership conversations.' Declaring this may raise the bar for how others see you. They might, perhaps, expect you to have some mastery of your discipline and to think, speak and act in a way that is congruent with it.

At this threshold we again encounter two energies: growing confidence, certainty and belief encourage us to cross the threshold, while the weight of other people's expectations and judgements hold us in the safer space of simply showing up. As we continue to show up, we develop a consistency of practice, and in the end I believe this moves us to cross the threshold to maintain our integrity and coherence.

This threshold feels like a big step. For example, I have an interesting dilemma as I bring T'ai Chi practices into leadership development work. I am showing up through my Pause for Breath leadership retreat and through using embodied work in my dialogue practice development groups and coaching work. However, I have a crisis of confidence; am I good enough to occupy the ground?

The truth is that I'm not particularly good at T'ai Chi, despite the years I have been doing it. How will my fellow T'ai Chi practitioners judge me? To balance this doubt, I know that my T'ai Chi is good enough to bring the principles skilfully to leaders who have little or no experience of embodied work. But one day I may come across a leader who is a martial artist and then what?

Occupying the ground

The third learning container, occupying the ground, is again self-explanatory. Your practice now is led by values, beliefs and conviction. You are unself-conscious about what you stand for and the way you do things. You are congruent in your practice, embodying the principles and values of it. You have developed a settled sense of presence in this field or discipline. Your practice is now something you inhabit, rather than something you remind yourself to do.

To occupy the ground and say, 'this is who I am and what I stand for' requires enough consistency of practice, and enough centre, to be able to stand in this declaration, whatever others might think. To occupy the ground you need commitment to your practice, and mind, body and spirit need to be aligned around it. However, you may feel somewhat alone and exposed if, in your organisational system, you are a pioneer in what you are espousing and practising. You cannot occupy the ground alone without becoming isolated, and so the consistency and impact of your practice needs to be attracting others, inviting them to be curious about how they might join you.

In another example, I believe I began to occupy the ground of supporting dialogue practice development when working with my third group. With the first group, I was showing up – I wanted to develop my own dialogue practice and also to develop my capacity to support others in this work. All the members of my first group had been on at least one of Peter Garrett's programmes, whilst I had been on three or four, so was slightly 'first among equals.' I learned how to host a dialogue practice group with the four members of that first group.

The second group was much larger, and I was able to gain confidence, becoming surer that what I was doing was skilful rather than simply lucky. In the third group, no-one had encountered dialogue practices except through me, and in supporting them I felt I began to cross the threshold to occupy the ground. My fourth open group is currently underway, alongside two in-house groups; my practice as a host for this work is embodied and consistent, and I continue to learn.

As we grow in our capacity to embody what we stand for, we approach another threshold, a gateway into the fourth container of affecting the field. Despite our presence and practice, we come to fully know that it is not enough. The influence of one person does not (usually) achieve wide-ranging change. The reach of one person is limited, but when joined by the voices of others, a collective energy for change may emerge.

At this threshold, we again encounter two energies: a sense of ownership, commitment and maturity encourage us to cross the threshold, while a sense of impatience with others may hold us in a solitary place of limited influence.

In occupying the ground month after month, year after year, we continue to hone our existing practice and to further develop our repertoire and presence. As we do so, we imprint our signature on our practice, developing a sense of ownership. This can separate us from others, as they do not share our signature.

For example, in my dialogue practice development work, my signature is to combine dialogue practices with embodied work, enabling others to have an energetic experience of the impact of advocacy, inquiry, conflict and influence. In focusing on energy and embodied work, I leave out some of the finer details of traditional dialogue theories and practices. And I am approaching a capacity threshold – I cannot do more work. How then, do I extend my reach? Can I trust others to help me? Is their practice deep enough?

Affecting the field

The fourth container of affecting the field, in which people are touched by a person's presence and work even though they have no direct contact. For example, in an organisational setting, consider the influence of the character and presence of a Chief Executive on employees they have never met. Or consider the reach of blogs and websites, as well as more traditional media of coaching, teaching and writing books.

To affect the field, we need to be changing the energy of those in the field. For example, when a coach works with a client, the client's energetic response to a colleague may change during a coaching session. When the client next meets their colleague, the colleague may experience a fundamental shift in their thinking, emotions or energy. The coach has, in a small way, affected the field, working directly with a client in a way which influences the client's colleague.

We often think we're affecting the field long before we actually do. This is because we get over-confident about our knowledge, skills, practice and power, as we become assured in occupying the ground. In its truest sense, affecting the field is something that happens when we are committed to occupying the ground; it is not something to separately aspire to. The very intent of aspiring changes our energy and moves our attention away from developing our practice and towards being recognised or celebrated for our leadership or our work. At least this is my personal risk – what is yours?

To affect the field, the focus of our practice development needs to be how we become accomplished and yet stay in contact with our essential frailty and humility. We can do this by cultivating our capacity for being centred and for inhabiting our finest leadership presence. This balances the part of us that wants to shine and be honoured for our brilliance. The foundations for affecting the field are to occupy the ground in our practice, and to develop our leadership presence, through increasing our capacity for connecting to, and recovering, centre.

Summary
Together the learning containers provide insight into a pathway for profound growth. The model articulates a process over time, from engaging with an idea for a new approach, to experimenting with it and embodying it. I've already touched on the fact that the pathway is not linear. I may be occupying the ground, or even affecting the field, in one aspect of my dialogue practice or leadership, whilst still only at the realising yourself or showing up stages in other aspects.

I sometimes liken change and learning pathways to an image of the daily change in the tide, ebbing and flowing. From a distance we see the tide rise or fall. Consider the image of the tide rising, coming in, as a metaphor for an overall direction of travel in our growth. If we go closer to the shore, we see that the tide advances as a wave of energy rolls in, crashes and retreats. There is forward and backward motion that might reflect practice. The overall motion is 'in,' but the transition is not smooth, consistent, or coherent. Our overall practice develops, but not linearly. I sometimes liken change and learning pathways to an image of the daily change of the tide ebbing and flowing.

If we go right down onto the shore and walk along the tideline, we see lots of tiny wavelets and ripples, moving at different speeds, tumbling over one another, impeding one another, rolling into one another in little surges. This is what change looks like close to the ground, where pebbles are rolled up and down the beach, caught in the force of energy.

In bringing the practices of mindfulness and dialogue to leadership conversations, where is your energy for change? How will you decide which practices to support? How will you support yourself as your early attempts at something new hit the shore, crash and recede, before gathering impetus again?

Returning to the metaphor of the tide, each tidal process has its own rhythm and time period, from the six hours it takes for a tide to come in, to the minutes it takes for a wave to form, to swell, to gain energy and hit the shore, and to the seconds it takes for the frontline tide to ripple over the beach and back. What might be the equivalent timeframes for your learning and practice development? When you step back, how long might it take to make changes in the mix of your current habits and new practices? Are you up for the longer journey of the tide coming in, or are you only up for playing in the ripples on the beach?

Of all the approaches outlined in this book, the aspect of practice which requires most time to inhabit is the capacity to recover centre under pressure. Developing this may include cultivating a regular practice of reflection, contemplation or meditation in order to steady our mind as well as our energy. In embarking on such a journey, it can be helpful to find a teacher and community within which to learn and practice.

The routes towards integrating mind, body and spirit and cultivating our presence are many. You may start, as I did, with a physical discipline or practice, such as a martial art, yoga, pilates or other mindful activity. You may start with a meditation practice, or with serious first-person inquiry and reflection of the kind that is required if you train to become a therapist or similar professional. You may start with developing your spirit, or through embodying your values.

As you deepen your practice to include mind, body and spirit, you will bring more clarity to your mind, more compassion to your heart, and more confidence into your physical being and sensing. These qualities don't appear overnight and one of the deepest challenges of this kind of slow development is how we measure progress. This is one of the reasons it can be daunting to adopt the spirit and discipline of practice.

I remember struggling with this in my T'ai Chi practice. When I started, it was easy to measure progress – I was taught new movements in each class, and over several months, the first form took shape. When the initial teaching was complete, I was left to practice. That's where things became more difficult; constant repetition felt dull and pointless. Then a senior student offered me the metaphor that each time we practice, we lay down a layer of rice paper. Viewed edge-on, each layer is almost invisible, but once you have a stack, you can see the difference. This metaphor for practice helps me keep faith with my continuing development, even though I can't see any immediate results from a single practice session. What do you need to put in place to sustain your commitment to growth, even when results are hard to see?

Practice 42 – taking stock

It is time to pause for breath and invite you to take stock of the theories, practices, self-inquiry and fieldwork you have encountered in this book.

Realising yourself
What has caught your attention? What excites and stimulates you? What might you like to take further in your learning and perhaps begin to 'try out?' Of these:

1. What do you easily 'get,' and already do naturally?

2. What have you tried once or twice with mixed results?

3. What currently seems out of reach?

Note two key things from question two and commit to practising them further.

Be thoughtful about how and where you might try these things out – don't choose your most important meeting or conversation. Be kind to yourself in finding something that matters, but is not too high profile or risky. Commit to stepping over the threshold to show up with one of your two key things.

Finally, choose one thing from question three and set an intent that you will develop your capacity for this over time. Be clear in this intent but take no direct action.

Showing up
What is already part of your conversational repertoire, and has been illuminated and affirmed by what you have read and discovered? Of these:

1. What are you already doing with sufficient presence that you can effortlessly do more?

350

2. What are you trying out regularly but still with feelings of clumsiness or self-consciousness?

3. What currently seems out of reach as something you might do regularly, consistently and well?

Note two key things that you already do naturally and well, and simply bring them more into awareness. Practice them deliberately, consciously, mindfully.

Note two key things from question two and commit to practising them further. Be thoughtful about how and where you might do this. Start to gently raise the bar and practice in settings with higher stakes. Commit to stepping over the threshold to occupy the ground with one of these things.

Finally, choose one thing from question three and set an intent that you will develop your capacity for this over time. Be clear in this intent but take no direct action.

Occupying the ground
Where might you already occupy the ground? Where are your mind, body and spirit already aligned? Where is your practice already effortless and centred? What do you need to acknowledge in yourself as accomplished and congruent? Of these:

1. Where is your practice already acknowledged by others as being consistent and influential?

2. What are you in the process of adopting as practice, but not always implementing skilfully or sometimes forgetting to do at all?

3. What currently seems out of reach as something you might inhabit or embody?

Note two key things that you might acknowledge graciously as already *being part of 'how I do things' and resolve to inhabit this way of being even more often and with more presence.*

Note two key things from question two and commit to practising them more consistently, so that your presence begins to inspire others to join you.

Finally, choose one thing from question three and set an intent that you will develop your capacity for this over time. Be clear in this intent but take no direct action.

Notes and reflections

Chapter 43 Last touch

'When you meet your friend on the roadside or in the marketplace,
let the spirit in you move your lips and direct your tongue.
Let the voice within you speak to the ear of his ear;
For his soul will keep the truth of your heart
as the taste of wine is remembered.
When the colour is forgotten and the vessel is no more.'
Kahlil Gibran

As I have made this journey of searching, both internally and externally, for a deeper grasp of dialogue, I have become clear that dialogue is not, for the vast majority of us, 'more of the same' in terms of conversation. Dialogue is what one of my clients calls a 'higher, deeper, wider conversation.' The development process for dialogue seems to be about finding the 'edges' of our conversational range, the boundaries we bump up against and the limits we impose, through choice or because we don't, or won't, learn new skills or cultivate new ways of being. Having found our current edges, we can search for, and experiment with, ways of moving beyond them.

Dialogue is about good contact. With a strong kinaesthetic sense, I'm drawn to having an embodied sense of what I mean by dialogue. In being centred and present, I am in good contact with myself and with others. If, collectively, we are centred and present, we can be in good contact with the conversation that needs to emerge through us. Good contact is grounded, at ease, connected. It is mindful and open to whatever arises in the moment without preference. Good contact embraces wonder and curiosity; it is a living, breathing connection.

Dialogue is also fundamentally about generosity, about giving. We need to give time, space, energy and attention. We need to give our authentic voice, our own relevant truth, however challenging for us and for others. We need to give our respect to others and their truths. These aspects of dialogue reflect the word give as meaning 'to offer.' If we can learn to offer our advocacy rather than wield it, to extend it rather than smite with it, our conversations will become more open, more expansive and potentially more fruitful.

There is, though, another meaning for give. To give is to yield, to surrender, as a mattress gives to our weight when we lie on it. In martial arts this sense of yielding is well known. It doesn't mean to collapse or to give way. It refers to blending with your partner to access your combined energy. In this way inquiry is yielding. It's not the soft and floppy option: it's holding your own form, views and energy whilst blending with the form, views and energy of another, in service to what can be created together.

These qualities of good contact and generosity come naturally when we are centred, and in my view, cultivating the capacity to be present to ourselves and others in this way is more important than knowledge, skills or techniques. When we are centred, we are able to access our full awareness and be mindful of our intent; what is our honest motivation as we take part in a conversation, or respond to the words of another? Most of us don't routinely take the time to clarify this, we simply react. The message of this book is that if we pause for breath and centre, we will disengage from our habitual self and create the space to make more mindful choices. Dialogue emerges naturally from this practice of becoming present.

I leave you with a story of profound dialogue from *Rivers and Tides,*[30] a DVD in which the artist Andy Goldsworthy is on a beach making a stone pine cone. He is under deadline from the incoming tide. He creates the cone by constructing layers of stone that fit together in a circular shape, their weight and form connecting and balancing as the pine cone shape grows outwards from the initial base. Three times his work collapses inwards; three times he clears the space and begins again. There is a fourth collapse, and in its wake the film records his response. He speaks, softly, equably:

> *'The moment when something collapses, it is intensely disappointing…and this is the fourth time it's fallen. And each time I got to know the stone a little bit more, and it got higher each time – so it grew in proportion to my understanding of the stone.'*

This reflects my sense of what happens when a group of people who have something important to talk about share a collective intent to make dialogue. They are almost certainly under deadline from some metaphorical incoming tide. As they fashion their words together, their conversation will almost certainly collapse at times. The question is whether they have the calm energy to clear the space and begin again? If individual voices are the material from which the art form of dialogue is crafted, then each time we set out to make dialogue, we will get to know the material of each other's voices a little better and our conversation will, perhaps, get higher, deeper and wider with each attempt.

Thank you for travelling with me – I wish you a fulfilling onward journey.

Practice 43 – pause for breath

This foundation practice appears at the end of each section of the book.

Sit in a comfortable upright posture, so that your feet are firmly planted on the floor and you are supporting your own back, rather than leaning against a chair. Rest your hands on your thighs, palms down.

Become aware of the contact between your feet/shoes and the floor. Become aware of the contact between your hands and your thighs. Become aware of the contact between your thighs and the chair. Become aware of the sitting bones, the bones at the base of the pelvis, pressing into the chair seat.

Notice your strong base, formed by your feet and sitting bones, and allow your spine to grow to its full length by gently imagining each vertebra lifting slightly from the one below. Sense lightness and spaciousness in your spine. Notice that your neck becomes long at the back, your chin tilted slightly towards your chest.

Now bring your attention to your breath. On each inhale, imagine your breath seeping into the spaces in your spine, allowing it to lengthen just a little bit more. On each exhale, imagine your breath flowing down through your chest and belly, softening any tension. Follow your breath for a few moments.

Now mentally scan your body and notice any places of tension, aching or discomfort. Choose one and, for a few breaths, imagine your inbreath soaking into this place and, on a longer exhale, imagine your outbreath dissolving any discomfort and carrying it out into the air around you, letting you rest.

After a few breaths, become aware of the contact between your sitting bones and the chair, between your hands and thighs, and between your feet and the ground.

Rise gently and stretch. You are ready to re-engage with the world.

Acknowledgements

How many people does it take to publish a book? Many more than I ever imagined. I was held afloat by the generosity of those who invested time and energy in challenge and/or support. Thank you.

For contributions of insight and wisdom on reading early drafts: Colby Adams, Joyce Campbell, Ray Charlton, Tom Crum, Marianne Dee, Kieran Docherty, Moira Foster, Joanne Frame, Peter Garrett, Roger Gibbins, Daryl King, Steve Marshall, Edna Murdoch, Dr Karen Niven, Wendy Palmer, Julia Parker, Michele Seymour, Susan Szpakowski, Portia Tung, Jill Young, and the many others who offered moral support and cheered me on.

For those from whom I learned 'on-the-job:' my coaching and supervision clients, members of my dialogue practice development groups and participants in my Pause for Breath retreats.

Acknowledgements

For giving me William Isaacs' book, which sparked my interest in dialogue: Caroline Gardner

For asking me, 'what is your message?' after reading some very early musings: Peter Mackenzie

For her inspirational artwork: Barbara Bash

For practical contributions in navigating an unknown process: Bek Pickard, Jane Tulloch and Gareth Pierce.

For her unstoppable enthusiasm and relentless optimism: Murielle Maupoint.

References

1 Dialogue and the Art of Thinking Together, William Isaacs, Doubleday
2 The Art of Loving, Erich Fromm, Thorsons
3 www.dialogue-associates.com
4 The World Café – Shaping Our Futures Through Conversations That Matter, Juanita Brown with David Isaacs and the World Café Community, Berret-Koehler Publishers
5 Theory U – Leading From the Future as it Emerges, C Otto Scharmer, Society for Organisational Learning
6 The Art of Thinking Together – Dialogue in Action, Fieldguide, DIA·Logos Incorporated
7 Difficult Conversations, Stone, Patton, Heen, Penguin
8 Why Good Leaders Make Bad Decisions, Campbell, Whitehead, Finkelstein, Harvard Business Review, February 2009
9 www.ross-smith.com
10 The Fifth Discipline Fieldbook, Senge et al, Nicholas Brealey Publishing
11 Tools for Thinking – Modelling In Management Science, Mike Pidd, Wiley
12 The Mindful Way Through Depression, Jon Kabat-Zinn et al, The Guilford Press

References

13 Switch: How to Change Things When Change is Hard, Chip and Dan Heath

14 Three Deep Breaths – Finding Power and Purpose in a Stressed-Out World, Thomas Crum, Berret-Koehler Publishers Inc

15 The Intuitive Body – Discovering the Wisdom Of Conscious Embodiment and Aikido, Wendy Palmer, Blue Snake Books

16 Executive Coaching with Backbone and Heart – A Systemic Approach to Engaging Leaders with Their Challenges, Mary Beth O'Neill, Jossey Bass

17 The 7 Habits of Highly Effective People, Stephen R Covey, Simon & Schuster

18 Authentic Happiness – Using the New Positive Psychology to Realise your Potential for Lasting Fulfilment, Martin EP Seligman, Phd, Nicholas Brealey Publishing

19 www.heartmath.org

20 Tao Te Ching – The Book of the Way, Lao-Tzu, Translated by Stephen Mitchell, Kyle Cathie Limited

21 The Art of Thinking Together – Dialogue in Action, Fieldguide, DIA·Logos Incorporated

22 After the Ecstasy, the Laundry – How the Heart Grows Wise on the Spiritual Path, Jack Kornfield, Rider

23 Paradoxical Theory of Change, Arnold Beisser

24 My Lover, Myself – Self-Discovery Through Relationship, David Kantor, Riverhead Books

25 On Dialogue, David Bohm, Routledge

26 The Invitation, Oriah Mountain Dreamer, Thorsons

27 Harry Potter and the Philosopher's Stone, J K Rowling, Bloomsbury

28 Bringing Life to Organisational Change, Margaret Wheatley and Myron Kellner-Rogers, www.berkana.org

29 Trust – A New Vision of Human Relationships for Business, Education, Family and Personal Living, Jack Gibb, Newcastle Publishing Co, Inc.

30 Rivers and Tides, A Goldsworthy and T Riedelsheimer, Germany/Scotland: Artificial Eye

Lightning Source UK Ltd.
Milton Keynes UK
UKOW041359071111

181651UK00002B/6/P